"Rodes has provided an excellent review of who influenced Wesley, how Wesley—with his usual eclectic gleaning—transformed the covenant theology of the Reformed tradition, and why the 'faith of a servant and faith of a child' metaphor is key to understanding Wesley's concept of the way of salvation. Thoroughly researched and intelligently argued, *From Faith to Faith* is a new and unique contribution to the field of Wesley Studies. A definitely needed addition to the academic's and the pastor's library."

—Diane Leclerc
NORTHWEST NAZARENE UNIVERSITY

From Faith to Faith

DISTINGUISHED DISSERTATIONS IN CHRISTIAN THEOLOGY

Series Foreword

We are living in a vibrant season for academic Christian theology. After a hiatus of some decades, a real flowering of excellent systematic and moral theology has emerged. This situation calls for a series that showcases the contributions of newcomers to this ongoing and lively conversation. The journal *Word & World: Theology for Christian Ministry* and the academic society Christian Theological Research Fellowship (CTRF) are happy to cosponsor this series together with our publisher Pickwick Publications (an imprint of Wipf and Stock Publishers). Both the CTRF and *Word & World* are interested in excellence in academics but also in scholarship oriented toward Christ and the Church. The volumes in this series are distinguished for their combination of academic excellence with sensitivity to the primary context of Christian learning. We are happy to present the work of these young scholars to the wider world and are grateful to Luther Seminary for the support that helped make it possible.

Alan G. Padgett
Professor of Systematic Theology
Luther Seminary

Beth Felker Jones
Assistant Professor of Theology
Wheaton College

www.ctrf.info
www.luthersem.edu/word&world

From Faith to Faith

John Wesley's Covenant Theology and the Way of Salvation

STANLEY J. RODES

☙PICKWICK *Publications* • Eugene, Oregon

FROM FAITH TO FAITH
John Wesley's Covenant Theology and the Way of Salvation

Distinguished Dissertations in Christian Theology 8

Copyright © 2013 Stanley J. Rodes. All rights reserved. Except for brief quotations in critical publications or reviews, no part of this book may be reproduced in any manner without prior written permission from the publisher. Write: Permissions, Wipf and Stock Publishers, 199 W. 8th Ave., Suite 3, Eugene, OR 97401.

Pickwick Publications
An Imprint of Wipf and Stock Publishers
199 W. 8th Ave., Suite 3
Eugene, OR 97401

www.wipfandstock.com

ISBN 13: 978-1-62032-544-5

Cataloguing-in-Publication data:

Rodes, Stanley J.

From faith to faith : John Wesley's covenant theology and the way of salvation / Stanley J. Rodes, with a foreword by T. A. Noble.

xx + 250 pp. ; 23 cm. Includes bibliographical references and indexes.

Distinguished Dissertations in Christian Theology 8

ISBN 13: 978-1-62032-544-5

1. Wesley, John, 1703–1791. 2. Covenant theology—History of doctrines—18th century 3. I. Noble, Thomas A. II. Series. III. Title.

BX8495.W5 R622 2013

Manufactured in the U.S.A.

*To all called of God
to be "fishers of men"*

Press on by all possible means . . . "from faith to faith";
from the faith of a servant, to the faith of a son.

JOHN WESLEY

Contents

Foreword by T. A. Noble xi
Preface xv
Acknowledgments xvii
Abbreviations xix

Introduction 1

1 John Wesley's Imaging of Covenant Theology 14
2 The Ancestry of Wesley's Covenant Theology 37
3 Wesley's Amendment of Covenant Theology 59
4 Wesley's Covenant Theology and Holy Scripture 77
5 Wesley's Covenant Theology in Context: I. The Evangelical Revival and the Conversation on Good Works 90
6 Wesley's Covenant Theology in Context: II. The Conversation on Divine Favor 109
7 The Salvific Sufficiency of the Covenant of Grace 133
8 The Holy Spirit and the Salvific Perfection of the Covenant of Grace 154
9 "From Faith to Faith": John Wesley's Pastoral Application of Covenant Theology 181
10 Epilogue 216

Bibliography 225
Name Index 243
Scripture Index 247

Foreword

THE EARLY YEARS OF the twenty-first century have seen belated recognition of a global revolution in world Christianity. Although many secular commentators were blinded by the decline of the Christian church in Europe and the rise of a fairly militant secular opposition to the church in North America, the Christian church as a whole is in a period of enormous growth, particularly in the southern hemisphere and in some parts of Asia. Historians from Latourette to Walls tell us that this global expansion of the church is a consequence of the sowing of the seed during "great century" of missionary endeavor in the nineteenth century, and that that sacrificial commitment to the mission of the church to "preach the gospel to every creature" was in turn rooted in the Evangelical Revival of the eighteenth century.

Right at the heart of the Evangelical Revival was the figure of John Wesley. There were of course other major figures. Jonathan Edwards was not only the key figure in the beginnings of the revival in New England, but his account of it influenced the subsequent revival throughout what were then the British dominions. Edwards also must be recognized as the greatest theologian of that awakening, and indeed perhaps of the eighteenth century. George Whitefield was the great preacher whose spell-binding oratory electrified mass congregations in England, Scotland, and the New World, and whose ability to communicate was envied even by the great Shakespearian actor, David Garrick. A host of other figures contributed: Charles Wesley, possibly the greatest hymnist of Christian history; Daniel Rowland and Howel Harris in Wales; Ebenezer and Ralph Erskine, William McCulloch, James Robe, and later Thomas Chalmers in Scotland; William Grimshaw, William Romaine, Samuel Walker, Henry Venn, John Fletcher, John Newton, and later Charles Simeon in England; and in the British colonies which became the United States, Gilbert Tennent, William Robinson, Samuel Davis, Daniel Marshall, and Francis Asbury. Among significant lay people we could also mention Lady Huntingdon, William Cowper, Isaac Milner, William Wilberforce, Hannah More, and Zachary Macaulay. Nor must we forget the continuing influence of Pietism in Germany from Spener and Francke to Zinzendorf and Rothe, not least in their spearheading of the world missionary movement, and crucial figures such as William Carey who link the revival of evangelical faith directly with the world missionary movement.

But the leading figure in the Evangelical Revival who arguably had the most widespread influence through five or six decades of consistent ministry was John Wesley. Where other evangelists such as Whitefield bemoaned the loss of many converts, Wesley's gift for administration in building up his Methodist Societies, his innovations in including lay people in the care of converts, and his sheer perseverance and personal organization over those decades laid firm foundations for the continued growth of the Methodist movement. Today the World Methodist Council comprises denominations with a world membership of around eighty million, a figure comparable to seventy-seven million Anglicans, seventy-five million Presbyterians, sixty-six million Lutherans, forty-seven million Baptists in the World Baptist Alliance, and forty-eight million in the largest Pentecostal denomination, the Assemblies of God.

But while John Wesley has been revered as an evangelist and church builder, even Methodists paid little attention to his theology until the twentieth century. But the work of George Croft Cell, Albert Outler, Colin Williams, Thomas Oden, Randy Maddox, and Kenneth Collins, among many others, has produced a rediscovery of Wesley the theologian. Part of the story is the recovery of the understanding that Christian Theology is not primarily a matter of intellectual system building for the academy, but an exploration of the coherence of the Christian faith for the sake of the mission of the church. Therefore while Outler may have described Wesley as a "folk theologian," it is recognized today that it is not only the writing of Christian Dogmatics which constitutes a "theologian" (although that remains crucial for mission!), but that the primary articulation of Christian theology is in sermons and letters and occasional writings to meet the need of the hour.

John Wesley, the Oxford scholar who abandoned the groves of academe to preach to the poor in the fields and streets, and who engaged in a lifetime of publication for his preachers and people, must therefore be accounted one of the great theologians of his century. And although he produced no Systematic or Dogmatic Theology, his consistent thinking in the area of pastoral theology for "the cure of souls" is second to none. His doctrinal structure was, as befits a presbyter of the Church of England, somewhat eclectic, or to use another term, ecumenical. But he stood solidly in the creedal tradition of the Fathers and the evangelical tradition of the Reformers, and particularly within that Anglican tradition influenced by Luther and Calvin but which rejected the later extremes of Calvinism articulated in the five-point scheme of the Synod of Dort. Wesley eventually adopted the term "Arminian" when he started to publish the *Arminian Magazine*, but while he stood in a tradition which was close to James Arminius himself, he had little in common with the later Dutch Arminianism that veered off in the direction of Socinianism and "free will." He was, in Herbert McGonigle's apt phrase, an "Evangelical Arminian," although in fact the so-called Arminian tradition within the Church of England owed more to the Greek Fathers. And indeed as Charles Simeon, the architect of Anglican evangelicalism, recognized, he and Wesley had a common bond in their understanding of the gospel besides which their differences were minor. But of course evangelicals of the Simeon tradition were said to be Arminian in the pulpit, but Calvinist on their knees! And while it is surely largely owing to Wesley that global evangelical Christianity today is more Arminian than Calvinist, it would perhaps be better to say that those terms are somewhat misleading and that there is hope of a resolution of that longstanding debate which will reflect the irenic spirit of both Simeon and Wesley.

It is therefore timely that this new book by Dr Stan Rodes highlights one major way in which Wesley's theology had much in common with the broader Reformed tradition. Classic Anglican theology stands more in the Reformed than in the Lutheran tradition, and among the structures of thought developed in Reformed theology through the seventeenth century was the elaboration of the "federal" scheme. This tried to bring unity to Christian thinking about grace and law by developing the biblical notion of the covenant (*foedus*). While Calvin himself wrote of the one covenant of God and that the covenant made with the patriarchs was "one and the same" in "reality and substance" as the covenant made with us (*Institutes*, II, x, 2), Ursinus, Olevieanus, and Cocciecus developed the differentiation between the covenant of works and the covenant of grace which was given the status of the standard Reformed view in the Westminster Confession. For the late seventeenth century and early eighteenth century, this federal or covenant terminology therefore became standard, even among those who rejected Calvinism.

Surprisingly, despite the fact that this language appears in Wesley (in, for example, the opening paragraph of Sermon 6, "The Righteousness of Faith"), the standard introductions to Wesley's theology have paid little

Foreword

attention to his theology of covenant. It has received some attention recently from Jason Vickers in *The Cambridge Companion to John Wesley*, but Dr Rodes has presented us with the first full-scale examination of this underlying structure of Wesley's thought. It was my privilege to take over the supervision of his doctoral research at Nazarene Theological College, Manchester, when my colleague Dr Herbert McGonigle was forced by health to suspend his work. The resulting thesis was a work of meticulous scholarship, investigating what Wesley meant by his double metaphor contrasting "the faith of a servant" with "the faith of a son." This book based on that research now focuses on what that research uncovered about the significance of covenant theology in Wesley's thought. It is an original contribution not only to Wesley Studies but to the place of Wesley within the broader Reformed tradition. Despite the sad history of past disputes between so-called "Calvinists" and so-called "Arminians," it may help to promote that greater understanding of Wesley's theology, which may promote greater unity within evangelical Christianity around the globe.

T. A. Noble,
Senior Research Fellow in Theology
Nazarene Theological College, Didsbury, Manchester

Preface

You may be reading this because you recognized the name John Wesley in the title of this book and are curious to learn more about him. Or perhaps the words "covenant theology" piqued your interest either because it is something you know something about or relatively nothing about, or because you've never actually seen "John Wesley" and "covenant theology" appear in such close proximity to each other. These are good reasons to keep reading. But if what lured you in was "the way of salvation" then you have arrived at ground zero of what motivated the research leading to his volume.

Having spent a good deal of my life listening to people tell the story of their lives, I almost always am listening with this question milling about in my mind: "Just where is this person on their spiritual journey?" The answer to that question matters. It has always mattered, especially to those entrusted with the spiritual care of others. And since it has always mattered, it seemed worthwhile to see what might be learned from someone of honorable and historic stature who spent a good deal of his life thinking about and responding to this same question. Enter John Wesley.

I began my research simply as an investigation into a rather curious distinction Wesley made among those to whom he gave spiritual counsel. Some people, he said, have "the faith of a servant"; others have "the faith of a son." That distinction seemed to be a thoughtful conclusion he had reached in his own pursuit of an answer to the question that must have lingered in his mind, too, as he heard and read the stories of real, every-day people over the course of his long ministry. And perhaps more importantly, it seemed to be his confident answer to the question posed to *him* by these same people—the question they themselves pondered in their own hearts and minds, "Just where *am* I on my spiritual journey?"

It was in the thick of my research on Wesley's distinction that the imprint of covenant theology on his theological thought came to the fore. The more I investigated, the more I realized how powerfully his soteriology was impacted by it, and how significantly and creatively he adapted it to the template of his evangelical Arminianism. In the end, the original research was cast in a doctoral thesis examining the distinction between the faith of a servant and the faith of a son. This volume represents a reconfiguration of that research in order to highlight Wesley's covenant theology, with the metaphors of servant and son serving as "Exhibit A" of its profound influence on his theological thought.

Because the whole idea of a real connection between Wesley's theological thought and covenant theology seems to be somewhat foreign, I am hopeful that the material in this volume will be convincing enough to compel a new attentiveness in the reading and researching of the Wesley corpus. There are, for example, a number of instances where reading the term "Christian" in light of Wesley's covenant theology (rather than as a generic term opposed to "pagan") will fundamentally impact the theological meaning of the passage. My aim in this volume is to present a comprehensive introduction to the influence of covenant theology on Wesley that will be taken seriously and, in the end, further a more accurate understanding of his theological thought.

I would hope, too, that it would incite further investigation into the subject. There are many aspects needing further research and implications waiting to be pondered. If my fellow Wesleyans gain from learning of the contributions of covenant theology to Wesley's theological formulations, and those from other theological traditions discover the same, that is a significant gain. Above all, a major personal goal of this study will have been accomplished if it proves to be a helpful resource to those entrusted with the spiritual care of others, or inspires applications in practical theology that turn out to be an asset to them. And if we all are encouraged to advance "from faith to faith" in our walks with God, that is best of all.

Acknowledgments

IN THE PROCESS OF completing this volume, I have often thought of Wesley scholar and friend, Herbert B. McGonigle. His love for God, passionate interest in John Wesley, incredible ability to recall almost everything he had ever read, and early investment in me as a scholar at Nazarene Theological College, Manchester, England combined to whet my appetite for the research that led to the discoveries set forth in this volume. I am hopeful he will find some delight in this effort. I am grateful to Thomas A. Noble who graciously stepped in alongside Dr. McGonigle as my supervisor during the last half of my doctoral work and whose genuine interest in my research was and remains a great encouragement. I am also grateful to the faculty, staff, and students of Nazarene Theological College who contributed kindness and helpfulness, and encouragement and direction along the way. I particularly appreciate the efforts of librarian Donald Maciver and the work of Geordan Hammond in guiding the development and acquisition of resources at the Manchester Wesley Research Centre located on the campus. It was also a constant delight to conduct a portion of this research at the Methodist Archives and Research Centre at The John Rylands University Library, The University of Manchester. Peter Nockles, Gareth Lloyd, and the Reading Room staff exhibited professionalism and kindness, making the experience a delight. I wish to thank the library staff of Northwest Nazarene University as well for partnering with me in this research by going the extra mile in assisting me in obtaining the needed literary resources. Finally, I am thankful for friends and family who have prayed for and encouraged me, first in the completion of my doctoral degree at The University of Manchester (Nazarene Theological College) and now in the completion of this volume. I am also indebted to the members of the Wesleyan Theological Society who recognized my work with the 2011 Outstanding Dissertation Award and to Robin Parry of Wipf and Stock for giving me the opportunity to publish my findings on this topic that was heretofore largely untouched in Wesley Studies. I am particularly thankful for my father who, until his final breath, exhorted

Acknowledgments

me to carry this project on to completion. I must also express my deep appreciation to my mother, Alberta Rodes; my in-laws, Don and Beverly Toland; my siblings and siblings-in-law; and certainly for my children, Stephanie (and Tim) Knapp and Scott (and Marisa) Rodes. Above all, I have no words to express my deep gratitude for my wife, Cindy, who has been steadfast in love, support, and prayer despite enduring many quiet evenings, long absences, and postponed plans. And above all, thanks be to God who gave sufficient strength from day to day.

Abbreviations

AM	*Arminian Magazine*
WTJ	*Wesleyan Theological Journal*
ACL	*A Christian Library: Consisting of Extracts from, and Abridgement of the choicest Pieces of Practical Divinity which have been published in the English Tongue,* 50 vols. (Bristol: F. Farley, 1749–55).
ACL (Jackson)	*A Christian Library: Consisting of Extracts . . . in Thirty Volumes,* edited by Thomas Jackson (London: Printed by T. Cordeux for T. Blanshard, 1819).
DNB	*Oxford Dictionary of National Biography,* edited by H. C. G. Matthew and Brian Harrison (Oxford: Oxford University Press, 2004. Online edition, 2008). http://www.oxforddnb.com.
ENNT (xxxx)	*Explanatory notes upon the New Testament. By John Wesley, M. A. Late Fellow of Lincoln-College, Oxford.* (London: publisher unnamed, 1788). All citations reference this edition unless specified otherwise with the year of a prior edition inserted parenthetically.
Letters	*The Letters of the Rev. John Wesley, A.M.,* Edited by John Telford. Standard edition. 8 vols. (London: Epworth, 1931).
Minutes, xxxx (Bennet)	*John Ben[n]et's Manuscript Minutes of the Early Methodist Conferences,* 1744–48. Methodist Archives. The University of Manchester (1977/429). The Conference year referenced varies from citation to citation.

Abbreviations

Minutes, xxxx (Jackson)	"Some Late Conversations between the Rev. Mr. Wesleys and Others," *The Works of John Wesley*, edited by Thomas Jackson, Volume 8 (London: Methodist Publishing House, 1831). The Conference year referenced varies from citation to citation.
Minutes (WMC, 1770)	*Minutes of several conversations between the Reverend Messieurs John and Charles Wesley, and others* (London: Wesleyan Methodist Church Conference, 1770).
Works (BE)	*The Bicentennial Edition of the Works of John Wesley*, edited by Frank Baker and Richard P. Heitzenrater (Nashville: Abingdon, 1976–).
Works (Jackson)	*The Works of the Rev. John Wesley, A.M.*, edited by Thomas Jackson, 14 vols. (London: Methodist Publishing House, 1831).

Introduction

THE VERY TITLE OF this volume makes a claim and extends an invitation. Simply put, the claim is this: John Wesley was an adherent of covenant theology. The invitation is to investigate Wesley's thought in light of this claim. Accepting this invitation is not without risk, as well-established conclusions regarding Wesley's thought may need to be revised and their implications for praxis reconsidered. But neither is it without reward: namely, a new and deeper appreciation of the substantial theological underpinnings of his pastoral convictions and counsel.

As a leading figure of the Evangelical Revival in eighteenth-century England, John Wesley labored to define, clarify, and communicate "the Successive Conquests of Grace, and the gradual Process of the Work of God in the Soul."[1] To this end he corresponded frequently with numerous leaders and laity, travelled incessantly, and published extensively as he monitored the growing number of Methodist societies, engaged in controversy, and set pen and voice to persuasive proclamation. In the face of difficulties in his personal life, conflict, and disappointments, Wesley wrestled like Epaphras for the souls of his hearers that they might "stand firm in all the will of God, mature and fully assured."[2] This was his pastoral task and passion, driven and sustained by a vision of the way of salvation that pushed him past parish boundaries and protocols and into the fields and beyond.[3]

From time to time over the course of more than fifty years as Methodism's leader, Wesley made an intriguing and instructive distinction between those who have "the faith of a servant" and those who have "the faith of a son." And in sermons, correspondence, and various publications, he applied this distinction as a way of helping those he led

---

1. Wesley and Wesley, *Hymns and Sacred Poems* (1740), iv.
2. Col 4:12 (NIV 1984).
3. It was in defense of his field-preaching that Wesley declared, "I look upon all the world as my parish; thus far I mean, that in whatever part of it I am, I judge it meet, right, and my bounden duty, to declare unto all that are willing to hear the glad tidings of salvation." Wesley, *Works* (BE), 19:65–66. See also ibid., 19:46.

understand and chart their way forward spiritually. There is no question he viewed the distinction as a helpful summary of convictions that belonged to the core of his soteriology.

There have been many questions, however, as to what this distinction reveals about the substance of those convictions. Indeed, the conclusions reached by respected scholars about what Wesley intended to say by his use of the metaphors have been not only divergent but sometimes diametrically-opposed to each other. It is noteworthy that the one thing these diverse conclusions have in common, beyond the servant-son distinction itself, is that none of them indicate any recognition of the relationship between the metaphors and Wesley's appropriation of classic covenant theology. A short tour of these conclusions tells the story best.

In *John Wesley's Theology Today* Colin Williams concluded that the distinction between servant and son indicates that Wesley understood justification to have two movements: "Preliminary faith, which includes the free response to God's prevenient grace and a desire to please him but is still only the 'faith of a servant'" and "Justifying faith proper, which is a sure trust and confidence in Christ bringing a conviction of forgiveness, this being 'the faith of a son.'"[4] Bernhard Holland, however, suggested that John Wesley "finally came to accept that there are *three* kinds of faith which suffice to give acceptance with God: *suppliant faith* (the effort to keep God's law and a pleading for a deeper faith); *justifying faith* (an assurance that "Christ died for me"); and *saving faith* (an assurance of God's pardon)."[5] He further contends that while Charles Wesley viewed suppliant faith—the faith of a servant—as justifying faith, and believed that "the act of supplication itself . . . is met by God's saving response," John Wesley did not equate the two and thus gave no such encouragement to those having "only the faith of a servant."[6]

On the basis of his proposal that John Wesley's theological thought in his later years was more akin to that of Eastern Christianity than to the dominating juridical concerns of Western Christianity, Randy Maddox concludes that "Wesley came to emphasize that there was a crucial degree of regeneration prior to the New Birth: the universal

---

4. Williams, *John Wesley's Theology Today*, 65.

5. Holland, "The Conversions of John and Charles Wesley," 49.

6. Ibid., 53. The great weakness of Holland's argument is that he entrusts too much to Melvill Horne's interpretation of John Wesley's views in Horne's early-nineteenth-century controversy with Thomas Coke concerning the witness of the Spirit, and deals too little with Wesley's own correspondence and publications. See Melvill Horne, *An Investigation of the Definition of Justifying Faith*.

nascent regenerating effect of Prevenient Grace."⁷ This involves Maddox in making an important shift, conceiving of the continuum of grace⁸ as a continuum of regeneration. Accordingly, he concludes that Wesley understood faith to be "justifying from its earliest degree—i.e., the mere inclination to 'fear God and work righteousness.'" However, lacking "clear assurance," this "nascent faith was not yet the fullness of Christian faith" but was "the faith of a 'servant.'"⁹ Thus, the difference between servant and son is not a matter of whether one is justified but is simply a matter of whether one has a sense of assurance regarding her salvation.

Kenneth Collins takes exception to Maddox's conclusion: "Though Wesley did at times link the phrase 'fear God and work righteousness' with justification, he most often associated it with *preparation for* the forgiveness of sins and thereby maintained an important distinction between prevenient grace and justifying grace."¹⁰ For Collins, then, those having the faith of a servant lack assurance precisely because they are neither justified nor regenerated, though they have embarked on the way of salvation. Those having the faith of a son, on the other hand, have been justified and enjoy a sense of pardon as well as a discernible measure of freedom from the power of sin.¹¹

Some Wesley scholars have determined that the distinction between servant and son centers not on the question of justification at all but on the matter of the degree of one's progress in the Christian life. Like Maddox, Theodore Runyon declares unequivocally, "Wesley places the encounter with divine grace and love in Christ, testified to in the Lutheran doctrine of justification, within the context of the Eastern understanding of the transforming power of the Spirit both within us and through us."¹² However, he takes up the servant-son metaphor in

---

7. Maddox, *Responsible Grace*, 159.

8. For the phrase "continuum of grace" see Wynkoop, "Theological Roots," 95. The phrase is used here to refer to the various workings of God's grace as distinguished by Wesley in his sermon, "On Working Out Our Own Salvation": preventing grace, convincing grace, and saving grace. Wesley, *Works* (BE) §II.1, 3:203–4. Wesley does not use the phrase "saving grace" in the sermon but the terminology is commonly supplied to summarize the distinction he describes. See, for example, Williams, *John Wesley's Theology Today*, 40.

9. Maddox, *Responsible Grace*, 127.

10. Collins, "Recent Trends," 68–69.

11. Collins, *The Scripture Way of Salvation*, 55, 58. The views of both Maddox and Collins stand opposed to that of Scott Kisker who suggests that Wesley associated justifying faith with the faith of a servant and regeneration itself with the faith of a son. See Kisker, "Justified but Unregenerate?," 44–58.

12. Runyon, *The New Creation*, 214.

his discussion of Wesley's doctrine of assurance and asserts that Wesley relied on the distinction between servant and son primarily "to point to the advantages which the direct witness of the Spirit brings."[13] Richard Heitzenrater, in his essay "Great Expectations: Aldersgate and the Evidences of Genuine Christianity," treats Wesley's use of the servant-son metaphor simply as one of several descriptions used by Wesley to mark progress on the *via salutis*:

> [Wesley's] later distinctions between two orders of Christians, between the faith of a servant and of a child of God, between the young convert and the mature Christian, between faith and assurance (and allowing for various degrees of both), are all the result of his finally differentiating between justification and sanctification as theologically and experientially distinguishable steps on the spiritual pilgrimage.[14]

Laura Felleman's view falls along the lines of Heitzenrater's. "'Full' or 'Proper' Christian faith," she writes, "refers to the promises of assurance and Christian Perfection. The servant of God has experienced justification, but this degree of faith does not include the full promise of sanctification. . . . The difference between the infant state and the mature state seems to be that those with the faith of a child of God sense the witness of the Spirit."[15] And Wesley Tracy, based on his evaluation of Wesley's extensive correspondence with Ann Bolton, has proposed that Wesley called upon the servant and son metaphors in order to distinguish between those who have been justified and the justified who have gone on to perfection.[16]

The conclusions of Heitzenrater, Felleman, and Tracy were anticipated by Umphrey Lee in *John Wesley and Modern Religion*, published in 1936. By 1770, Lee asserts, Wesley "had adopted the theory of the infinite grades of faith and of assurance which he set forth to more than one correspondent" and "had decided on the division of Christian experience into two stages, the condition of a servant and the condition of a son, which is part of his mature doctrine of Christian Perfection."[17]

---

13. Ibid., 69.

14. Heitzenrater, *Mirror and Memory*, 148.

15. Felleman, "John Wesley and the 'Servant of God,'" 79–80.

16. Tracy, "John Wesley, Spiritual Director," 148–62. Evidence from the available correspondence between Wesley and Bolton, as well as Bolton's own recollection, argue strongly against Tracy's conclusion which relies too uncritically on John Banks' reconstruction of Bolton's spiritual journey. See Banks, *Nancy Nancy*.

17. Lee, *John Wesley and Modern Religion*, 166–67.

Lee is not alone in suggesting that the distinction between the faith of a servant and the faith of a son was a relatively late development in Wesley's theological thought.[18]

This diversity of conclusions might easily be dismissed as par for the course in terms of the nature of scholarly debate. However, such a dismissal is problematic in view of the fact that apparently both Wesley and his reading and listening audience understood the distinction well enough that it rarely needed a lengthy, theological explanation. *Something* important and clarifying was being communicated by Wesley, and that something was specific, pertinent, and reasonably accessible to his recipients.

This observation suggests that inquiries into the servant-son metaphor have looked past, or have overlooked altogether, this important contextual question: what is it about the metaphor that made it theologically amenable to Wesley and accessible to his audience? That is, what was already in place theologically—below the surface, so to speak—when the Methodist Conference in 1746 distinguished between "a Jewish faith" and "the proper Christian faith," and described someone with a Jewish faith as "a servant of God" and someone with a "proper Christian faith" as "a child of God"?[19] Why was this explanation acceptable as an accurate and effective response to the question that had been raised? Fast-forward a couple of decades and the same questions arise. When Wesley wrote to Ann Bolton in 1768, what theological framework gave him the confidence that she would be able to make sense of his affirmation, "[God] has already given you the faith of a servant. You want only the faith of a son"?[20] And twenty years after this, in 1788, what common ground was accessed in his sermon "On the Discoveries of Faith" when Wesley admonished his readers to advance "'from faith to faith'; from the faith of a *servant* to the faith of a *son*"?[21]

Responding to the contextual question, this study demonstrates that Wesley's contrasting of the metaphors of servant and son provided both him and his audience a definitive narrative of the way of salvation, and that this narrative is grounded in his covenant theology. Indeed, it is

---

18. Felleman, for example, suggests the summer of 1766 as a turning point and as the time frame during which Wesley jettisoned Peter Böhler's teaching on the instantaneous blessings of faith. Felleman, "John Wesley and the 'Servant of God,'" 86. M. S. Fujimoto argues that the metaphor signals a late and significant shift in Wesley's view of justification. Fujimoto, "John Wesley's Doctrine of Good Works," 257–59.

19. *Minutes*, 1746 (Jackson), Q. 9–11, 8:287–88.

20. Wesley, "John Wesley to Ann Bolton, April 7, 1768," *Letters*, 5:86.

21. Wesley, *Works* (BE) §14, 4:35.

this imaging (i.e., the servant-son metaphor) of the narrative that acts as a point of entry for the discovery and exploration of Wesley's covenant theology and serves as the focus of this study.

But what, exactly, *is* covenant theology? As Peter Lillback points out, covenant theology is "an elastic term" whose "varying definitions demonstrate its complexities and vast scope."[22] That being said, getting a handle on what this term means in relation to our present purposes might begin with considering its broadest sense. Covenant theology, says J. I. Packer, is "a hermeneutic . . . a way of reading the whole Bible."[23] Similarly, Michael Horton describes covenant theology as "an architectonic structure" that "holds together the structure of biblical faith and practice."[24] Lillback himself adopts Jürgen Moltmann's description of covenant theology as "a theological method which utilizes the biblical theme of the covenant as the key idea for a) the designation of the relationships of God and man, and b) the presentation of the continuity and discontinuity of redemptive history in the Old and New Testaments."[25]

Yet, while the idea of covenant as an overarching theme surely informed Wesley's theological understanding, this broad sense does not accurately portray the contours of his covenant theology. The reason is that it fails to account for key developments in the century before Wesley that had hued covenant theology into a more sculpted theological construct. By Wesley's time the superstructure of covenant theology that was generally recognized and accepted consisted of two covenants: the covenant of works and the covenant of grace. Upon these two covenants, the basis for and nature of relationship between God and humanity were delineated. The progressive nature of the covenant of grace, culminating in the revelation of Christ and the outpouring of the Holy Spirit, came to be identified in terms of various "moments" (dispensations) of God's redemptive activity. This superstructure is also referred to as theological federalism, emphasizing Adam and Christ as the representative heads, respectively, of these two covenants.[26]

Admittedly, the idea of linking Wesley with covenant theology seems a bit suspect when laid alongside a declaration like Horton's that "*Reformed* theology is synonymous with *covenant* theology."[27] Without

22. Lillback, "The Continuuing Conundrum," 45–46.

23. Witsius and Packer, *The Economy of the Covenants*, 1:np.

24. Horton, *God of Promise*, 13.

25. Lillback, "The Continuuing Conundrum," 46.

26. Some scholars would argue that federal theology is an outgrowth of covenant theology. See Weir, *The Origins of the Federal Theology*.

27. Horton, *God of Promise*, 11.

doubt, the family tree of covenant theology has a Reformed likeness to it. As J. I. Packer notes, "Historically, covenant theology is a Reformed development: Huldreich Zwingli, Henry Bullinger, John Calvin, Zacharias Ursinus, Caspar Olevianus, Robert Rollock, John Preston, and John Ball, were among the contributors to its growth, and the Westminster Confession and Catechisms gave it confessional status."[28] To Packer's shortlist we must certainly add Johannes Cocceius, one of the most influential covenant theologians of the seventeenth century.[29] But this roster of Reformed divines tells only part of the story.

A careful inspection of the historical development of covenant theology discloses that it is something more than Reformed theology. In other words, the inverse of Horton's declaration is considerably less defensible. As the subsequent examination will show, Wesley maintained the superstructure of covenant theology apart from the predestinarian template of Reformed theology that was part and parcel of its historical development. Still, the home field advantage never was Wesley's, as an essentially Reformed perspective remained strongly influential despite the failure of the Puritan experiment of the mid-seventeenth century. In recognition of the established and integral relationship between Reformed theology and covenant theology, in this study "Wesley's covenant theology" means Wesley's *appropriation* of covenant theology.

Still, questions remain concerning the claim of the influence of covenant theology in Wesley's theological thought. Among the various strands of covenant theology, of which was Wesley an adherent? How does knowing this and accounting for it influence our understanding of his soteriology? And if this truly is of significance, hasn't this already received adequate and focused attention by the numerous and noteworthy scholars who have contributed discerning explorations of Wesley's theological thought?

These important questions will certainly be engaged in the following chapters. However, the last question merits some consideration here at the outset. The short answer is that Wesley's covenant theology has received surprisingly little attention. Yet, this is not because his acquaintance with covenant theology has gone wholly unrecognized. In his extensive work on John Wesley's sermons in the Bicentennial Edition of *The Works of John Wesley*, Albert Outler identified covenant theology as part of Wesley's theological heritage. However, the implications of

---

28. Packer, "Introduction," *The Economy of the Covenants*, 1:np.

29. Packer does acknowledge Cocceius but discounts the worthiness of his contribution." Ibid., 1:np.

this for Wesley's thought are left unexplored.[30] Other than this, only Robert Monk and Jason Vickers present specific discussions of the interface of covenant theology with Wesley's theological thought.[31] However, Monk's study, *John Wesley: His Puritan Heritage*, is restricted by the confines of his primary objective and suffers, at points, from a limited understanding of covenant theology in that phase of its development. Vickers' contribution acknowledges the fact of Wesley's acquaintance with covenant theology and introduces aspects of how the theological currents of the day influenced the way his thought interfaced with it. Although Vickers' treatment is necessarily brief, it is, nonetheless, a valuable aid to this neglected area of Wesley Studies.

Aside from Outler, Monk, and Vickers, mention of the relationship of covenant theology to Wesley's theological thought is scarce to non-existent.[32] But why is this? What has side-lined serious investigation of Wesley's covenant theology? While any response to this question is necessarily somewhat speculative, I suggest that the following four factors have contributed toward obscuring the imprint of covenant theology on Wesley's thought.

First, even though Wesley openly articulates the core convictions of covenant theology, at no point does he explicitly speak to its influence on him. However, the significance of this fact is not so much that he *didn't* acknowledge this influence, but that he *didn't have* to draw the connection. The reality is that covenant theology was the dominant dialect of theological discourse in his day[33] and its essential features were woven into the very fabric of his theological thought. At times he clarified aspects of his covenant theology and, frequently, he applied it; but it no more needed to be announced and identified as such than did the fact that he breathed air like everyone else in his audience. Perhaps

---

30. Outler, "Introduction," *Works* (BE), 1:80–81; 1:203 n. 2; 3:175 n. 42. Thomas A. Noble also acknowledges Wesley's acquaintance with covenant theology, noting that in the sermon "The Righteousness of Faith," "Wesley adopts the scheme of federal Calvinism." However, the sense of the observation seems more a recognition of Wesley's making use of the schema of covenant theology rather than an intimation of its integral role in his theological thought. Noble, "John Wesley as a Theologian."

31. See Monk, *John Wesley: His Puritan Heritage*, 96–106 and Vickers, "Wesley's Theological Emphases," 190–206.

32. Rupwate, "The Covenant Theology of John Wesley," 79–90. Though promisingly titled, Rupwate's interest is in Wesley's theology of covenant in relation to Wesley's Covenant Service.

33. Jason Vickers highlights this fact as well, noting that "Anglican theologians in the long eighteenth century . . . spoke a common theological language—namely, the language of covenant." Vickers, "Wesley's Theological Emphases," 191.

for this very reason its persistent voice in Wesley's theological thought has faded from our attention like nondescript white noise, despite its pronounced influence on his vision of the way of salvation. However, as we shall see, the evidence clearly reveals covenant theology was deeply embedded in his theological thought and played an integrative role that left a clear imprint on his soteriology.

A second factor that seems to have come into play might be described as doctrinal profiling. Given the fact that covenant theology, in terms of its historical development, is so entwined with defining a theological framework for the predestinarian views of Calvinism in particular, there seems to be an unspoken and untested assumption that Wesley, as an Arminian, simply would find no common ground with the core theological components of covenant theology.[34] Consequently, it is further assumed that covenant theology really has little if anything to add to a truly Wesleyan understanding of God's redemptive activity in the world.

Yet, it is important to recognize that some difficulty lay in the phrase, "Wesley, as an Arminian." With this epithet comes a whole string of conclusions that make perfect sense for dismissing the influence of covenant theology on Wesley's thought; that is, until considered in light of the historical evidence. Certainly, he was opposed to hyper-Calvinism's Five Points "when these were argued in an absolute sense," as Herbert McGonigle notes.[35] Wesley, however, "believed that his convictions found a place within the framework of Reformed thought and [that] his difference with the Calvinists did not threaten the foundations of Protestant orthodoxy."[36] His rejection of Calvinism was not a wholesale rejection, but reflected a critique of Calvinism in the vein of the rejection of what Ellen More describes as "the more rigid aspects of Calvinist theology" that had emerged from within the culture and polity of English nonconformity during the middle and second-half of the seventeenth century.[37] John Goodwin (1595–1666) is a prime example of this critique from within, and is important to this discussion because he

---

34. There are some notable exceptions to the view that Arminianism and covenant theology are exclusive of one another. See, for example, Blacketer, "Arminius' Concept of Covenant in Its Historical Context," 193–220 and Lettinga, "Covenant Theology Turned Upside Down," 653–69. While Wesley's covenant theology is not a direct reflection of either of these views, these examples are indicative of the breadth of the influence of covenant theology.

35. McGonigle, *Sufficient Saving Grace*, 2.

36. Ibid., 1.

37. More, "John Goodwin and the Origins of the New Arminianism," 51.

had been thoroughly Calvinistic and a solid adherent of covenant theology. And while he ultimately drifted into a rationalistic Arminianism with which Wesley himself would *not* have concurred,[38] it is noteworthy that he retained the elements of covenant theology.[39] Nevertheless, with all of this overlooked—as it seems to have been, for the most part, at least in Wesleyan circles—the superstructure and language of covenant theology has consequently received so little consideration that Wesley's own overt references to his covenant theology are rarely detected much less contemplated.

A third factor is the accumulation of appraisals of Wesley's theology that are thoughtful and compelling *apart* from any consideration of his covenant theology.[40] Over time, this formidable array of studies seems to have inoculated Wesley scholars to the influence of covenant theology on his theological thought. There is nothing intentional or academically-suspect about these very significant contributions to Wesley Studies. Rather, the point here is to call attention to what seems to have been, over the long history of scholarly investigations of Wesley's theological thought, a momentum of assumptions and perspectives that has pushed to the edges the importance of the influence of covenant theology on Wesley.

Lastly, a fourth factor—and perhaps the greatest contributor to the general neglect of covenant theology in relation to Wesley's theological thought—is John Fletcher's "dispensational" understanding of God's saving activity. Fletcher is frequently perceived as Wesley's theological spokesman, largely because Wesley, in the wake of the firestorm created by the publication of the minutes of the 1770 Conference, opted to defer to Fletcher to carry the weight of responding to the fury of the critics of the minutes. And respond Fletcher did, with a passionate and voluminous defense in which he incorporated his own unique understanding of the various dispensations of God's redemptive work. However, the distinctiveness of his views is generally overlooked. W. R.

---

38. McGonigle distinguished Wesley's Arminianism as "evangelical Arminianism" in contrast to the Arminianism that typically embraced rationalism and latitudinarianism. McGonigle, *Sufficient Saving Grace*, 7–9.

39. More, "John Goodwin and the Origins of the New Arminianism," 70. Notably, in his debate with hyper-Calvinist James Hervey, Wesley attached his rejoinder to an extract of Goodwin's *Treatise on Justification* which Goodwin had written in 1642, just as his own critique of high Calvinism was taking shape.

40. Two examples of comprehensive studies of Wesley's thought that immediately come to mind are Kenneth Collins' *The Theology of John Wesley* and Randy Maddox's *Responsible Grace*.

Davies, for example, describes Fletcher's covenant theology as "reminiscent of seventeenth-century covenant theology."[41] While this is true in some respects, the difficulty with Davies' assessment is that it suggests a greater theological continuity than was actually the case. In reality, Fletcher developed a kind of dispensational construct that was *not* a feature of mainstream seventeenth century covenant theology, a fact easily obscured by the tendency to assume that similarity in terminology constitutes equivalence in meaning. Fletcher himself seems to have made just such an assumption, claiming in his unpublished essay on the new birth that both John and Charles Wesley "hold the doctrine of dispensations" in common with him.[42] This, however, would be true only in a general sense. In actual fact, there is no evidence in Wesley's published writings or correspondence that he espoused or subscribed to Fletcher's particular conception of dispensations. In fact, Fletcher's conception of dispensations was the basis of his identifying entire sanctification with Pentecost, a view with which Wesley disagreed.[43]

Nevertheless, it is the case that, by and large, the attention given in Wesley Studies to the idea of dispensations has been almost if not entirely dominated by Fletcher's distinctive views. This may be attributed in part to Fletcher's much more extensive use of the terminology of covenant theology. But even this is dependent on the assumption that Fletcher's views are Wesley's, an assumption rooted in what Peter Forsaith identifies as a perception of Fletcher that is deeply entrenched in a "pro-Wesley historiography."[44] This historiography, contested only relatively recently, appears to find support in Wesley's own *A Short Account of the Life and Death of the Rev. Mr. John Fletcher* (1786) and in his acknowledgement of Fletcher's declension of covenant theology in the opening paragraphs of his (Wesley's) sermon, "On Faith." However, the *Short Account* was motivated not by Wesley's interest in defending Fletcher's rendition of covenant theology but by his concern to portray Fletcher as "the Arminian dogmatic champion and exemplar of Christian perfection."[45] And with respect to the sermon, to take Wesley's appreciation for Fletcher's contribution as Wesley's endorsement of Fletcher at all points is assuming more than the evidence can support. There is merit to Richard Watson's *caveat* that "Mr. Fletcher's writings are not to be considered, in

---

41. Davies, "John William Fletcher of Madeley as Theologian," 222.
42. Fletcher, "An Essay on the Doctrine of the New Birth," 35–56.
43. Raser, *Our Watchword and Song*, 29–30.
44. Forsaith, *Unexampled Labours*, 6.
45. Ibid., 4.

every particular, as expressing the views of Mr. Wesley, and the body of Methodists."[46]

Nevertheless, the promotion of Fletcher's writings especially among American Methodists[47] along with Luke Tyerman's 1882 biography of Fletcher, Wesley's *Designated Successor*, have furthered acceptance of Fletcher as Wesley's theological spokesman. Consequently, Wesley's concept of the dispensations of the covenant of grace—which generally reflects the superstructure of seventeenth-century Reformed covenant theology—has been overrun by Fletcher's. As a result, Wesley's appropriation of covenant theology, if detected at all, has been made to appear embryonic and uneventful in his theological thought. That is, Fletcher is made out to be the one with a developed covenant theology. However, as the ensuing study will demonstrate, there is convincing textual evidence that long before Fletcher added the force of his pen to the Methodist cause, Wesley held a well-developed and thoughtfully nuanced covenant theology and that this significantly shaped his soteriology and informed his pastoral guidance.

Yet, despite Wesley's occasional use of the technical terminology of covenant theology, its pivotal role in his theological thought is not particularly obvious. As it turns out, its imprint and influence on him is evidenced in less direct though no less convincing ways. And as this investigation reveals, there may be no marker of its presence at the core of his thought that is more captivating or more summative of his soteriology than the distinction he made repeatedly between the faith of a servant and the faith of a son.

Accordingly, the opening chapter takes a closer look at the occurrences of this imaging in the John Wesley corpus. By examining the emergence and the momentum of the metaphor in Wesley's sermons, correspondence, and his various other writings, a clearer picture is gained of its value to him. The following chapter explores the ancestry of his covenant theology. For the benefit of having some sense of direction as we delve into this subject, Outler's assertion that Wesley came by covenant theology by way of William Perkins, William Ames, and the Westminster Confession will serve as a guide.[48]

---

46. Watson, *The Life of the Rev. John Wesley*, 70. Watson's statement appears as a footnote in the course of his description of the fall-out of the 1770 Minutes.

47. Wood, "John Fletcher as the Theologian of Early American Methodism," 189–204.

48. Wesley, *Works* (BE), 1:203; fn 2.

Based upon what is discovered about the ancestry of Wesley's covenant theology, chapter 3 examines both Wesley's coherence with and departure from classic covenant theology. Distinctives of his covenant theology come into view and a foundation is laid for the assessment of his soteriology in the final chapter. How covenant theology functions as a hermeneutic for Wesley in his exegesis of scripture is the emphasis of chapter 4, "John Wesley's Covenant Theology and Holy Scripture." The influence of non-Puritan sources on his covenant theology becomes evident in this part of the study.

Chapters 5 and 6 together bring to light the broader historical context of soteriological concerns that influenced the shape of Wesley's covenant theology. Long-standing conversations concerning the role of good works and the question of the divine response to the "responsive unregenerate" are introduced, and Wesley's own engagement on these pivotal matters is considered. The significance of these conversations for Wesley's appropriation of covenant theology becomes increasingly evident in the remainder of the study.

The final chapters focus all of the foregoing on the implications of Wesley's covenant theology for his vision of the way of salvation. Chapters 7 and 8 present his understanding of the salvific sufficiency of the various dispensations of the covenant of grace, introducing his conception of the covenant of grace as multi-dimensional and contrasting his soteriology with what characterized the predominantly Calvinistic covenant theology of his day. Extensive attention is given to his understanding of the role of the Holy Spirit in light of his covenant theology. Chapter 9 illustrates Wesley's appropriation of covenant theology at the pastoral level, providing a rich and intriguing view of his understanding of the way of salvation and his conscientious endeavor to draw out the role of human response while holding firmly to the Reformation doctrines of *sola gratia* and *sola fidei*. The way Wesley's covenant theology functioned in his theological thought is seen in the capacity of the servant-son metaphor to carry forward this agenda. This is highlighted with specific examples from his dealings with rank and file Methodists. And finally, an epilogue concludes this volume with some observations on the findings of this study and with some initial reflection on the implications of Wesley's covenant theology in helping his Methodists find their place in the unfolding story of their salvation: the story of a servant, the story of a son—the story of encounter with the God of all grace and the divine invitation to advance "from faith to faith."[49]

---

49. Wesley, "On the Discoveries of Faith," *Works* (BE) §14, 4:35.

CHAPTER 1

John Wesley's Imaging of Covenant Theology

When John Wesley compiled and published *A Collection of Hymns, for the Use of the People Called Methodists* in 1780, he saw to it that the hymns were "not carelessly jumbled together, but carefully ranged under proper heads, according to the experience of real Christians."[1] A glance at the table of contents is revealing. Wesley traces "the experience of real Christians" from start to finish—from before their first setting foot on the way of salvation to mourning under conviction of sin to groaning for and experiencing "full Redemption."[2] Paul Ricoeur describes such a portrayal as emplotment: "the capacity to set forth a *story*" in which events are configured into a meaningful totality.[3] Without doubt, Wesley intended that with this hymnbook in hand his Methodists would be able to both gauge and further their progress on the way of salvation. Yet in no way did he envision this story as a story of his own making. Rather, as we shall discover, he conceived of what had transpired in the lives of these "real Christians" in terms of the storyline of God's reconciling humanity to himself as revealed in Scripture. And in his view (though certainly not in his view alone) covenant theology both configured that storyline into "a meaningful totality" and provided a biblically-rooted framework from which the complexities of "the work of God in the Soul" might be parsed.

---

1. Wesley, *A Collection of Hymns*, §4, iv.

2. Wesley should likely be understood to mean that the gamut represented has been distilled from the testimonies of those who have progressed on the way of salvation to now being, in his estimation, "real Christians." However, this qualification is still subject to Wesley's quite elastic use of the phrase, as discussed later in this volume.

3. Ricoeur, *Figuring the Sacred*, 11–12. The comments above belong to Mark Wallace in his introduction to this anthology of Ricoeur's work.

As was noted earlier, Wesley does not explicitly address the matter of the role of covenant theology in his theological thought. For him, covenant theology is a given—a fact easily overlooked by those of us so far removed in so many ways from the setting in which he labored. Thus, his repeated distinction between those who have "the faith of a servant" and those who have "the faith of a son" appears to present-day readers of Wesley as something of an enigma, as evidenced in the array of conclusions drawn as to what he intended to communicate by it.[4] On closer inspection, however, Wesley's distinction is a clarion marker of covenant theology's presence in his theological thought. And as such, to speak in terms of servant and son as being a distinction made by Wesley is a bit misleading in that it suggests that it originated with him. There is, in fact, compelling evidence that this is not the case. But neither is it the case that the distinction is nothing more than a matter of his tapping into these metaphors on account of their presence in Scripture. It *is* this, but it is far *more* than this; for these metaphors had come to embody soteriological affirmations central to covenant theology and to represent its very superstructure. Furthermore, this embodiment was already generally familiar to his audience; and Wesley, seizing upon this established imaging of covenant theology, strategically employed it in his correspondence, sermons, and publications.

Yet, however convincing—or, at least, enticing—these assertions may be, it remains to demonstrate their credibility. And this is the aim of the remainder of this study. But to begin, our attention turns in earnest to the examination of the servant and son metaphors in Wesley's theological thought. This imaging is of great importance to him for it summarizes foundational elements of his soteriology, something Wesley himself acknowledges in two late sermons.[5] Becoming acquainted, then, with his use of the servant-son metaphor is essential and also provides opportunity to become more familiar with the terminology and theological superstructure of covenant theology in general. Our examination opens with an abbreviated chronological survey of the occurrences of the metaphor in the John Wesley corpus, and is followed by an assessment of this textual evidence. But before proceeding, attention must be given to three considerations critical to a proper evaluation of Wesley's use of the metaphor.

First, it is crucial that the servant and son metaphors be understood as metaphors. This may seem obvious, but inattentiveness on this point

---

4. See the Introduction.
5. The sermons "On Faith" and "On the Discoveries of Faith" were written in 1788.

has contributed to shuttering the view of Wesley's covenant theology that comes to light in his use of these metaphors. According to Aristotle, Ricoeur notes, "the power of metaphor . . . is 'to set before the eyes.'"[6] It accomplishes this mission by "presenting one idea under the sign of another that is more striking or better known."[7] Thus, when Wesley writes in his August 29, 1777 letter to Alexander Knox, "You are not yet a son, but you are a servant"[8] an image is set before Knox's eyes. Knox is not a servant, literally; but the twist of the literal meaning produces a characterization.[9] And it does this by transposing an entire realm (the realm of servant-master relationships) into the place where another realm normally governs[10] (for example, Knox's actual life setting). As a result, when Knox reads "You are a servant" the properties of servant-master relationships now take the driver's seat as he contemplates his life—and specifically in this context, his spiritual journey. Of course, this has a substantially different meaning for Knox than the meaning that very *same* realm of servant-master relationships held for those who heard Wesley describe George Whitefield as a servant when he preached his sermon, "On the Death of George Whitefield."

To be able to distinguish between multiple meanings attached to the same metaphor, says Samuel Guttenplan, is to be "metaphor-sighted": to understand what characteristics are to be emphasized and which are to be suppressed.[11] Thus, when Wesley speaks of Whitefield as a servant of God, one subset of those features associated with "servant" (faithful, loyal, diligent) is given priority, whereas with Knox, another subset is given priority (doubtful, fearful, without the privileges and comfort of a son). The point here is that metaphor is far more than mere substitution. To regard it as substitution is to reduce metaphor to nothing more than wrapping to be torn away.[12] However, rather than to *rename* (i.e., merely substitute), the function of metaphor is to *characterize* what is *already* named and, through the re-description of reality that occurs in the characterization, to actually confer an insight.[13]

6. Ricoeur, *The Rule of Metaphor*, 235.
7. Ibid., 99.
8. Wesley, *Letters*, 6:272–73.
9. Ricoeur, *The Rule of Metaphor*, 272.
10. Ibid., 278.
11. Guttenplan, *Objects of Metaphor*, 21.
12. Ricoeur, *The Rule of Metaphor*, 93.
13. Ibid., 99, 101. Part of this re-description is the power of metaphor to reach beyond evoking new understanding to infusing the feeling attached to the transposed realm. See Ibid., 224, 269.

The second consideration follows from this; namely, treating metaphors as literary objects that can be reduced to one-to-one correspondence like a scale model[14] is a simplification that obscures the very insight they are intended to deliver. Consider, for example, the commonly-held conclusion that the central issue addressed by Wesley in his use of the metaphors is the matter of assurance of pardon. In this view, when Wesley says, "You are only a servant" he is saying, "You do not yet have an assurance of pardon"; and when he says, "You are a Son," he is saying "You *do* have an assurance of pardon."[15]

But what possible advantage would Wesley hope to gain by *not* speaking with Knox on the matter of assurance in a more direct manner, as he does with others on this very subject? Surely, such a view suffers from regarding the metaphor as purely ornamental, to use Ricoeur's term;[16] and the end result is to *obscure* meaning rather than to confer insight! The same may be said of investigations that reduce Wesley's use of the metaphor to the single question, "Is the person with the faith of a servant justified or not?" This certainly is an intriguing and important question, but answering it does not appear to be the primary motive behind Wesley's employment of the servant and son metaphors. Indeed, he passed up many opportunities to answer this particular question unequivocally. In the end, regarding metaphor as merely ornamental turns Wesley's use of the servant-son metaphor into a clever (and confusing!) ploy when in reality it reflects a rich and carefully nuanced application of his appropriation of covenant theology.

Third, it is helpful to recognize that Wesley knowingly used the servant and son metaphors in both a *synthetic* and *antithetic* sense. His commentary on the opening phrase of Jude 1 ("Jude, a servant of Jesus Christ") provides a concise orientation to these two uses. He notes that after the sending of the Son, the term "servant" signifies one "having the spirit of adoption" and describes "the fruit and perfection of being . . . a son."[17] Thus, although each metaphor effectively retains the force of its respective, diverse subset of human relations (servant-master/

---

14. Ibid., 283.

15. While both Maddox and Collins arrive at different conclusions on the question of whether or not Wesley viewed the servant as one who was justified, both of them, in the end, reduce the metaphor to being primarily representative of Wesley's view of assurance. Collins, *The Theology of John Wesley*, 131–36 and Maddox, *Responsible Grace*, 124–27.

16. Ricoeur, *The Rule of Metaphor*, 24.

17. Wesley, *ENNT*, 803.

child-parent), they are, in this case, *synthetic*;[18] that is, their relation is both-and or complementary—two sides of the same coin, we might say.

In the *antithetic* use of the metaphors, on the other hand, "servant"—which when taken in the context of "the old Covenant, was adapted to the spirit of fear and bondage"[19]—is intended *solely* to stand in *contrast* to "son" (which describes one who has received the spirit of adoption). In this use, the metaphors stand in either-or relation to each other. Additionally, they characteristically appear together (or, if not together, with the missing metaphor implicitly present) and make a theological statement *as a couplet*. For this reason, in this study the two metaphors will often be referred to as the servant-son metaphor. This antithetic sense is exemplified in Wesley's letter to Alexander Knox discussed above. And, *it is exclusively in this antithetic sense that Wesley makes use of the metaphors in his imaging of covenant theology.*

Yet, while this antithetic relationship of "servant" and "son" is inherent to Galatians 4:1–7, one of the foundational biblical texts of covenant theology, it is not the case that every *antithetic* use of these terms by Wesley necessarily images his appropriation of covenant theology. The fact is that he found the metaphors of servant and son quite adaptable in providing biblical support for various theological affirmations. In his preface to *Hymns and Sacred Poems* (1740), for example, Wesley appealed to the Galatians passage in order to encourage those who had a "sure trust and confidence" of being "'reconciled to the Favour of God'" but who are not born of God "in the full sense."[20] These persons are not children of the devil, he declared; rather, they are under-aged children who, for that reason, "differeth nothing from a Servant." Nevertheless, he goes on to argue, they are heirs, and, for *this* reason, are—even as servants—"yet Lord of all."[21] Here he underscored the *continuity* between servant and son that is found in their status as heir.

Conversely, in his sermon, "Christian Perfection" (1741), Wesley appealed to the same passage to accentuate the discontinuity between servant and son and conveyed this *discontinuity* as exemplary of "the wide difference there is between the Jewish and the Christian dispensation."[22]

---

18. The term is used here in the broad sense of its root meaning (= to place together) and strictly to emphasize conceptual proximity.

19. Wesley, *ENNT*, 803.

20. Wesley would later ascribe to entire sanctification the characteristics of being born again "in the full sense."

21. John Wesley and Charles Wesley, *Hymns and Sacred Poems* (1740), viii.

22. Wesley, *Works* (BE) §II.11, 2:110.

It is this discontinuity that stands at the heart of his argument that while from Adam to Christ "there was *then* no man that sinned not," it *now* is made possible, since the giving of the Holy Spirit, that "He that is born of God sinneth not."[23] In the context of this sermon, Wesley's emphasis is upon the distinction between the giving of the Holy Spirit and "his sanctifying graces" (a spiritual advance reserved for the Christian dispensation) and "the miracle-working power" of the Spirit (that which exemplified the extent of the Spirit's work within the confines of the Jewish dispensation and was evident in the lives of the Apostles).[24] What is significant here is that this antithetic use of the metaphors with its sharp emphasis on the *discontinuity* between servant and son is consistent with the enduring association of the metaphors with the superstructure of covenant theology.[25] However, despite this connection, Wesley's use of the metaphors in this particular instance anticipates but is not representative of what would become their more *characteristic* role in voicing the soteriological affirmations of his appropriation of classic covenant theology.

It was not long, though, before Wesley came to more clearly distinguish sanctification from justification;[26] and with this development the metaphors seem to have settled into a more specifically-defined role in his soteriology. His use of the metaphors continued to reflect the correlations found in Galatians 4: the servant metaphor with fear and the spirit of bondage, and the son metaphor with love and the spirit of adoption. However, from the mid-1740s to the end of his life, Wesley's employment of these metaphors was more consonant with their place in classic covenant theology where they represented defining moments in God's redemptive activity in and for the world as well as a pattern of the experience of the "gradual process of the work of God" in the lives of "real Christians."

---

23. Ibid., §II.10, 14, 2:109, 111.

24. Ibid., §II.11, 2:110. The emergence of a clearer distinction between justification and sanctification contributed toward some re-shaping the role of the servant-son metaphor in his theological thought.

25. Ibid., §II.10, 2:109. The distinction between the Jewish and Christian dispensations is part of the well-established technical terminology of covenant theology. Wesley's familiarity with this terminology is further evident in his identifying the Jewish dispensation with "the infant state of the church."

26. Heitzenrater, *Mirror and Memory*, 147.

Wesley's Deployment of the Servant-Son Metaphor

The first documentable appearance of this more characteristic use of the servant-son metaphor by Wesley occurs in 1746, eight years after his Aldersgate experience and a relatively short but significant distance from the earliest days of the Revival. It is clearly referenced in the minute record of the Conference held in May at the New-Room in Bristol. At this conference deliberations at the Conferences in 1744 and 1745 on justification continued and centered on the nature of justifying faith. Early on in the discussion the experience of one of the conferees, Jonathan Reeves, was taken up as a case study on the point:

> Q. 9. By what faith were the Apostles clean before Christ died?
>
> A. By such a faith as this; by a Jewish faith: For "the Holy Ghost was not then given."
>
> Q. 10. Of whom then do you understand those words, 'Who is among you that feareth the Lord, that obeyeth the voice of his servant, that walketh in darkness, and hath no light?' (Isaiah [50].10.)
>
> A. Of a believer under the Jewish dispensation; one in whose heart God hath not yet shined, to give him the light of the glorious love of God in the face of Jesus Christ.
>
> Q. 11. Who is a Jew, inwardly?
>
> A. A servant of God: One who sincerely obeys him out of fear. Whereas a Christian, inwardly, is a child of God: One who sincerely obeys him out of love . . . .[27]

That same year, this same use of the servant-son metaphor appears in Wesley's sermon, "The Spirit of Bondage and of Adoption." The language of this sermon closely resembles that of the Conference minutes:

> St. Paul here speaks to those who are the children of God by faith. . . . "Ye have not received the spirit of bondage again unto fear"; but "because ye are sons, God hath sent forth the Spirit of his Son into your hearts." "Ye have received the Spirit of adoption, whereby we cry, Abba, Father." The spirit of bondage and fear is widely distant from this loving Spirit of adoption. Those who are influenced only by slavish fear cannot be termed the *sons* of God. Yet some of them may be styled his *servants*, and "are not far from the kingdom of heaven."[28]

---

27. *Minutes*, 1746 (Jackson), 8:287–88.
28. Wesley, *Works* (BE) §1–2, 1:249–50. Emphasis mine.

Later in the sermon, Wesley declares: "One who is . . . without fear or love, is in Scripture termed 'a natural man.' One who is under the spirit of bondage and fear is sometimes said to be 'under the law.' . . . But one who has exchanged the spirit of fear for the spirit of love is properly said to be 'under grace.'"[29] After distinguishing these three states—labeled the natural, the legal, and the evangelical[30] later in the sermon—Wesley draws upon the metaphor again as a way of clarifying the seriousness of the situation for those who are in the natural state:

> Have you the Spirit of adoption, ever crying, "Abba, Father"? Or do you cry unto God as "out of the belly of hell," overwhelmed with sorrow and fear? Or are you a stranger to this whole affair, and cannot imagine what I mean? Heathen, pull off the mask. Thou hast never put on Christ. Stand barefaced. Look up to heaven; and own before him that liveth for ever and ever, thou hast no part either among the sons or servants of God.[31]

While there is no indicator that the servant-son metaphor was any differently conceived or of any less importance to Wesley over the intervening years, it is not until the first edition of his *Explanatory Notes Upon the New Testament* in 1755 that the metaphor again appears in the John Wesley corpus. In three passages of scripture in particular, it exerts a marked influence on the commentary. On John 17:24 Wesley follows very closely the commentary of J. A. Bengel whose *Gnomon of the New Testament* he relied upon as one of his primary sources. Though the verse reads simply, "Father, I will that these also whom thou hast given me, be with me where I am," Bengel brings into play the metaphors of servant and son. Wesley follows suit but reconfigures Bengel's comment in two ways: first, he preserves not only the antithetic relationship of servant and son, but strengthens the idea of progression (from servant to son)—a notion clearly evident in the 1746 uses of the metaphor; and second, he generalizes Bengel's comment in a way that emphasizes the privileges that accrue to *all* those who are sons of God and not servants only.[32]

---

29. Wesley, *Works* (BE) §5, 1:250.
30. Ibid., IV.1, 1:262.
31. Ibid., IV.1, 1:263.
32. Wesley, *ENNT* (1755), 276–77. Bengel, *Gnomon*, 2:15–16. In the first instance of his reconfiguring of Bengel's comment, Wesley reverses the order in which Bengel references the metaphors. And in the second instance, whereas Bengel had particularized "the Son," Wesley makes the designation anarthrous thus emphasizing the position and privilege of sonship in general rather than the unique place of Jesus as the Son of God.

A second passage where the metaphor appears in Wesley's commentary is Romans 1:7, "To all that are in Rome, *who are* beloved of God, called *and* holy, Grace to you, and peace from God the Father, and the Lord Jesus Christ."[33] Replicating Bengel's comment on the last portion of the verse, Wesley writes: "This is the usual way wherein the Apostles speak, 'God the Father,' 'God our Father' . . . In the Old Testament indeed, the holy men generally said, The Lord our God. For they [the holy men] were then as it were *Servants*; whereas now they [the Apostles] are *Sons*. And Sons so well know their Father, that they need not frequently mention his proper Name."[34]

Jude 1 is the third appearance of the metaphor in his New Testament *Notes*. Commenting on "servant," Wesley takes opportunity, as noted above, to explain how this particular use of the term relates uniquely to the primary terminology of the metaphor:

> V. 1. *Jude, a servant of Jesus Christ* . . . The word *Servant*, under the Old Covenant, was adapted to the Spirit of Fear and Bondage that clave to that Dispensation. But when the time appointed of the Father was come, for the sending of his Son to redeem them that were under the Law, the word *Servant* (used by the Apostles concerning themselves and all the children of God) signified one that having the Spirit of *Adoption* is made *free* by the Son of God. His being a *Servant* is the Fruit and Perfection of his being a Son. And whenever the Throne of God and of the Lamb shall be in the new Jerusalem, then will it be indeed that *his Servants will serve him*, Rev. xxii.[35]

There are two important observations regarding these three occurrences of the metaphor in Wesley's New Testament *Notes*. First, there is nothing inherent in any of these biblical texts themselves that requires exposition in terms of the servant-son metaphor. Indeed, in only one instance—that of Jude 1—does there even appear a term common to the metaphor. Second, and most significantly, Wesley's comment on Jude 1 appears to be entirely his own rather than borrowed from any of his sources. This is an indication that he considered the metaphor to be of sufficient theological value to preserve certain critical distinctions and relationships, as evidenced by his integrating portions of two Pauline texts (Rom 8:15–16 and Gal 4:1–7) into his very brief excursus on the servant-son metaphor included in his comment on Jude 1. What

33. Wesley, *ENNT* (1755), 382.
34. Ibid. Brackets and emphasis mine. Compare Bengel, *Gnomon*, 2:16.
35. Wesley, *ENNT* (1755), 688.

is important about this fact is that both of these texts were appealed to as the biblical basis of theological affirmations central to covenant theology. Wesley's commentary on Jude 1, then, also suggests a conscious decision on his part to include rather than ignore Bengel's employment of the servant and son metaphors in his commentary on John 17:24 and Romans 1:7.

Explicit occurrences of the metaphor in Wesley's correspondence first appear in the late 1760s. As a result of his preaching to the "large and deeply attentive" congregation at Witney, Oxfordshire as early as January 1764,[36] Wesley became acquainted with a young woman named Ann Bolton, establishing what John Telford describes as "one of the closest friendships and most sustained correspondence of Wesley's life."[37] He first references the metaphor in a letter to Bolton written at Liverpool on April 7, 1768:

> Indeed, my dear sister, the conversation I had with you at London much increased my affection for you and my desire that you should not fall short of any blessing which our Lord has bought for you with His own blood. Certain it is that He loves you. And He has already given you the faith of a servant. You want only the faith of a child.[38]

The correspondence continued in a similar vein the remainder of that year and throughout the next. On August 12, 1770, Wesley wrote to her yet again. This letter must be noted for it revisits essential features of the metaphor using expressions that reappear in the declarations of Wesley's sermon "On Faith," eighteen years later:

> "He that feareth God," says the Apostle, "and worketh righteousness," though but in a low degree, is accepted of Him; more especially when such an one trusts not in his own righteousness but in the atoning blood. I cannot doubt at all but this is your case; though you have not that joy in the Holy Ghost to which you are called, because your faith is weak and only as a grain of mustard seed.[39]

By this time, two years and nine months had elapsed since the first record of correspondence between Wesley and Miss Bolton, and perhaps

---

36. Wesley, *Works* (BE), 21:441–42.

37. Wesley, *Letters*, 5:80.

38. Ibid., 5:86. In keeping with its usage in Wesley's day, the term "want" should be read as "need" or "lack."

39. Ibid., 5:197.

six years since their first encounter. At this point, Wesley makes a second explicit application of the metaphor. In a letter dated at London on November 16, 1770, he writes, "I am glad you are still waiting for the kingdom of God: although as yet you are rather in the state of a servant than of a child. But it is a blessed thing to be even a servant of God! You shall never have cause to be ashamed of His service."[40] Though Wesley continued corresponding with her, this letter was the last in which he employed the metaphor in relation to her spiritual progress.

A few years later, in 1774 and 1775, Wesley published two new editions of his *Works*. In each of these editions Wesley clarified—even corrected—several journal entries with the help of the servant-son metaphor.[41] In the original assessment of his own spiritual condition described in his journal entry of January 29, 1738, Wesley listed the righteous deeds that might have been viewed as commending him to God, and then concluded: "If the oracles of God are true, if we are still to abide by 'the law and the testimony,' all these things, though when ennobled by faith in Christ they are holy, and just, and good, yet without it are 'dung and dross,' meet only to be purged away by 'the fire that never shall be quenched.'"[42] Wesley now clarified this early evaluation of his spiritual state by inserting the words, "I had even then the faith of a *servant*, though not that of a *son*" after the phrase "ennobled by faith in Christ."[43] The addition appears only in the *errata*, the printer having failed to add the footnote as Wesley had instructed.

Wesley's original journal entry had continued the condemnatory assessment: "This then have I learned in the ends of the earth, that I am 'fallen short of the glory of God'; that my whole heart is 'altogether corrupt and abominable,' and consequently my whole life . . . ; that 'alienated' as I am 'from the life of God,' I am 'a child of wrath,' an heir of hell."[44] Prompted to bring this conclusion in line with his amendment of the sentence just previous, Wesley added, "I believe not" immediately after the word "wrath." This addition, too, also appears only in the *er-*

---

40. Ibid., 5:207.

41. See Wesley, *Works* (BE), 24:350–51 and 18:214–16, the notes to the text of the journal. These references to the metaphor added to the journal entry of January 29, 1738 are replicated as footnotes in Jackson's edition of Wesley's *Works* but do not reflect omissions found in the 5th edition (1775). These omissions are retained by Joseph Benson in his 1809 edition but the footnotes appended to the January 29, 1738 entry are not included. See John Wesley, *Works* (Benson), 1:250–52.

42. Wesley, *Works* (BE), 18:214–15.

43. Ibid., 18:215.

44. Ibid.

rata. The metaphor continues to come into play as Wesley moves on to declare his spiritual aspirations:

> If it be said that I have faith (for many such things have I heard, from many miserable comforters), I answer, So have the devils—*a sort* of faith; but still they are strangers to the covenant of promise. So the apostles had even at Cana in Galilee, when Jesus first "manifested forth his glory"; even then they, in a sort "believed on him"; but they had not then "the faith that overcometh the world." The faith I want is, "a sure trust and confidence in God, that through the merits of Christ my sins are forgiven, and I reconciled to the favour of God."[45]

Here as well, the erratum of the 1774 edition indicates that "the faith of a *son*" was to have been added so that the final sentence in the preceding quote should have begun, "The faith I want is the faith of a *son*, 'a sure trust and confidence in God . . .'"[46]

For yet a third time in Wesley's detail of his spiritual course during this period of his life, he solicits the servant-son metaphor for the purpose, it appears, of clarifying the Methodist morphology of conversion. His journal entry recounting the last several days of April 1738 read, "Accordingly, on Tuesday 25, I spoke clearly and fully at Blendon, to Mr. Delamotte's family, of the nature and fruits of faith. Mr. Broughton and my brother were there. Mr. Broughton's great objection was, he could never think that I had not faith, who had done and suffered such things."[47] At this point in the text, Wesley added a footnote as follows: "He was in the right. I certainly then had the faith of a *servant*, though not the faith of a son."[48]

Near this same time period, Wesley entered into correspondence with another whose spiritual course he came to describe in terms of the servant-son metaphor and its primary themes. Alexander Knox was eight years of age when his father, Alexander Knox, Sr., hosted Wesley when he visited Londonderry, Ireland in 1765.[49] Eleven years later, on January 27, 1776, Wesley's correspondence commenced with his identifying Alexander's prolonged illness as evidence of the divine initiative in the young man's life.[50] It is in his letter written at Penrhyn on August

---

45. Wesley, *Works* (BE), 18:215–16.
46. Ibid.
47. Ibid., 18:234–35.
48. Ibid.
49. Wesley, *Works* (BE), 21:507 and 22:2.
50. Wesley, *Letters*, 6:204–5, 212.

29, 1777 that Wesley profiles the spiritual condition of Alexander Knox in terms of the servant-son metaphor:

> You should read Mr. Fletcher's *Essay on Truth*. He has there put it beyond all doubt that there is a medium between a child of God and a child of the devil—namely, a servant of God. This is *your* state. You are not yet a son, but you are a servant; and you are waiting for the Spirit of adoption, which will cry in your heart, "Abba, Father."[51]

Over the next five years, themes frequently associated with the metaphor continue to emerge in Wesley's admonitions to Alexander Knox.[52]

Yet another occurrence of the metaphor is found in a letter from one with whom Wesley had conversed most likely in May 1778 while in Sligo, a town eighty-five miles southwest of Londonderry. While the correspondence does not appear to have been extensive, it was sufficiently significant to Wesley for him to eventually publish in the *Arminian Magazine*. The letter, written at Belfast on July 22, 1779, carried the news that the correspondent, a Methodist preacher from Ireland, would not be making the journey to London to discuss with Wesley his "present state of mind" and offered the following explanation:

> When I told you my state in Sligo, you observed, it was that of a servant, and not of a son. It is no better with me since. I feel my bondage great through unbelief, and such deadness of soul that I cannot mourn with those who mourn, nor rejoice with those who rejoice. Hence my zeal is very low, and I am condemned for doing the Lord's work so negligently. . . . I refer it to you whether it would not be better to decline so public a character, until I have experienced a larger degree of grace.[53]

Just seven years later, the metaphor again appears in one of Wesley's sermons. At Wakefield on the morning of May 1, 1786 Wesley finished his sermon, "On Friendship with the World." In his strong admonition that his hearers live wholly aligned to "'the good, and acceptable, and perfect will of God,'"[54] Wesley found it helpful to call upon the

---

51. Ibid. 6:272–73.

52. See Wesley's letters to Alexander Knox dated April 2, 1778; July 11, 1778; December 23, 1779; and December 23, 1780. Ibid. 6:309, 315, 364; 7:44.

53. "Letter CCCCLXXXVII [From Mr. A. B. to the Rev. J. Wesley]," *AM* (March 1789), 162.

54. Wesley, *Works* (BE), 3:127–28.

metaphor as a way of establishing a minimum standard for believers contemplating marriage:

> Above all we should tremble at the very thought of entering into a marriage covenant, the closest of all others, with any person who does not love, or at least, fear God. . . . "Be not unequally yoked with an unbeliever." Nothing can be more express. Especially if we understand by the word "unbeliever'" one that is so far from being a believer in the gospel sense—from being able to say, "The life which I now live, I live by faith in the Son of God, who loved me and gave himself for me"—that he has not even the faith of a servant: he does not "fear God and work righteousness."[55]

This is the first appearance in his sermons of this particular way of phrasing the metaphor (i.e., "faith of a servant").[56]

Less than two years later, Wesley wrote "On Faith." The phrasing of the metaphor in this sermon is the same used in his 1786 sermon noted above and also appears in another sermon written that same year, "On the Discoveries of Faith." In the latter sermon Wesley continues his effort of making certain that Methodists are "sufficiently apprised of the difference between a servant and a child of God":[57]

> But still let it be carefully observed (for it is a point of no small importance) that this faith is only the faith of a servant, and not the faith of a son. Because this is a point which many do not clearly understand, I will endeavour to make it a little plainer. . . . Whoever has attained this, the faith of a servant, "feareth God and escheweth evil"; or, as it is expressed by St. Peter, "feareth God and worketh righteousness." In consequence of which he is in a degree (as the Apostle observes), "accepted with him". Elsewhere he is described in those words, "He that feareth God, and keepeth his commandments." Even one who has gone thus far in religion, who obeys God out of fear, is not in any wise to be despised, seeing "the fear of the Lord is the beginning of wisdom." Nevertheless he should be exhorted not to stop there; not to rest till he attains the adoption of sons; till he obeys out of love, which is the privilege of all the *children* of God.
>
> Exhort him to press on by all possible means, till he passes "from faith to faith"; from the faith of a *servant* to the faith of a

---

55. Wesley, *Works* (BE) §12, 3:132.

56. The very first appearance of this phrasing was in Wesley's letter to Ann Bolton on April 7, 1768 shown above.

57. Wesley, "On Faith," *Works* (BE) §I.11, 3:497.

son; from the spirit of bondage unto fear, to the spirit of childlike love. He will then have "Christ revealed in his heart," enabling him to testify, "The life that I now live in the flesh I live by faith in the Son of God, who loved *me*, and gave himself for *me*"— the proper voice of a child of God.[58]

This is the last explicit occurrence in Wesley's correspondence and published writings prior to his death on March 2, 1791.

The Absence, Emergence, and Gathering Momentum of the Servant-Son Metaphor in the Wesley Corpus

The textual evidence is both striking and puzzling. For the metaphor to have made appearances over so long a span of time and to have received so much attention late in Wesley's life, speaks clearly of its value to Wesley for articulating critical aspects of his soteriology.[59] Yet, relative to the number of years from the first occurrence of the metaphor to its last, the frequency of such occurrences is not only surprisingly low but is conspicuously absent from contexts where its appearance might have been most expected. For example, the metaphor is missing in action in those very sermons where it would seem likely to have been found: "Salvation by Faith," "The Almost Christian," "Scriptural Christianity," "Justification by Faith," "The Witness of the Spirit" (Discourses I and II), "The Circumcision of the Heart," "The Marks of the New Birth," "The Great Privilege of Those That are Born of God," "The Scripture Way of Salvation," and "The New Birth" to name a few. In addition to its absence in the vast majority of Wesley's sermons, there are numerous other places where explicit occurrences of the metaphor would seem to have been in order, especially in those contexts speaking to a Methodist understanding of salvation: for example, the two *Appeals* (1743 and 1745), *The Principles of a Methodist Farther Explained* (1746), *A Plain Account of the People Called Methodist* (1748), and *A Short History of Methodism* (1765). It is also noteworthy that explicit occurrences of the servant-son metaphor appear with relative infrequency in Wesley's correspondence even on those occasions when matters are discussed that are clearly and closely associated with it.[60]

---

58. Wesley, "On the Discoveries of Faith," *Works* (BE) §13–14, 4:35–36.

59. Outler states that the metaphor became "a Wesleyan commonplace." Wesley, *Works* (BE) 1:250 n. 4.

60. One such example would be the so-called John Smith correspondence in the mid- to late-1740s in which there is an extensive discussion of Wesley's understanding of

Wesley also does not explicitly reference the metaphor in his commentary on passages of scripture he particularly related to the metaphor. Perhaps most notable is its complete absence from his commentary on Acts 10, the story of Cornelius and the Gentile Pentecost,[61] and particularly on Acts 10:35, "But in every nation, he that feareth him, and worketh righteousness, is accepted of him."[62] Although in later years Wesley enlists this verse as part of the biblical foundation of the metaphor, his extensive commentary on verse 35 includes no discernible incorporation of the servant-son metaphor in *any* of the editions of his New Testament *Notes*. Rather, his comment on the passage remains strictly within the scope of the text itself. It is also absent from his commentary on Romans 8:15–16 and Galatians 4:1–7. With respect to the former passage, while the elements of the passage are clearly present both in his 1746 sermon, "On the Spirit of Bondage and of Adoption" and his 1788 sermons "On Faith" and "On the Discoveries of Faith," Wesley again chooses not to use the commentary as a platform for explaining, introducing, or even alluding to the metaphor.[63] As for Galatians 4:1–7, the metaphor is absent in the sense that there is nothing in the commentary that is *dependent* on the metaphor (in contrast, for example, to his commentary on Jude 1). This is not to say that his commentary on the passage does not exhibit components that are critical to the metaphor, such as the very terms "servant" and "son." However, these terms belong to the text itself and, here again, Wesley's commentary remains within the general scope of the text.

Yet another example of its absence is in the minutes of the Conferences held in 1744 and 1745. There is no record of any reference to the servant-son metaphor throughout the Monday evening discussion on justification during the 1744 Conference, even though this subject was the context of its first appearance in the minutes of the 1746 Conference. This is likewise the case in 1745 when discussion of the same doctrine was taken up again as the conferees responded affirmatively to the proposal "to review the minutes of the last conference with regard to justification."[64] The conversation ranged from a consideration of the role of faith (and included a reading of Richard Baxter's *Aphorisms on*

---

perceptible inspiration. The correspondence consists of twelve letters in all, dated from May 1745 to March 1748.

61. Acts 10:1—11:18. Wesley, *ENNT*, 383–89.
62. Wesley, *ENNT*, 386.
63. Ibid., 484–85.
64. *Minutes*, 1745 (Bennet), 26. See also *Works* (Jackson), 8:281.

Justification) to the nature, certainty, and necessity of assurance, and the matter of the role of good works. While the question of whether or not Cornelius was in the favor of God before he believed came up as a point of discussion, this prompted no introduction of the servant-son metaphor. Interestingly, the brief focus of attention on Cornelius' standing before God centered on Acts 10:2 rather than Acts 10:34–35.

The preceding recital of the absence of explicit occurrences of the metaphor raises questions about its emergence in Wesley's theological thought. Does his use of the servant-son metaphor signal a new development in his theological understanding or does it betray his longstanding theological convictions? And what does its emergence tell us about the theological cargo Wesley entrusted to the metaphor? Or, perhaps the better question is, what does it tell us about the theological cargo Wesley perceived the metaphor to have entrusted to *him*? In order to lay the groundwork for the more extensive exploration of Wesley's use of the servant-son metaphor in the following chapters, it will be helpful to evaluate the chronology of its appearances more closely with respect to the question of emergence.

It is sometimes assumed that the metaphor was part of the nomenclature of Methodist proclamation from the late 1730s.[65] This assumption is normally based on Wesley's comments in his 1788 sermon, "On Faith." At pains in this late sermon to set the record straight regarding the Methodist morphology of conversion, he makes an intriguing reference back to the earliest days of the Revival: "Indeed nearly fifty years ago, when the preachers commonly called Methodists began to preach that grand scriptural doctrine, salvation by faith, they were not sufficiently apprised of the difference between a servant and a child of God."[66] A casual reading of this comment might suggest that the servant-son metaphor was incorporated into the earliest proclamation of Methodists. However, all that can be said with certainty on the basis of Wesley's critique is that it reveals a general failure among early Methodist preachers[67] to communicate what he considered, in his reflection on the matter in 1788, as an accurate understanding of "the work of God in the soul."[68]

---

65. See, for example, Laura Bartels Felleman, "John Wesley and the 'Servant of God,'" 78.

66. Wesley, "On Faith," *Works* (BE) I.10, 3:497.

67. Wesley may have included himself and his brother Charles in this charge. In his 1787 sermon, "The More Excellent Way," Wesley specifically identifies his own tendency in the early days after Aldersgate to be more harsh in his judgments. See *Works* (BE) §I, 3:267. See also Robert Southey, *The Life of Wesley*, 1:295.

68. John Wesley and Charles Wesley, *Hymns and Sacred Poems* (1740), iv.

Its appearance in 1746 in his sermon "The Spirit of Bondage and of Adoption" and in the Conference at its meeting in May seems to be of particular importance. The fact that the metaphor did not come into the picture during the earlier deliberations on justification at the Conferences in 1744 and 1745 suggests at least that the metaphor came to enjoy greater prominence theologically among these early Methodists in 1746 than it had previously. Of course, it must be noted that Wesley had preached from Romans 8:15 (the text of "The Spirit of Bondage and of Adoption") thirteen times *before* publishing this particular sermon in 1746.[69] It is impossible to establish with absolute certainty whether or not he had made use of the metaphor in this particular way when preaching from that text on occasions prior to publishing this sermon. There are, however, indications that the mid-1740s was a formative season in Wesley's theological thought. Aside from the fact of the widening doctrinal divide between Wesley and the Moravians during this period of time and the series of early conferences on soteriological themes, five of the eight sermons Wesley composed or published in 1746 were written on texts from Romans. Outler notes: "This is not accidental, for these are the sermons in which Wesley has distilled the essence of his gospel of justification."[70] The possibility remains that the metaphor—if not a new or newer addition into Wesley's thought—may have gained greater attention in his thinking during this time, thus becoming of sufficient import to him to prompt the publication of this particular sermon on this important text.

There is further evidence, albeit circumstantial, lending support to the mid-1740s as the general time-frame during which the metaphor began to find its place in Wesley's theological thought. As noted above, Wesley seems to have been particularly attuned to J. A. Bengel's emphasis on the distinction between servants and sons, making it a point in his New Testament *Notes* to include Bengel's contrasting of servants and sons even when the biblical texts themselves did not necessitate the comparison.[71] Although Wesley did not publish his New Testament *Notes* until the mid-1750s, both he and his brother Charles appear to have been familiar with Bengel well before that time. This is evidenced by the fact that Bengel appeared on the reading list for students at the

---

69. See Albert Outler's introductory comment on the sermon. Wesley, *Works* (BE), 1:248–49.

70. Ibid.

71. For a close inspection of specific texts where Bengel's influence is clearly evident in Wesley's New Testament *Notes*, see chapter 4.

Kingswood School as early as 1748.[72] That a work (or perhaps several) by Bengel makes it onto the list in the very year the school was founded strongly argues for the familiarity of Wesley (and, most likely, of the others attending the conference) with Bengel and his notable contributions as a biblical scholar.[73] It is certain that Wesley had obtained some of Bengel's works before 1748.[74]

Stronger evidence of Wesley's acquaintance with Bengel's scholarly contributions—and perhaps with his *Gnomon* in particular—dates from September 1747 in a letter to Charles Wesley "at the Foundery," the Wesleys' London headquarters, from a Mr. J. Robertson, who appealed to Charles for help in obtaining various works of Bengel's.[75] Robertson specifically noted that he already owned a copy of Bengel's *Gnomon* and *Ordo Temporum*. Though Bengel's *Gnomon* had been published just a few years earlier in 1742, this example of the attention Bengel's work was commanding within the network of persons associated with the Wesleys gives credence to the likelihood that John Wesley, too, was acquainted with the work by as early as the mid-1740s. It is very possible that Bengel's use of the metaphor contributed to Wesley's coming to appreciate its value in conveying his own soteriological convictions. This connection is all the more important, as we shall see later in this study, in light of Bengel's adherence to a strand of covenant theology distinct from that which dominated mid-eighteenth-century English Calvinism.

It does *not* appear, however, that the metaphor itself was new to Wesley. The fact that Wesley references the servant-son metaphor and integrates aspects of Galatians 4:1–7 and Romans 8:15–16 into his commentary on Jude 1 demonstrates that the metaphor had received considerable attention from Wesley for some time. As noted in the survey above, Wesley's commentary on Jude 1 neither restates nor adapts any of the sources Wesley relied upon in producing his New Testament Notes.

72. Only the name Bengelii appears on the reading list for "the 6th class" included in John Bennet's manuscript minutes for Thursday, June 3 of the 1748 Conference, but no reference as to precisely what work is noted. *Minutes*, 1748 (Bennet), np.

73. Wesley's lifelong confidence in Bengel's scholarly work with the biblical text is evident in his reliance on Bengel's detailed notes on the textual problems of 1 John 5:7 when writing his sermon, "On the Trinity" in 1775. See Outler's introductory comment on the sermon in *Works* (BE), 2:373–74.

74. Randy L. Maddox, "John Wesley's Reading," 118–33. See also Maddox, "Remnants of John Wesley's Personal Library," 122–28.

75. "From J. Robertson at Pitcomb near Bruton, Somerset, to the Foundery (September 23, 1747)," *London Letters Chiefly Addressed to the Rev. C Wesley*, DD/Pr 1 (MARC), 67. The letter included an extensive list of Bengel's works which the author of the letter hoped to obtain with Charles Wesley's assistance.

Furthermore, indications are that the metaphor was not foreign to those attending the 1746 Conference or to those reading (or listening) to Wesley's sermon, "The Spirit of Bondage and of Adoption." Indeed, one of the outstanding features of *each* occurrence of the metaphor—particularly those occurrences prior to Wesley's 1788 sermons "On Faith" and "On the Discoveries of Faith"—is that it consistently appears with minimal, if any, orientation of the reader *within the text itself.* In fact, its appearance in the minutes of the 1746 Conference gives no indication as to who proposed the metaphor as helpful in expressing the conclusions of the Conference, but only that it was apparently understood by and met the approval of the conferees.

Therefore, rather than conceiving the servant-son metaphor as emerging into Wesley's *awareness* at this point in time, the evidence suggests that the metaphor—already a familiar concept—began to *resonate* with Wesley on a new level. Thus, it is on account of this resonance that the metaphor secured a determinately more consequential and influential place in his theological thought by the mid-1740s. The occurrences of the metaphor in the footnotes and *errata* of the 1774 and 1775 editions of Wesley's *Works* argue the point convincingly, indicating the emergence of such resonance at a date *later* than the early stages of his post-Aldersgate engagement with the Revival. His editing also accentuates the metaphor's continued importance to Wesley, prompting him to clarify for his readers some of the entries in his earliest journals.

It is precisely this lasting and influential role that occasions a final observation with respect to the textual evidence: *the gathering momentum of the metaphor.* As noted in the chronological survey, there is a nine-year gap between the explicit uses of the metaphor by Wesley in 1746 and its next appearance in 1755. After this it is another thirteen years before the next explicit occurrence of the metaphor. However, over the twenty years from 1768 to 1788 there are at least nine such occurrences, not including the multiple occurrences in his 1788 sermons "On Faith" and "On the Discoveries of Faith."

It is possible that this record of the increased frequency of explicit occurrences during the last third of Wesley's life may be, in part, a function of the limits of the Wesley corpus presently available for inspection. In addition, restricting the foregoing survey to explicit occurrences of the metaphor excludes consideration, for the moment, of those occasions where the theological overtones of the metaphor may be present despite the absence of the metaphor itself. Nevertheless, there does seem to be a crescendo in Wesley's use of the metaphor from 1768, not only in terms of a greater frequency of occurrence but also in a broadening of the contexts of those occurrences: first, his correspondence with individuals, then in footnotes to later editions of his journals intended for a general audience, and finally in sermons penned late in life—the last two written only weeks apart. In the very least, it must be admitted that the metaphor was not only alive and well but also at the forefront of Wesley's theological thought late in his life.

This last point is particularly evident in the fact that Wesley not only included the two 1788 sermons in an edition of *Sermons on Several Occasions* published that same year, but also in issues of the *Arminian Magazine* published in late 1788 and in the summer of 1789. Clearly this is an effort to expose a greater number of his Methodists to his exegesis of the metaphor. This is further accentuated by Wesley's publication of the letter he received from a Mr. A. B. in 1779 in the March 1789 issue of the magazine. The Methodist preacher's admission to his spiritual state provides for Wesley not only an exemplary portrait of "integrity and candour" among spiritual leaders but also highlights for his readers that the spiritual realities to which the metaphor points are of such gravity for the spiritual life that it warrants honest and serious reflection by every Methodist. Wesley's encouragement to his readers on this matter is his tacit affirmation that "a larger degree of grace" awaits any who find themselves in the state of a servant.[76]

The gathering momentum of the metaphor raises an important question: Why the relative absence of the metaphor in the earlier years and its more pronounced presence in later years? Indeed, one might have expected just the opposite: that the resonance of the metaphor with Wesley and his associates as they labored to articulate their understanding of justification at the 1746 Conference would have resulted in a greater frequency of its use in the years immediately following, but would have faded over the ensuing years as the initial energy of this valuable theological asset was spent.

One answer suggested by several Wesley scholars is that the lively place of the metaphor during Wesley's later years coincides with new

---

76. Wesley, *AM* (March 1789), 162. The letter poignantly points to such realities, describing Mr. A. B.'s yet unimproved "present state" (the state of a servant) in the strongest of terms: bondage, unbelief, and deadness. On these matters, the letter speaks for itself. Wesley's editorial comment reads simply, "We see here a notable instance of that integrity and candour which influence the most common Preachers among the Methodists. Is it not much to be wished that such a spirit was found in all the Ministers of the Church of Christ?"

developments in his soteriology during the closing two and a half decades of his life. Some cite the metaphor as evidence of a rather radical about-face by the mature Wesley.[77] However, as the following chapters demonstrate, reading Wesley in light of the influence of covenant theology on his soteriology indicates not a new *development* in his theological thought in the last twenty-five years of his life, but a shift in *emphasis* as he articulates *longstanding* theological views in response to new developments around him. It might be argued that a shift in emphasis may itself, on occasion, precipitate or further contribute to a real and new development in thought. Yet, the fact that a spotlight normally does not equally illuminate everything on a theater's stage does not mean that whatever may be in the shadows at a given moment is not on the stage at all. And this seems to more accurately describe what the case is for Wesley. The textual evidence argues that with the shift in emphasis elements that had been in the background began to take a more prominent place while those previously in the foreground receded to a degree.

Nevertheless, much of the scholarly attention paid the metaphor thus far has opted to bypass any serious consideration of the question of how the metaphor originated in Wesley's thinking. As a result, this question is largely, if not wholly, set aside as materially inconsequential to understanding the metaphor itself and how it functioned in his theological thought. To expand the analogy of the theater stage, bypassing the question of how the metaphor originated in Wesley's thought has resulted in at least two missteps: a) treating the metaphor as merely a prop, and b) giving the impression that Wesley himself introduced the metaphor to the stage.

Alternatively, entertaining the question of the metaphor's origination in Wesley's thought allows the possibility outlined in the opening pages of this chapter; namely, that Wesley's use of the metaphor reveals the *existing* infrastructure of his theological thought. Thus, it is not that Wesley's soteriology occasioned his use of the metaphor, but that his use of the metaphor reveals covenant theology to be a constituent element of his theological thought that, in turn, profoundly influenced the development and articulation of his soteriology. The metaphor, then, is Exhibit A of the imprint of covenant theology upon Wesley's vision of the way of salvation outlined in the emplotment he described and

---

77. Felleman, "John Wesley and the 'Servant of God,'" 72–86. See also Maddox, *Responsible Grace*, 157–58. Felleman contends for a radical about-face by Wesley whereas Maddox suggests a discernible but less dramatic development.

exegeted in letters and sermons as well as in various other publications, such as *A Collection of Hymns* mentioned at the outset of this chapter.

Seeing the servant-son metaphor in this light raises a number of questions. How might this covenant theology have become so embedded in his theological thought? And what covenant theology was it? Was it the covenant theology of the Westminster Confession or that of Amyraut or Coccaeus or of the Arminianism that challenged the excesses of the Commonwealth? And in what ways did Wesley's appropriation of covenant theology shape his soteriology? These are critical questions salient to discerning the contours of the imprint of covenant theology on Wesley's theology, and answering them requires investigating its ancestry in his thought.

CHAPTER 2

The Ancestry of John Wesley's Covenant Theology

ONE OF THE MOST direct introductions to the ancestry of Wesley's covenant theology appears in his sermon "The Righteousness of Faith" published in 1746. His text was Romans 10:5–8, a text from which he had preached at least as early as 1740 and from which he would preach as late as 1789: "For Moses describeth the righteousness which is by the law, The man who doth these things shall live by them. But the righteousness which is by faith speaketh thus, . . . The word is nigh thee, even in thy mouth, and in thy heart; that is, the word of faith which we preach."[1] The opening paragraph of the sermon is an intriguing and abrupt immersion into the core components of covenant theology:

> The Apostle does not here oppose the covenant given by Moses to the covenant given by Christ. If we ever imagined this it was for want of observing that the latter as well as the former part of these words were spoken by Moses himself to the people of Israel, and that concerning the covenant which then was. But it is the covenant of grace which God through Christ hath established with men in all ages (as well before, and under the Jewish dispensation, as since God was manifest in the flesh), which St. Paul here opposes to the covenant of works, made with Adam while in paradise.[2]

This beginning is significant to this study on several counts. First, it highlights Wesley's familiarity with the superstructure of covenant theology. Second, it is a compelling testimony to the fact that Wesley perceived his audience to be so oriented to covenant theology that it would

---

1. Wesley, *ENNT*, 496.
2. Wesley, *Works* (BE) §1, 1:202–3.

be the lens through which his sermon would be read. Consequently, the first order of business was to make a clarification so as not to put the rest of the sermon at risk doctrinally. Third, while the basics of covenant theology seem to have been generally understood and accepted, his comment indicates there were diverse conceptions within the bounds of covenant theology that were theologically significant. Therefore, and fourthly, Wesley's clarification suggests that he himself was committed to a particular understanding of covenant theology which shaped his theological thought and, he hoped, would shape that of his audience.

It is worth noting that Wesley's publication of this particular sermon coincides with the conclusions of the 1746 Conference that distinguished between "a believer under the Jewish dispensation"—subsequently described as "a Jew, inwardly" and "a servant of God"—and "a Christian, inwardly" who is "a child of God."[3] These key terms and distinctions also appear in Wesley's commentary on Galatians 4:1–7 which provided the biblical underpinning for his use of the servant-son metaphor. Of course, the terms "servant" and "son" belong to the biblical text, as do the metaphor-related terms "bondage" and "adoption." But what deserves special attention here is Wesley's opening comment on Galatians 4:1, "*Now*—to illustrate by a plain similitude the pre-eminence of the Christian over the legal dispensation, *the heir as long as he is a child*—As he is under age, *differeth nothing from a servant*—not being at liberty either to use or enjoy his estate, *though he be lord*—Proprietor *of* it *all*."[4] The term "dispensation" along with the adjectives "Christian" and "legal" belong to the technical language of covenant theology.[5]

In light of Wesley's obvious familiarity with covenant theology, these words can hardly be regarded as an incidental carry-over from his dependence on John Guyse's *The Practical Expositor* in preparing his New Testament *Notes*.[6] Rather, in choosing to retain Guyse's comment, Wesley not only signals his acquaintance but his purposeful and sustained alignment with core components of covenant theology. And, most significantly, he sets the whole passage under the general theological framework of covenant theology. Wesley does not alter this theologi-

---

3. *Minutes*, 1746 (Jackson), 8:287–88.

4. Wesley, *ENNT*, 604. Typically, Wesley italicized the words of Scripture so as to set them off from his own comment on the passage. Wesley's comment on this passage is taken virtually *verbatim* from the paraphrase of Gal 4:1 offered by Guyse. See Guyse, *The Practical Expositor*, 4:337.

5. The terms "legal" and "Jewish" are often used interchangeably in the language of covenant theology.

6. Wesley, *ENNT*, v.

cal orientation to the passage in any of his editions of his New Testament *Notes* and echoes the same terminology in relationship with his use of the servant-son metaphor in his late sermons, "On Faith" and "On the Discoveries of Faith." Clearly, covenant theology is the habitat—the theological setting or environment—in which the servant-son metaphor dwells, as it were, and from which it draws its life.

It is true, of course, that the metaphors of servant and son belong to the sacred text of the Christian canon first and foremost. And in view of Wesley's high regard for the very words of Holy Scripture, this fact alone not only legitimizes his use of the servant-son metaphor but obligates him to account for it theologically. Without doubt, to some extent this explains the continued vibrancy of the servant-son metaphor in his correspondence, sermons, and publications over the course of his life as the leader of Methodism. For this reason, his understanding of the biblical underpinnings of the metaphor is critical to this study and merits close inspection subsequently. However, attention must first be given to covenant theology not only because it constitutes the theological habitat of the metaphor but because it is a determinant in Wesley's exegesis both of the sacred text and of the experience of those on the way of salvation.

The question is where to begin in order to gain such an acquaintance. In a footnote concerning Wesley's comments in the opening paragraph of "The Righteousness of Faith" discussed above, Outler states that Wesley would have come by covenant theology through the Puritans William Perkins and William Ames; and, he adds, "*especially* the Westminster Confession."[7] However, to infer from Outler's assertion that the Puritan covenant theology mediated to Wesley *is* the covenant theology operative in Wesley's theological thought places a burden on Outler's assertion greater than it can bear under the weight of the evidence. For one, as we shall see, there were voices outside of English Calvinism—other strands, as it were, of covenant theology—to which Wesley was exposed and that influenced his thought and impacted his use of the servant-son metaphor.[8] And for another, the covenant theology mediated by *Wesley* to *his* audience reflected the reality of the fundamental doctrinal divide between him and the Puritans over the question of predestination. Thus, in the least, Outler's assertion calls for some

---

7. Wesley, *Works* (BE), 1:203; n. 2.

8. Outler was aware of these voices and states specifically that the federal theology of Johannes Cocceius had influenced both Wesley and Jonathan Edwards. See Outler's introductory comments in Wesley, *Works* (BE), 1:81, and his critical notes on "The Righteousness of Faith" and "On Divine Providence" in *Works* (BE) n. 2, 1:203 and n. 7, 2:536, respectively.

discovery of what covenant theology might look like when separated from the predestinarian template which, historically, is indigenous to it.

Nevertheless, the covenant theology of English Calvinism as represented by Perkins, Ames, and the Westminster Confession provides a defensible starting point in exploring the ancestry of Wesley's covenant theology. The Puritans were, after all, a vigorous voice for this theological framework and contributed toward its coming to serve as a given in theological discourse in the seventeenth and eighteenth centuries particularly. As early as the late 1500s, as Jens Møller has argued convincingly, "the covenant idea seems in England to have become almost exclusively the preserve of the Puritans" having been practically avoided by Anglican theologians.[9]

This is not to say that the ancestry of Wesley's covenant theology was void of any Arminian influence. The evidence of the nature of Wesley's spiritual endeavors prior to Aldersgate suggests that the holy living tradition arising out of the anti-Calvinist Anglicanism of the seventeenth century was a formative influence as well. Parish priest and royal chaplain Henry Hammond stands out as one representative of Caroline Anglican moralism who presented an Arminian take on covenant theology.[10] Hammond wrote and, in 1644, published *A Practical Catechism* while the Westminster Assembly was in session. Neil Lettinga describes the work as an implicit "attack on puritan theology." Although "the idea of the covenant of grace was a fundamental doctrine for both Hammond and the puritans," Hammond "turned puritan Covenant Theology upside down" by rejecting the notion that the covenant of grace was meant only for the elect. Hammond argued that "God offered the covenant of grace to all who were baptized, but required 'renewed, sincere, honest, faithful obedience to the whole Gospel' as 'consideration' to validate the contract."[11] Traces of Hammond's reconfiguration of covenant theology

---

9. Jens G. Møller, "The Beginnings of Puritan Covenant Theology," 57–58.

10. Jeffrey Chamberlain argues that the charge of moralism leveled against Anglicans by Methodists in the train of the Methodist revival is the result more of caricature than of actual fact, and notes the emphasis on obedience as a corrective action by Anglican divines who nonetheless upheld the reformed standard of free grace (though Chamberlain notes the very real doctrinal differences that existed). However, Chamberlain's own example of Archbishop Sharp's dismissing the necessity of "a sensible change of Mind" suggests that, whatever doctrinal claims to the contrary, the charge of moralism leveled against rank and file Anglicans by some Methodists may not have been wholly unfounded. See Chamberlain, "Moralism, Justification, and the Controversy over Methodism," 652–78.

11. Lettinga, "Covenant Theology Turned Upside Down," 658.

may be evident in Wesley's.[12] However, Wesley—particularly after Aldersgate—was not willing to grant as much salvific latitude to sincerity as was championed by Anglican divines, despite their assertion that such sincerity was not without the assistance of divine grace.

The presence of an Anglican voice like Hammonds' in the ancestry of Wesley's covenant theology notwithstanding, Wesley's own family might be suggested as the earliest and most proximate source from which covenant theology would have been mediated to him. His Puritan family history can be traced to his maternal grandfather, Samuel Annesley, and before him to his two great-grandfathers, Bartholomew Westley and John White, both of whom were "recognized Puritans active during the period of the Commonwealth."[13] While aspects of this notable legacy of Puritanism may have been muted to some degree with both of Wesley's parents (before their marriage) having left Dissent to join the Church of England, it certainly was not muted altogether.[14] In fact, the influence of Puritan theology on Wesley is confirmed by Wesley himself in his largely affirmative comments on Puritan writings he selected for *A Christian Library*.[15] And, in 1760 Wesley emphasized a significant point of theological affinity with English Puritanism in a letter to the editor of *Lloyd's Evening Post*. The occasion was his response to the charge leveled against him that "'No Protestant Divine ever taught your doctrine of assurance.'" As part of his rebuttal, Wesley provided a list of Protestant Divines, including William Perkins, with whom, he contended, his own views on assurance were aligned.[16] As for the influence of William Ames, the presence of a revised edition (1648) of Ames' *Medulla theologiae* among the holdings of the Kingswood School is of interest.[17] Ames'

12. See below the discussion of Wesley's editing of John Preston's *The New Covenant; or, the Saints' Portion*.

13. Monk, *John Wesley: His Puritan Heritage*, 16.

14. Ibid., 22–23.

15. See Wesley, 'Preface,' *ACL*, 7:np.

16. Wesley, "December 20, 1760," *Works* (Jackson), 3:29–31. Wesley's claim was not without merit. See Keddie, "The Doctrine of Assurance in the Theology of William Perkins," 230–44. According to Outler, Perkins and Ames are among "the great Puritans" that Wesley read "in Oxford, and maybe before" and knew as well as "the Anglican titans." See Wesley, *Works* (BE), 1:79–80. Wesley, however, does not mention the works of either Perkins or Ames in his diaries or among his record of acquisitions noted in his financial accounts from the Oxford period (1725–35). Heitzenrater, "John Wesley and the Oxford Methodists," 493–526.

17. Maddox, "Kingswood School Library Holdings," 342–70. The title appears in the catalogue of the library holdings compiled by Cornelius Bayley in 1775. If Ames' book was added to the library by John Cennick during his days as headmaster of the

covenant theology is plainly evident in Wesley's at points,[18] making it plausible that Wesley's acquaintance with Ames' works was immediate rather than secondary and remote, and strengthening the argument that Wesley was acquainted with and, in large measure, subscribed to the core components of classic covenant theology.

Beyond this direct connection to Wesley, the covenant theology of English Calvinism as represented by Perkins, Ames,[19] and the Westminster Confession also serves as a backdrop against which the distinctive influence of *other* strands of covenant theology upon Wesley become evident, and against which his own appropriation of covenant theology more clearly comes to light. Yet, it comes to light only if the reading of Wesley is undertaken with a fairly good grasp of the core theological features of what might be fairly described as classic covenant theology. With this knowledge, it is then possible to detect not only how deeply influential covenant theology was on Wesley's thought but also to discern how profoundly his distinctive appropriation of covenant theology shaped his soteriology.

The following survey begins with a thorough consideration of key aspects of the covenant theology of Perkins and Ames, bringing to light their respective treatment of core components and concerns of covenant theology in general. From there, other developments in the evolution of this formative theological construct are explored, including a brief introduction to the place of the covenant theology of Johannes Cocceius in the family tree of Wesley's theological thought.

---

school before his break with Wesley in early 1741, it is unlikely that the book remained in the collection as an undetected tribute to Cennick's turn toward Calvinism. Given Wesley's lifelong disappointment with Cennick, his high regard for the practical divinity of the Puritans and his close attention in 1768 to the Kingswood school's library holdings, it is more likely that the book remained with Wesley's knowledge and blessing. For a brief orientation to Cennick's relationship with Wesley and then with Calvinistic Methodism, see Evans, "The Relations of George Whitefield and Howell Harris," 179–90.

18. Compare, for example, Wesley's tracing the establishment of the moral law back before the creation of humankind to the creation of angels with Ames' description of the same. See *Wesley*, "The Original, Nature, Properties, and Use of the Law," *Works* (BE) §I.1–2, 2:6 and Ames, "Speciall Gubernation about intelligent Creatures," *The Marrow of Sacred Divinity* §32, 50–55.

19. R. T. Kendall frames his presentation of the Calvinism of William Ames within a larger discussion of the theological influence of the Netherlands. See R. T. Kendall, *Calvin and English Calvinism to 1649*, 151–64. While Ames' tenure as a professor at Franeker was certainly influential, it is nonetheless the case that his voice, theologically, was clearly that of English Calvinism.

William Perkins and the Two Covenants

Although it is true that Wesley did not include an extract of any of William Perkins' works in his *A Christian Library*, this fact, as Karl Ganske notes, speaks more to the matter of how Perkins' works fit Wesley's agenda as the editor of the *Library* than to the level of his acquaintance with Perkins' theological thought.[20] And this observation would certainly apply with respect to Perkins' role as one of the mediators of Puritan covenant theology to Wesley. The widespread influence of Perkins' *A Golden Chaine* is well-attested. First published in 1591,[21] Møller describes the work as "a systematic treatment of the theological meaning of the covenant" that was "extremely popular and influential both in England and on the Continent."[22] Perkins, a strict supralapsarian, first introduces God's decree of predestination "by which he hath ordained all men to a certain and euerlasting estate . . . either to saluation or condemnation," and then declares that "the meanes of accomplishing Gods Predestination are twofold: the creation, and the fall."[23] That is, the decree anticipates the eventuality of a subject to predestinate (thus, the creation of humankind) and an occasion for such predestinating (thus, the fall).

Beginning with his description of God's dealings with humanity, Perkins identifies being in subjection to God as one feature of the Adamic estate of innocence. Being thus subject to God (and therefore obligated[24] "to performe obedience to the commandements of God") Perkins then specifies two commandments unique to Adam *prior* to the fall: "God's commandement concerning the trees, . . . ordained to make examination, and triall of mans obedience" and "God's commandement concerning the observation of the Sabboth." Perkins includes as the sev-

---

20. Ganske, "The Religion of the Heart and Growth in Grace," 230–31.

21. *Armilla Aurea*, Perkins' original version written in Latin was published in 1590. See Jinkins, "Perkins, William (1558–1602)," *DNB* (http://www.oxforddnb.com).

22. Møller, "The Beginnings of Puritan Covenant Theology," 58–59. Edward Hindson describes Perkins' work as "a basic guide to Puritan theology and preaching" representative of "Reformed doctrine as generally interpreted by the Puritans." Hindson, *Introduction to Puritan Theology*, 138.

23. Perkins, *A Golden Chaine* (1600), 10.

24. Perkins uses the term "bound" but the context clearly shows that this was meant in the sense of being obligated as opposed to being coerced, as Perkins makes very clear in his description of the fall having occurred "without constraint": "For wee must not think that mans fall was either by chance, or God not knowing it, or barely winking at it, or by his bare permission, or against his will: but rather miraculously, not without the will of God, but yet without all approbation of it." Ibid., 15.

enth and final attribute of this "excellent estate of innocencie" Adam's "free choice, both to will, and performe the commandement of the two trees, and also to neglect and violate the same."[25]

To some extent, the essentials of a covenant-bound relationship are evident: commandments, obligation to perform, and outcomes in accordance with whether the commandments are observed or violated. Despite these features, Perkins does not use the word "covenant" to describe the nature of God's relationship to Adam in his innocency.[26] In this regard, his presentation of covenant theology aligns with that of Heinrich Bullinger (1504–75) whose *A Brief Exposition of the One and Eternal Testament or Covenant of God*, first published in 1534, came to serve as the blueprint of covenant theology.[27] While Bullinger spoke of God having given a *law* to Adam in paradise prior to the fall, the one and only *covenant* "for the restitution of the human race" was made with Adam upon the occasion of the fall and is encapsulated in Genesis 3:15, "'the first promise and the authentic gospel.'"[28]

At the heart of this distinction between law and covenant was the contention that the character of the primordial relationship lacked an ingredient essential to covenant: the explicit promise of reward for obedience. Instead, there was only the threat of punishment, placing the relationship in the category of law rather than covenant.[29] Perkins, too, reserves "covenant" to describe the nature of the governance of God's relationship with humanity *after* the fall, and explains: "there are two kinds of this couenant[;] the couenant of workes, [and] the couenant of grace."[30] The notion of double covenant—a covenant of works and a

---

25. Ibid., 13.

26. Ibid., *A Golden Chaine*, 12–13. Indeed, Perkins does not use the word "covenant" until after his description of the fall of angels and men, the nature and distinction of original and actual sin, the just punishment of sin, and extensive discussions of Jesus Christ (the foundation of election) in the distinction and unity of his two natures.

27. Bullinger was well known among the English clergy, von Rohr notes, "due at least in part . . . to Archbishop Whitgift's order that Bullinger be purchased and studied." See John von Rohr, *The Covenant of Grace in Puritan Thought*, 31.

28. McCoy and Baker, *Fountainhead of Federalism*, 24–26.

29. Von Rohr, *The Covenant of Grace in Puritan Thought*, 37. Von Rohr notes that discussion over this technical "'difference persisted well into the next century. Richard Baxter described the terms governing the relationship as a Law in one respect, and a Covenant in another.'"

30. Perkins, *The Golden Chaine*, 36. Perkins' commitment to Ramist logic is clearly evident in this passage where Perkins is compelled to begin with the most general definition of covenant and then work to the specifics. Jens Møller, "The Beginnings of Puritan Covenant Theology," 59.

covenant of grace—is important in the historical development of covenant theology.[31] However, at this point in the development of the idea, the covenant of works is, like the covenant of grace, postlapsarian. Indeed, it *must* be postlapsarian. Since both creation and Adam's fall must occur *before* the *execution* of the decree, covenant—being the divinely-appointed outward means of the execution of the decree[32]—does not (indeed, cannot) come into play until *after* the fall.[33]

While Perkins alludes to an Edenic connection in his commentary on Galatians 4:24–25, he firmly fixes the covenant of works *as* the Mosaic Law: "The two Testaments are the Couenant of workes, and the Couenant of grace, ... The law, or couenant of workes, . . . was written on tables of stone, the Gospel on the fleshly tables of our hearts. . . . [T]he law was in nature by creation: the Gospel is aboue nature, and was reuealed after the fall. . . . [T]he law hath Moses for a Mediatour, *Deut.* 5.27, but Christ is the Mediatour of the new Testament."[34]

In this he follows his contemporary, Dudley Fenner, who, according to Michael McGiffert, was the first to formally connect the double decree (the elect to salvation; the non-elect to reprobation) with the teaching of the double covenant. Whereas the covenant of grace functions *solely* in behalf of the elect, the covenant of works performs a *dual* function: on the one hand, it is the instrument whereby the *elect* are incited to "flie vnto Christ" who delivers them into the provisions of the covenant of grace; on the other hand, it is the means whereby the decree

---

31. This is a significant development in that, as McGiffert notes, "Zwingli, Tyndale, Bullinger, and Calvin accepted no other general covenant than that of grace, commencing after the Fall." McGiffert, "From Moses to Adam," 133.

32. Perkins, *A Golden Chaine* (1600), 24.

33. The use of the word "covenant" in relation to Adam *does* appear in Perkins' "A Faithfvll and Plaine Exposition Upon the Two First Verses of the 2 Chapter of Zephaniah." In this exhortation to repentance, Perkins declares, "What couenant God made with [Adam], was made for himselfe and for vs: what God promised him, and he to God, he promised for himselfe and for vs." Nevertheless, rather than indicating that Perkins used the term as an equivalent for "the covenant of works" (thus suggesting a covenant of works made with Adam in the time of his innocence), it indicates in this instance that he is using the term synonymously with "Law" in the general sense in which Bullinger used *that* term. In his exposition on Zephaniah, Perkins is not discussing the two covenants but is seeking to establish "that euery man that came from *Adam*, sinned in the sinne of *Adam*." Perkins, *Workes*, 1:415.

34. Perkins, *A Commentarie upon the Epistle to the Galatians*, 306. See also McGiffert, "From Moses to Adam," 145–46. Given developments in covenantal theology subsequent to Perkins' publication of *A Golden Chaine*, it is feasible that Perkins may be acknowledging the argument for an Edenic connection without relinquishing his view of the Mosaic Law as the covenant of works.

of reprobation is executed upon the *non-elect*. Unavoidably, the Mosaic Law is substantially separated from the covenant of grace, an outcome Wesley consistently rejected.

William Ames and the Two Covenants

Whereas Perkins avoids using the term "covenant" to describe God's relationship to Adam in his *innocence*, William Ames applies the term in precisely this way in his *Medulla Theologiae* (*The Marrow of Sacred Divinity*) published in 1627.[35] In a chapter entitled "Of speciall Gubernation about intelligent Creatures," Ames describes God's governance of humanity as an extension of his dealings with man *in his innocence*: "the Law and covenant of God with man in the *Creation* was, *Doe this, and thou shalt live*: If thou doe it not, thou shalt dye the death."[36] Ames refers to this law—made with both angels and Adam in the time of creation—as "the Law of nature."[37] The phrase may indicate something of the extent of the influence upon Ames of developments in covenant theology among German theologians.[38] The term appearing in the work of Zacharias Ursinus (1534–83) is *foedus naturale*—a covenant of nature originating with the creation of the world.[39] While Ursinus does not develop the idea to the point of correlating the covenant of nature with the covenant of works,[40] it is significant that within a very short

---

35. An abbreviated version was published in 1623. See Sprunger, "Ames, William (1576–1633)," *DNB* (http://www.oxforddnb.com).

36. Ames, *The Marrow of Sacred Divinity*, 55.

37. Ibid., 54.

38. Commenting on the international texture of covenant theology, Møller observes: "And as Dutch theologians learned from their English-speaking colleagues, so did English theologians from the Germans. This theological relationship between Continental and English theologians can be demonstrated from both internal and external evidence. . . . Perkins knew the first Calvinist dogmatic treatise based on the idea of the covenant—Olevian's *De substantia foederis gratuity inter Deium et electos* (1585)." As further evidence, Møller notes the similarity of Fenner's definition of covenant to that of Gomarus. Møller, "The Beginnings of Puritan Covenant Theology," 58.

39. From Ursinus' *Opera Theologica* cited by Visser, "The Covenant in Zacharias Ursinus," 539. Perkins also spoke of the law being in nature by creation. See Perkins, *A Commentarie upon the Epistle to the Galatians*, 306.

40. See Visser, "The Covenant in Zacharias Ursinus," 540, and McGiffert, "From Moses to Adam," 133. McCoy and Baker relate Ursinus' covenant of nature to the emergence of the concept of "double covenant" (a term McCoy and Baker use to reference a covenant made at creation and a covenant made after the fall). Though he was first to mention a covenant before the fall, Ursinus did not draw out the implications that would come to characterize covenant theology as it developed after him. McCoy and Baker, *The Fountainhead of Federalism*, 35–36.

period of time it was precisely this correlation that was made and, in fact, that came to be a settled affirmation of covenant theology. The following definition of "covenant of works" appearing in Thomas Wilson's (1563–1622) *A Christian Dictionarie* published in 1612, gives evidence of this development: "*Couenant of workes*: Is a league [or agreement] touching the sauing of some [on] condition of their perfect obedience. This was made with Angels and *Adam* before their fall: and since that time, it is propounded in Scripture to conuince vs of sin, and to prepare vs to Christ. *Rom.* 3, 20. *Galat.* 3, 24. *The Law is our Schoolemaister to Christ.* Leuit. 18.5. *The Man that doth these things, shall liue.*"[41]

This definition highlights two important developments. First, while the covenant of works itself is singular in nature, its salvific role is duplex and defined by its relation to the fall. *Prior* to the fall, the covenant is sufficient to save; contingent, of course, upon the fulfillment of the condition of perfect obedience. *After* the fall, the salvific role of the covenant of works is referential only—pointing to Christ as alone sufficient to save. Second, not only does the Mosaic Law embody the covenant of works, but the Mosaic Law is given a lineage reaching back to Adam in the time of his innocence.[42]

Ames, too, conflates the covenant made with Adam (prior to the fall) with the Mosaic Law. Outlining nine distinct ways in which the old and new covenants (the Law and the gospel) differ from each other, he describes the old covenant as *both* a "covenant of friendship between the Creator and the creature" (the covenant with Adam in his innocency) *and* "a dead letter, and deadly to a sinner."[43] For Ames, it is his understanding of the moral law that forms the basis for conflating the covenant made with Adam with the Law given to Moses. The Law of God is the moral law, unchanged by the fall and replicated at Sinai: "the Law prescribed to Men and Angells, was the same as touching the Essence of it: namely morall, the summe whereof is in the Decalogue."[44]

---

41. Wilson, *A Christian Dictionarie*, 69.

42. In the dictionary's entries for the word "Law," the moral law is listed under the heading, "Abrogation of Moses Law." Ibid., 287–88.

43. Summarizing the difference "in the effects" between the old and new covenants, Ames declares, "Hence [the old covenant] never brought salvation to any man, neither could bring any thing to a sinner, but onely death[;] but [the new covenant] doth not properly and of it selfe bring death or condemnation to any, but it brings assured salvation to all those of whom it is received." Ames, *The Marrow of Sacred Divinity*, 115.

44. Ibid., 54. Wesley would be in essential agreement with Ames insofar as understanding the Decalogue as a divinely given summation of the moral law.

The significance of this is twofold. First, the distinction between the law given to men and angels *before* the fall at the time of their creation and that same law written on tables of stone *after* the fall, is not found in the moral "Essence" of the law for its essence is ongoing and unchanged. Rather, the distinction lies in the *role* of the law as a basis for the relationship of God with humanity. Ames declares that the Law of God had "the power of justifying" only in the time of Adam's "state of integrity" or innocence (a power never experienced by Adam—nor, subsequently, by his posterity—on account of his having failed the "triall of obedience"). *Since* the fall, the Law of God has only "condemning power" with respect to the non-elect who, as it were, live irrecoverably in a "state of sinne."[45] Thus, for the non-elect, the covenant of works remains perpetually in effect. The result of this fact is that they remain under the requirement of the covenant of works ("Do this, and live"); and, on account of the fall, experience the unavoidable consequence of condemnation. For the elect, however, the role of the law *since* the fall is quite different: *both* the justifying and condemning power of the law have been abrogated by the covenant of grace, the covenant in which they—and they alone, on the basis of their election—are privileged to participate.[46]

This leads to the second aspect of the twofold significance of Ames' conflation of the covenant of works with the Mosaic Law: it is definitive for the *administration* of the covenant of grace in which the elect alone participate. While the substance of the covenant of grace is singular,[47] the "manner of administring is double: one of Christ to be exhibited" (i.e., that period of time leading up to the Incarnation), "and the other of Christ exhibited" (i.e., Christ having come in the flesh).[48] The administration of the covenant of grace *before* Christ's appearing involved, says Ames, "some representation of the Covenant of works" whereas the administration of the covenant of grace *after* Christ was exhibited differs in its "cleernesse"[49] and in its "freedome"—namely, that "the govern-

---

45. Ibid., 219.

46. Ames, however, does not regard the Law of God as inconsequential for the elect. Rather, it remains in effect and serves a distinct purpose for the elect: "[The Law of God] hath force and vigor, in respect of power to direct, and some power also it doth retaine of condemning, because it reproves, and condemnes sinne in the faithfull themselves, although it cannot wholy condemn the faithfull themselves; who are not under the Law but under Grace." Ibid., 219.

47. It "hath beene onely one from the beginning," Ames asserts. Ibid., 193.

48. Ibid.

49. What is more clear in the administration of the covenant of grace *after* Christ

ment of the Law, or mixing of the covenant of workes, which did hold the ancient people in a certaine bondage, is now taken away: . . ."[50] In short, the idea of a "representation of the Covenant of works" within the historical time-frame affirmed to belong to the covenant of grace appears to have been a generally accepted tenet of covenant theology by the time of Ames. However, the differences among covenant theologians as to *how* this might be were sufficient to spark significant controversy.

Other Developments in Covenant Theology

Amandus Polanus (1561–1610), for example, retained the conception of a single covenant of grace spanning the whole range of salvation history from the fall onward, but proposed that "God had 'repeated the covenant [of works] with the people of Israel through Moses'" so that there was an "'old covenant of grace' before Christ and 'the new covenant of grace' after Christ."[51] Church of Scotland minister and university principal, Robert Rollock (1555–99) also taught that God repeated the covenant of works to the people of Israel so that it is "set before euery one which is without Christ, seeking righteousnesse by the law and the works of the law, to this end, if it may be, that by the sense of sin [and] the feeling of his owne misery, he may be prepared to embrace the couenant of grace in Christ."[52] William Pemble (1590–1623) conceived of this not in terms of simple repetition but of two administrations of the covenant of works, the first with Adam before the fall and the second with Israel at Sinai.[53] Taking this point of view a bit further, the Salmurian theologian John Cameron had retained the idea of a basic unity in the covenant of grace but had identified the Mosaic covenant as a third covenant.[54] And

---

is exhibited is that the doctrine of grace and faith is "more distinct and expresse" and the need for types and shadows is no longer necessary now that the veil is lifted. Ibid., 199. This is primarily a *quantitative* rather than *qualitative* measure. Song, *Theology and Piety*, 28.

50. Ames, *Marrow of Sacred Divinity*, 199.

51. Pelikan, *Reformation of Church and Dogma*, 368–69.

52. Rollock, *A Treatise of Gods Effectual Calling*, 7, 10.

53. Pemble, *Vindiciæ Fidei*, 151–52. See also Thomas Boston's notes to Edward Fisher's *The Marrow of Modern Divinity*, originally published in 1645, where Boston states both the covenant of grace and the covenant of works were delivered to Israel at Mt. Sinai. He assures there was no confounding of the two since the covenant of works was made subservient to the covenant of grace although the former was "the most conspicuous part" (but not "the principal part") of "the Sinai transaction." Boston, *The Marrow of Modern Divinity*, 36–37.

54. Armstrong, *Calvinism and the Amyraut Heresy*, 144.

pushing beyond this, Moïse Amyraut (1596–1645) opposed the Mosaic Law to the covenant of grace in a more definite way, proposing three distinct covenants: "First, that which was contracted in the earthly paradise and ought to be called *natural*; secondly, the one which God transacted in a special way with Israel and is called *legal*; and thirdly, that which is called gracious and is set forth in the gospel."[55] Amyraut, however, still affirmed that the covenant of grace was initiated with Adam at the fall though it was greatly obscured, very rudimentary, and the promise (Gen 3:15) "very quickly 'almost completely extinguished.'"[56]

The Westminster Confession, reflecting Reformed orthodoxy, affirmed two covenants only: the covenant of works "wherein life was promised to *Adam*, and in him to his posterity, upon condition of perfect and personal obedience," and the covenant of grace "wherein he freely offereth ... Life and Salvation by Jesus Christ" to "all those that are ordained unto life." The Confession declared that the covenant of grace "was differently administred in the time of the Law" than in the time of the gospel and that "there are not therefore two Covenants of Grace, differing in substance, but one and the same, under various dispensations." However, while affirming the "Promises, Prophesies, Sacrifices, Circumcision, the Pascal Lamb, and other Types and Ordinances delivered to the people of the Jews" as "fore-signifying"[57] Christ to come, the Confession appears to be strangely silent on the long-held association of the covenant of works with the Decalogue and the question of how the demands of the Mosaic Law are to be regarded.

Whatever the case, the evidence suggests that this was a point of continuing lively discussion. In the year of Wesley's birth, the second edition of John Bunyan's *The Doctrine of the Law and Grace Unfolded* was published in which Bunyan unequivocally equates the Mosaic Law with the covenant of works.[58] It does not appear that the struggle over how best to understand the Mosaic covenant in relation to either the covenant of works or the covenant of grace had abated by the time Wesley

---

55. Quoted from Amyraut's "De tribus foederisbus divinis," Thesis 2 in *Theses Salmurienses*, 1:212 by Armstrong, *Calvinism and the Amyraut Heresy*, 144. Amyraut's concept of the developing revelation of God involved his assertion that whereas atonement was limited (to Israel) under the legal covenant, it was universal under the covenant of grace.

56. Armstrong, *Calvinism and the Amyraut Heresy*, 153–55.

57. The Westminster Assembly, *The Confession of Faith*, chap. VII, 20–22.

58. Bunyan declares, "The Covenant of Works, ..., is the Law delivered on Mount *Sinai*, to *Moses*, in two Tables of stone, in ten particular branches, or heads; ..." Bunyan, *The Doctrine of the Law and Grace Unfolded*, 5.

rose to prominence. John Guyse, for example, dubbed the Mosaic covenant "a 'temporary covenant of peculiarity' with the Jews"—describing it as "not merely the covenant of works" and "not merely the covenant of grace."[59] This label, "covenant of peculiarity" does not originate with Guyse, however. Matthew Henry, whose commentary on the New Testament preceded that of Guyse by almost two decades, also refers to the Mosaic covenant as "the Covenant of Peculiarity" though he is unwilling to explore Guyse's solution noted above. Henry declares: "The Body and Soul too of all Divinity (as some observe) consist very much in rightly distinguishing between the two Covenants, the Covenant of Works, and the Covenant of Grace, and between the two dispensations of the Covenant of Grace, that under the Old Testament, and that under the New." He then goes on to speak of the "old covenant" spoken of in Hebrews as "the old Dispensation of the Covenant of Grace."[60] Wesley's position is most akin to Henry's on this point.

The Covenant Theology of Johannes Cocceius

The influence of Johannes Cocceius (1603–69) on the historical development of covenant theology is difficult to overstate. When he enrolled in the Gymnasium Illustre in Bremen, he came under the instruction of Matthias Martini (1572–1630), rector and professor of sacred philology at the Bremen school. Martini had played a significant role as a moderating voice at the Synod of Dort in 1618 where the high Calvinists succeeded in gaining the condemnation of the Articles of Remonstrance but failed to gain unequivocal support for their supralapsarian view. Martini's more moderate Calvinistic views undoubtedly shaped Cocceius' as Martini became immensely influential in his life and academic development. Cocceius pursued rabbinical studies in Hamburg and then relocated from his German homeland to the University of Franeker in the Netherlands where he studied with the Orientalist, Sixtinus Amama, Maccovius, and William Ames who had been exiled from England.[61]

It is Cocceius' teaching career that expanded his influence along with his extensive works in the exegesis of scripture and in theology.[62]

---

59. Guyse, *The Practical Expositor* (1792–94) 5:339.

60. Henry, *An exposition of the several epistles* (1721–25), 6:564–65.

61. This overview is based on the account of Cocceius' academic upbringing by Baker and McCoy. See Baker and McCoy, *The Fountainhead of Federalism*, 70–72.

62. His major works include *Summa doctrinae de foedere et testamento Dei*, *Summa theologiae ex Sacris Scripturis repetita*, lectures and publications of his exegesis of each book of the Bible, and a Hebrew lexicon. Ibid., 72.

Having completed his studies at Franeker he returned to Bremen to teach in place of Martini and held that post for six years. In 1636 he returned to the University of Franeker where he taught for the next fourteen years until becoming professor of theology at Leiden, "perhaps the most distinguished university in Europe at that time"[63] where he remained until his death. "Students came from all over Europe to hear him and study with him," Baker and McCoy write, summarizing the extent of his influence. "In particular, in this period when English dissenters were not permitted to study in Oxford and Cambridge, Leiden was second only to Edinburgh as the university to which they flocked for university education. Cocceius thus became a focal point in connecting the development of federal theology in Germany, the Netherlands, and Great Britain."[64]

While this assessment of the magnitude of Cocceius' influence may be sufficient grounds to reasonably assume some influence on Wesley, the case is strengthened by the fact that the Württemberg scholar J. A. Bengel was profoundly influenced by Cocceius. While it is difficult to trace exactly *how* Cocceius' reconfiguration of covenant theology came to influence Wesley's, the fact that it *did* is clearly discernible as will be evident later in this study. Recalling Wesley's incorporation of the servant-son metaphor in his *Explanatory Notes Upon the New Testament* noted earlier, the debut of Bengel's covenant theology in Wesley's thought is certain. The relationship of this debut to the mediating of Cocceius' covenant theology to Wesley is not without basis. Peter Erb notes that "with the Lutherans at Halle, Bengel shared an interest in Reformed theology as it was applied to the study of Scripture, particularly the covenant theology of Johann Cocceius and the work of his follower Campegius Vitringa."[65] And Ernest Stoeffler has traced Bengel's exposure to and interest in Cocceius to Wolfgang Jäger's[66] "unabashed adoption of the federalist theology of Johannes Cocceius"[67] despite Johannes Brenz efforts in resisting the encroachment of Reformed theology in Württemberg.[68]

63. Ibid., 70–72.
64. Ibid., 72.
65. Erb, *Pietists: Selected Writings*, 17.
66. Jäger was a member of the faculty at Tübingen where Bengel carried on his work.
67. Stoeffler, *German Pietism*, 97.
68. Ibid., 96. A Lutheran orthodoxist, Brenz resisted the encroachment of the Reformed theology promoted by Halle. The resulting tension at Tübingen where Bengel had studied from 1703 until his graduation in 1707 resulted in a "theological atmo-

What is compelling about Bengel's use of the Servant-Son metaphor—and Wesley's subsequent choice to not only include it but to expand on it and to incorporate it into his correspondence from time to time—can best be understood in light of Coccejus' unique rendering of the idea of progression within the covenant of grace. Concerning Coccejus, Hans Frei notes: "The first to work out with thematic clarity the scheme of a 'federal theology,' he took the traditional reformed concept of a covenant between God and man and worked it into a notion of distinctive temporal stages operative in the history portrayed in scripture."[69] The key development here was not the introduction of historical distinctions within the covenant of grace. This is evident already in Ames' *Medulla Theologaie* published two decades before either of Coccejus' major works on covenant theology. Indeed, it may be the imprint of Ames' covenant theology that shapes the distinctions noted by his student, Coccejus. But what is of particular importance in Coccejus' work is his nuancing these distinctions into what Van Asselt describes as "one of the most remarkable constructs" in his theological system: "the doctrine of the so-called abrogations or annulments."[70]

Found in both his *Summa Doctrinae* (1648) and *Summa Theologiae* (1662), this doctrine "depicts five stages (*grades*) through which God leads humanity to eternal life, and in which the consequences of the violation of the covenant of works through sin are gradually nullified."[71] Coccejus, Van Asselt notes, "treats the covenant of grace from the perspective of the annulments of the covenant of works" based on the declaration of Hebrews 8:13—"'And what is becoming obsolete and growing old is ready to vanish away.'"[72] Coccejus describes this process as follows:

> The covenant of works is close to disappearing through a gradual obsolescence. . . . The abrogation of the law or of the covenant of works proceeds along the following steps:
>
> 1. The possibility of being made alive [is abrogated] because of sin.

---

sphere . . . fraught with a certain amount of confessional ambiguity" and created a theological climate affording a certain freedom that troubled many Lutheran orthodoxists. The situation benefited Bengel by giving him freedom to make use of Coccejus's approach to scriptural interpretation to shape the methodology of his own study of the Bible. Ibid., 97.

69. Frei, *The Eclipse of Biblical Narrative*, 46.
70. Van Asselt, *The Federal Theology of Johannes Coccejus*, 271.
71. Ibid.
72. Ibid.

2. The curse [is abrogated] through Christ, who is introduced in the form of the promise and who is appropriated by faith.

3. Terror or the effects of the fear of death and servitude [is abrogated] through the promulgation of the new covenant. After atonement for sin has been accomplished, the redeemed are under the law of the Redeemer. In this same way, the law that the Redeemer has abolished as a law of sin now becomes a law of the Savior that bestows righteousness on those who belong to him (Gal. 2:19; Rom. 7:4; 2 Cor. 5:15, 21).

4. The struggle against sin [is abrogated] through the mortification of the body.

5. All the consequences and effects of the covenant of works [are abrogated] through the resurrection of the dead.[73]

In this scheme, despite the abrogation of the covenant of works by Christ (the second abrogation), the after-effects of the covenant of works remain on account of the fact that the obligation of the covenant continues since it has been abrogated only insofar as the pact (*pactum de operibus*), as a way of salvation, has been nullified.[74] Thus,

> As long as Christ has not appeared "*realiter*" in time, the covenant of works continues to make its demands and in spite of the promise made of Christ's coming it goes on sowing unrest: It keeps the believers under the Old Testament dispensation in fear and servitude. Not until Christ has really appeared in the flesh is there freedom and joy, because what had been promised really happens and now becomes history. But even then the covenant of works . . . finds expression in the struggle between flesh and Spirit in the life of the believer (Rom 7). Not until death and resurrection in the eschaton have all the effects of the violation of the covenant of works been abrogated.[75]

Consequently, under the covenant of grace, each abrogation progressively addresses a specific "after-effect"[76] of the covenant of works: *condemnation* because of sin ("damnation"), *consequences* of the broken covenant ("terror"), *conflict* with sin ("the struggle against the remnants

---

73. Cocceius, *Summa Doctrinae* (1648), §58 cited by Van Asselt, *The Federal Theology of Johannes Cocceius*, 271–72. Bracketed inserts mine. See also Van Asselt, "The Doctrine of the Abrogations," 107.

74. Ibid., 109.

75. Ibid.

76. Ibid.

of the flesh"), and *all remaining consequences* (remaining as a result of the covenant of works having been broken).[77]

It is not surprising, then, that Cocceius, when speaking of the abrogations, uses terms that emphasize *both* the once-for-all nature of the abrogations *and* their gradual progression. The persistent encroachment of the after-effects of the covenant of works is met and gradually overcome by the activity of God's grace:

> The abrogation proceeds (*procedit*) by stages (*gradibus*), through which gradually (*paulatim*) and more and more (*magis magisque*) salvation is realized among believers. This suggests a process of deliverance in which one stage is left behind and progress is made toward the next step. This process of deliverance is amenable to description in terms of the covenant of works/covenant of grace schema: the elements of the covenant of works undergo a negative development, going from greater to lesser, while the elements of the covenant of grace undergo a positive development, progressing from lesser to greater.[78]

This clearly indicates development within salvation history. Van Asselt notes,

> Cocceius' theology is oriented not toward static states of affairs, but towards movement in history. This progression, of course, does imply a value judgment, an evaluative moment: more value can be attributed to subsequent stages in comparison to those that came before. This additional value, however, does not degrade the value of the preceding stage, but rather transforms it.[79]

There is, then, a *progression*, a development from lesser to greater. And further, this development takes place in history. Van Asselt, however, makes a convincing argument that, for Cocceius, *this development is not only salvation-historical but also is a development in terms of the experience of the believer.* He calls attention to the fact that the statement of each abrogation begins by "referring to the moment of knowledge of the believer and the condition or state of the believers connected with

---

77. In *Summa Theologiae*, Cocceius identifies what is abrogated as follows: "1. The possibility of justification and vivification, 2. Damnation, 3. Terror, 4. The struggle against the remnants of the flesh, 5. All the consequences (of the covenant of works)." Cocceius, *Summa Theologiae*, chap. 31, §1 cited in Van Asselt, *The Federal Theology of Johannes Cocceius*, 272.

78. Van Asselt, *The Federal Theology of Johannes Cocceius*, 276.

79. Ibid. 277. Emphasis mine.

it: damnation, fear, servitude, and struggle between flesh and Spirit."[80] Each of these conditions is answered by advancements in salvation history: "the *protevangelium*, the appearance of Christ, the Resurrection, eschaton."[81]

Thus, "the various degrees in the abrogations are moments in a movement"[82]—not only moments in the movements of God's saving activity over *time* (salvation history) but moments corresponding to developments within the *experience* of the believer in each dispensation. As a result, according the Cocceius, "salvation takes various forms in the various dispensations of the economy of salvation."[83] This general idea is not unique to Cocceius. Andreas Musculus (1514–81) held that "each succeeding convenantal dispensation amplifies the previous one" and associated these with the three stages of the development of the people of God (childhood, youth, and adulthood)."[84]

In Cocceius' view, the experience of faith under the dispensations prior to the gospel dispensation was qualitatively different on account of being oriented to the *promise* of Christ's coming rather than to the *revelation* of Christ, the distinguishing event of the gospel (or Christian) dispensation. Nevertheless, he emphasized that "those believing God's word of promise . . . are justified before God at all times"[85] on the basis that their faith is faith *in Christ*, though Christ is yet to be revealed. The notion that there was such a qualitative difference in the experience of faith of the elect depending on the dispensation under which they lived was an affront to many Calvinists, though Cocceius claims this idea originated with Beza and Cloppenburg. His promulgation of this view aroused the ire of Gisbertus Voetius (1589–1676), a Reformed systematic theologian known as "the *pater orthodoxiae* in Holland,"[86] who rejected the idea of there being such a qualitative difference in the experience of faith. In opposition to Cocceius, Voetius defended the conviction that "the believers under the old and the new dispensation" both "fully shared in divine pardon and grace"[87] on the basis of their being members of the

---

80. Van Asselt, "The Doctrine of the Abrogations," 108.

81. Ibid. 108.

82. Ibid. 110.

83. Van Asselt, *The Federal Theology of Johannes Cocceius*, 239.

84. Musculus related these stages to the three mediators of the covenant of grace: Abraham, Moses, and Christ. Blacketer, "Arminius' Concept of Covenant," 214.

85. Van Asselt, *The Federal Theology of Johannes Cocceius*, 239.

86. Van Asselt, "*Amicitia Dei* as Ultimate Reality," 36.

87. Van Asselt, "The Doctrine of the Abrogations," 113.

elect. Cocceius' distinction, together with the whole of his doctrine of abrogations, was also strongly rejected by Antonius Hulsius (1615–85) who termed the doctrine a *monstrosum dogma* in theology.[88]

It is evident from the foregoing survey that while covenant theology possesses certain identifiable theological components, it is quite variegated. On the one hand, there is a sense in which those components that are routinely present might reasonably be characterized as classic covenant theology. One such component that is consistently present is the centrality of the promise of Genesis 3:15 appearing in the pronouncement of judgment upon the serpent: "and [her seed] shall bruise thy head, and thou shalt bruise his heel." This "gracious promise," as Wesley describes it,[89] points to what Cocceius calls "the intervention of the Sponsor and Redeemer" [90] in behalf of fallen humanity. This intervention is what is affirmed by Wesley, and by covenant theologians in general, in his declaration that the covenant "had its force from the designed death of the great testator, the *Lamb slain from the foundation of the world.*"[91] Thus, Christ's victory on the Cross is the foundation of the covenant of grace, the inception of which coincides with the fall and with "the gracious promise" of Genesis 3:15.

On the other hand, gaining consensus on what constitutes classic covenant theology comes at the price of generalizing the theological content of at least some of those components to the point that critical theological nuances can be easily obscured or overlooked. For example, as the examination above reveals, it is possible—and accurate—to speak of the covenant of works as one of the basic conceptions of seventeenth century covenant theology. Yet, at the same time, *how* the covenant of

88. Ibid.

89. Wesley, *Explanatory Notes Upon the Old Testament*, I:17–18.

90. Cocceius, *Summa Theologiae*, cap. 31 §1 quoted in Van Asselt, *The Federal Theology of Johannes Cocceius*, 272–73. On the matter of the intervention of the Sponsor/Redeemer (Christ), Van Asselt notes that "Cocceius thinks in an infralapsarian way: The Fall as a historical fact calls for salvation. But because salvation is founded in eternity"—in the *pactum salutis*, the eternal pact between the Father and the Son—the second abrogation (Christ's intervention in the face of the curse) "is fed back to an event in eternity, which, however, is revealed and announced after the Fall in the primordial promise." Van Asselt, "The Doctrine of the Abrogations," 108.

91. Wesley, *Explanatory Notes Upon the Old Testament* (1762), 1:1. The words at the end of the sentence are emphasized by Wesley to differentiate them as belonging to Scripture (Rev. 13:8). The context of Wesley's use of the word "covenant" here is his introduction of the Old Testament to the reader. In this same context he describes the idea of covenant as "a declaration of the will of God concerning man in a federal way."

works is conceived is itself one of the most variegated elements of covenant theology; and, the implications of this variegation are theologically substantial. Or, as another example, even though the predestinarian template of covenant theology may be properly identified as a primary attribute of classic covenant theology, this element itself is hardly conceived in a uniform way—as Voetius' dispute with CoccEian covenant theology reveals.

So it is that the ancestry of Wesley's covenant theology is more complex than what might be suggested by the appearance of simplicity in Outler's assertion of the place of Perkins, Ames, and the Westminster Confession in that ancestry or in his passing references to the influence of Cocceius' doctrine of abrogations. With good reason, the ancestry of Wesley's covenant theology may best be understood as a reflection of much of the dynamic conversation within covenant theology itself over the course of the intense, formative season of its formal development beginning particularly with the latter part of the sixteenth century. The question is whether Wesley's covenant theology was an empty echo that remained largely external to his theological thought like barnacles to the hull of a ship, or if it was, as declared at the outset of this study, a core feature of the infrastructure of his thought which he knowingly and thoughtfully called upon in articulating his vision of the way of salvation.

CHAPTER 3

John Wesley's Amendment of Covenant Theology

WHAT WE KNOW OF John Wesley's covenant theology comes by way of the minutes of Conferences, the letters borne of controversy, counsel, and reflection, and the sermons, extracts, and journal entries comprising the Wesley corpus. These chronicle his encounter with the covenant theology instilled in the theological understanding of his companions, converts, and antagonists. One indicator of its status as the common currency of theological discourse is Wesley's confidence that his use of its technical terminology would be understood by his audience. And yet, as the opening paragraph of his sermon "The Righteousness of Faith" clearly demonstrates, he recognized that certain aspects of the covenant theology to which some of his audience subscribed bore the imprint of a covenant theology at odds at points with his own.

It is in piecing together the record of these encounters that Wesley's amendment of classic covenant theology comes to light and that we discover he was not a passive recipient of the covenant theology mediated to him. Instead, with theological precision he thoughtfully modified and revised what he had received. And what becomes clear upon close inspection of the evidence is that Wesley amended classic covenant theology at the level of its most basic component: the two covenants God has made with humanity—the covenant of works and the covenant of grace.

An exemplary case in point of this amendment may be found in his extract of *The New Covenant; or, the Saints' Portion*, a sermon by John Preston.[1] Expounding the phrase from God's declaration to Abram, "And I will make my covenant between me and thee" (17:2), Preston

---

1. Preston (1587–1628) was a Church of England clergyman, awakened under the preaching of the Puritan John Cotton and himself not infrequently accused of "'puritanisme.'" Moore, "Preston, John (1587–1628)," *DNB* (http://www.oxforddnb.com).

59

provides a succinct description of the two covenants in terms consistent with classic covenant theology. His original wording was as follows:

> You must know that there is a double *Couenant,* there is a *Couenant* of Works, and a *Couenant* of Grace: the Couenant of Workes runs in these termes, *Doe this, and thou shalt live,* and I will be thy God. This is the *Couenant* that was made with *Adam* and the *Couenant* that is expressed by Moses in the Morall Law, *Doe this, and live.* The second is the *Couenant* of Grace, and that runs in these termes, . . . *Thou shalt beleeue, and take my Sonne, and accept of the gift of righteousnes, and I will be thy God.* The difference between them you shall find, 2 Cor. 3. where you shall see 3. differences, . . .²

In his extract of Preston's work for *A Christian Library,* Wesley's additions and deletions to this paragraph are revealing:

> You must know that there is a double covenant; 1. A covenant of works; and 2. A covenant of grace. The covenant of works runs in these terms, "Do this, and you shall live, and I will be thy God." This is the covenant that was made with Adam ~~and the covenant that is expressed by Moses in the Moral Law, "Do this and live"~~ *in paradise.* The covenant of grace runs in these terms, "You shall believe, and take my Son, and accept of the gift of righteousness, and I will be thy God." Between these two covenants you shall find a threefold difference, 2 Cor. 3.³

By adding the words "in paradise" and deleting "and the covenant that is expressed by Moses in the Moral Law, 'Do this and live,'" Wesley is addressing an element consistently present in classic (Puritan) covenant theology with which he fundamentally disagreed: the conflation of the Mosaic Law with the covenant made with Adam.⁴ The point is

---

2. Preston, *The new covenant,* 317–38.

3. Preston, "The New Covenant," *ACL* (Jackson), 6:31. Wesley's additions appear in italics; strike-through text indicates words and phrases deleted by Wesley.

4. It is difficult to assess the influence on Wesley of his reading of the covenant theology of Henry Hammond in *A Practical Catechism* and William Beveridge in *Thoughts on Private Religion.* Wesley read both works, Heitzenrater notes, while at Oxford. *Heitzenrater,* "John Wesley and the Oxford Methodists," 497, 506. In his *Catechism,* Hammond instructs his imaginary catechumen that "The Judiacall law was not the first Covenant" for *that* covenant was "the law of unsinning perfect obedience made with Adam in innocency." However, Wesley specifically deletes from Preston the words Hammond next spoke to his catechumen: "The truth is, the Judiacall law did represent unto us the first Covenant." Hammond, *A Practical Catechism,* 10. Wesley seems to have had a specific interest in clarifying the point. See the discussion below on the distinctiveness of Wes-

of sufficient importance that it prompts the addition of the following explanatory note inserted parenthetically into the extract at this very point:

> In the passage of Scripture here referred to [2 Cor 3] the apostle is not contrasting the covenant of justice, or law of innocence, (termed not very properly the covenant of works,) made with man before the fall, and the covenant of grace made with man after the fall, but he is contrasting *the two last dispensations of the covenant of grace, the Mosaic and the Christian*, and showing, in a variety of particulars, the great superiority of the latter to the former.[5]

This point, in fact, is *so* important that it is pressed beyond Preston's reference to the Apostle Paul's discussion of covenant in the third chapter of 2 Corinthians:

> And when, in the epistle to the Galatians, chap. iii.10, he asserts that "as many as are of the works of the law are under the curse," he does not speak of the law given to our first parents before the fall, but wholly of the law of Moses, moral and ceremonial, signifying that as many as adhered to it, and confided in it for justification, rejecting the gospel, were under condemnation and wrath . . .[6]

Certainly, these distinctions indicate an important difference between classic covenant theology and the covenant theology operative in Wesley's theological thought. But what is at stake for Wesley? What does he gain or secure that warrants his taking such care to amend classic covenant theology on this point? There are, after all numerous points of correspondence between Wesley's covenant theology and classic covenant theology:

 a. The affirmation that God is a covenant-making God;

 b. The recognition of two covenants made with humanity (the covenant of works and the covenant of grace) and that the

---

ley's view of the perpetuity of the moral law.

5. Preston, "The New Covenant," *ACL* (Jackson), 6:31.

6. Ibid. It should be noted that while the changes to the text of Preston's sermon appear in the 50-volume first edition of *A Christian Library* [*ACL*, 10:81] published 1749–55, and in the edition published beginning in 1819, the extended explanatory note appears only in the later edition. Nevertheless, the extended clarification accurately reflects distinctions made by Wesley in his 1746 sermon, "The Righteousness of Faith," Wesley, *Works* (BE), 1:202–16.

inception of the covenant of grace may be traced to "the original promise made to [Adam] and his seed concerning the seed of the woman, who should 'bruise the serpent's head'" (Gen 3:15);[7]

c. The insistence that gaining righteousness by works is impossible for fallen humanity;

d. The concept of the double administration of the covenant of grace (one administration *before* Christ's coming, another *since* his coming);

e. The view that the administration of the covenant of grace before Christ's coming was progressive in nature; and

f. The declaration of the undiminished stature of the moral law and humanity's amenability to it.

Yet, the correspondence on these points is not exact. This is not surprising. Given the incompatibility between Wesley's evangelical Arminianism and the predestinarian template indigenous to covenant theology, some adaptation was inevitable. The question is, in what ways did Wesley amend covenant theology? The answer is discovered in surveying his understanding of the covenant of grace and his view of the perpetuity of the moral law.

The Covenant of Grace in Wesley's Covenant Theology

If there is any point where Wesley's amendment of the covenant theology mediated to him is most pronounced, it would be in the way in which the covenant of grace is conceived. This difference molds Wesley's covenant theology into the form exemplified in his sermons, correspondence, and other publications and follows the fault line created by his rejection of the Calvinistic doctrine of predestination—and of double predestination, in particular. It is important to note, however, that his conception of the covenant of grace aligns fully with two firmly established tenets of covenant theology: first, the *foundation* of the covenant of grace is Christ by virtue of his mediation as "the lamb slain from the foundation of the world" (Rev 13:8); and second, the *inauguration* of the covenant of grace is coincidental with the fall.

Of course, in the scheme of supralapsarian Calvinism everything flows from the divine decrees of election and reprobation. The covenant

---

7. Wesley, "The Righteousness of Faith," *Works* (BE) §I.7, 1:206.

of grace is the means of executing the decree in behalf of the elect; the foundation undergirding this covenant, says Perkins, is "Christ Jesus, called of his father from all eternitie, to performe the office of the Mediator, that in him, all those which should be saved, might be chosen."[8] This mediatorial work of Christ is a work on behalf of the elect of fallen humanity of *all* ages. Making this same point, Ames declares:

> Now such a Mediator is not given, for one age onely but for yesterday, to day, and for ever. *Hebr.* 13.8. Jesus Christ yesterday, to day and is the same for ever: *Rev.* 13.8. The Lambe slain from the foundation of the World. Although he was only manifest in the fullnesse of time. *Col.* 1.27. *Tit.* 1.2. 1 *Pet.* 1.20. For this Meditation [*sic*] was equally necessary in all ages: Also, it was sufficient, and effectuall from the beginning, by virtue of God's decree, promises, and acceptation.'[9]

Though John Deschner contends that Wesley did not subscribe to the distinction between *logos incarnandus* (Christ to be exhibited) and *logos incarnates* (Christ exhibited),[10] the textual evidence convincingly argues otherwise. In his sermon, "The Original, Nature, Properties, and Use of the Law" Wesley declares:

> But it was not long before man rebelled against God, ... And yet God did not despise the work of his own hands; but *being reconciled to man through the Son of his love*, he in some measure re-inscribed the law on the heart of his dark, sinful creature. "He" again "showed thee, O man, what is good" (although not as in the beginning), ... *And this he showed not only to our first parents, but likewise to all their posterity*, by "that true light which enlightens every man that cometh into the world."[11]

---

8. Perkins, *The Golden Chaine* (1600), 24.

9. Ames, *The Marrow of Sacred Divinity*, 80–81. Note: pages in this edition of the work are numbered incorrectly. Page numbering shown here reflects the correct numbering.

10. Deschner, *Wesley's Christology*, 72–73. The terms, *logos incarnandus* and *logos incarnates* are Deschner's. In a footnote, Deschner argues that Wesley denies this distinction, rejecting the idea of a pact between Father and Son and refusing to speak of "the Lamb who was slain form the foundation of the world," Ibid., 81–82. Certainly Deschner is correct in noting that Wesley rejected the idea of a prelapsarian pact between the Father and the Son. See Wesley's preface to his extract of John Goodwin's, *A Treatise on Jusification*, 15–16. However, the textual evidence is overwhelming that Wesley held firmly to the fundamental conviction of covenant theology that Christ's mediation is from the time of the fall as "the lamb slain from the foundation of the world."

11. Wesley, *Works* (BE) §I.4–5, 2:7. Emphasis mine.

For Wesley as for his Calvinist counterparts, every provision of grace throughout all ages flows only and always from the reconciling work of Christ. This is evidenced, in his view, by the re-inscription of the moral law[12] ("that true light which enlightens every man that cometh into the world") on the hearts of our "first parents" and "likewise to all their posterity." In "The Righteousness of Faith" Wesley underscores this point in words reminiscent of Ames: "But it is the covenant of *grace* which God through Christ hath established with men in all ages (as well before, and under the Jewish dispensation, as since God was manifest in the flesh) . . ."[13] Without feeling compelled to adopt "the horrible decree"[14] as his starting point, Wesley clearly retains in his own theological thought this essential element of covenant theology: that the mediatorial work of Christ is from the foundation of the world.

There may be no more clear affirmation of this by Wesley than in his October 15, 1756 letter to James Hervey in which he critiques Hervey's *Theron and Aspasio* published that same year. In a footnote Hervey contended that "the faithful *Jews* no more died under the Curse of the Law, than the faithful *Christians*."[15] Wesley cites a sentence from Hervey's footnote and declares his unequivocal agreement with him on this point: "'The *Death* of *Christ* procured the *Pardon* and *Acceptance* of Believers, even before He came in the Flesh.' Yea, and ever since. In this we all agree."[16] While the foundation of the covenant of grace is "the lamb slain from the foundation of the world" (Rev 13:8), the re-inscription of the law upon the hearts of "our first parents" clearly iterates the basic tenet of orthodox Reformed theology that the fall is the event that occasioned Christ's mediation and initialized the covenant of grace. However, though Wesley also held this view, it is in relation to this very affirmation that his covenant theology begins to distinguish itself.

The point of divergence is Wesley's conviction that not only is the *inauguration* of the covenant of grace coincidental with the fall, but so is the *termination* of the covenant of works. This conviction is of supreme importance for Wesley in facilitating an Arminian adaptation of

12. Ibid.

13. Ibid., 1:203. Emphasis mine. Wesley is in full agreement on this point with his friend turned antagonist, James Hervey: "Though he laid down his life in the Reign of Tiberias, He was a real Redeemer in *all Ages*." Hervey, *Theron and Aspasio*, 1:74.

14. The phrase was Wesley's epithet for the divine decrees of election and reprobation. See, for example, "Free Grace," *Works* (BE) §26, 3:556; and n. 65.

15. Hervey, *Theron and Aspasio*, 1:74.

16. See Wesley's preface in Goodwin, *A Treatise on Jusification: Extracted from Mr. John Goodwin, by Mr. John Wesley*, 7.

covenant theology—first, by reconfiguring the *reach* of the covenant of grace; and second, by disallowing any notion that there is a reinvigoration of the covenant of works beyond the fall.

On the first point, whereas the covenant of grace is treated by the Puritan divines only in terms of its provisions for the *elect*, Wesley declares unequivocally that *all* the sons of Adam were and are under the covenant of grace: "And who ever was under the covenant of works? *None but Adam before the fall.* He was fully and properly under that covenant, which required perfect, universal obedience, as the one condition of acceptance, and left no place for pardon, upon the very least transgression. *But no man else was ever under this*, neither Jew nor Gentile, neither before Christ nor since."[17]

This is nothing short of a declaration that the covenant of works, along with the provision of life attached to it, reached its terminus at the fall. And together with his view that the covenant of grace is the covenant "which God through Christ hath established with men in all ages,"[18] it is certain to Wesley that at no time *since* the fall has the covenant of works defined the terms of relationship between God and humanity.[19] The ramifications of this declaration are far-reaching and clearly signal Wesley's amendment of the covenant theology of Perkins, Ames, and the Westminster Confession.

The second aspect of Wesley's assertion that the covenant of works reached its terminus coincidental with the fall is his conviction that the Mosaic Law belongs fully and *only* to the covenant of grace; that is, the giving of the Law to Moses at Sinai signals *neither a continuation nor a reinvigoration of the covenant of works*. Wesley makes this point repeatedly in "The Righteousness of Faith," arguing against any discontinuity between "the former" and "the latter" words spoken by Moses to Israel as highlighted by the Apostle Paul in Romans 10:5–8, the sermon's text: "The Apostle does not here oppose the covenant given by Moses to the covenant given by Christ. . . . But it is the covenant of *grace* which God through Christ hath established with men in all ages."[20]

---

17. Wesley, "The Law Established Through Faith: Discourse I," §II.3, *Works* (BE), 2:27. Emphasis mine. This echoes the affirmation of the 1746 Conference. See *Minutes*, 1746 (Jackson) Q.24, 8:289.

18. Wesley, "The Righteousness of Faith." *Works* (BE) §1, 1:202–3.

19. See Wesley's 1784 sermon, 'On Patience,' *Works* (BE) §10, 3:174–75.

20. Wesley, *Works* (BE) §1, 1:202–3. "The latter" refers to those words spoken by Moses to Israel at Moab as recorded in Deuteronomy 30:11–14; "the former" refers to Moses' words to Israel at Horeb (Lev 18:5).

In making this point, Wesley is voicing his opposition to the notion that the words spoken by Moses at Moab were themselves "another covenant" rather than the covenant given at Mount Sinai in Horeb. Thomas Goodwin seems to have espoused such a view: "'The apostle pertinently quotes the words of this last great sermon of Moses, to distinguish the covenant of works and the covenant of grace.'"[21] Wesley counters that, rather than arguing for a kind of synonymy between the Mosaic Law given at Sinai (in Horeb) and the covenant of works, the Apostle Paul references Moses' words in illustrative fashion in order to connect *both* the former and the latter words with the covenant of grace and thereby to *contrast* them with the covenant of works.

Of course, in the view of classic covenant theology, treating the Mosaic Law as a continuation of the covenant of works did not detract from its function as an instrument of grace *for the elect*. Indeed, by means of the re-encounter with the covenant of works and the impossibility of meeting its demand of perfect obedience, the effect of the Mosaic Law on the elect was to incite them to "flie unto Christ" and thus to deliver them into the provisions of the covenant of grace. This, however, was not the effect upon the so-called non-elect. Rather, they are wholly and irrecoverably segregated from the covenant of grace having been sentenced by divine decree to miss the pedagogical purpose of the Mosaic Law ("to train us up for *Christ*"[22]), and, consequently, sentenced to the impossibility of establishing a righteousness of their own. In Wesley's view this is unacceptable because it obscures the fact that God's redemptive initiative extends to *all* of humanity—a certainty secured by the fact that the Mosaic Law belongs fully and only to the covenant of grace:

> [The Jews] were ignorant that "Christ is the end of the law for righteousness to everyone that believeth"; that by the oblation of himself once offered he had put an end to the first law or covenant (*which indeed was not given by God to Moses, but to Adam in his state of innocence*), the strict tenor whereof, with-

---

21. Goodwin's comment is cited by Guyse, *The Practical Expositor*, 486. Wesley also steers clear of Guyse's own view that Moses explained the strict demands of the law "as a covenant of works" in contrast to "The language of the gospel-doctrine of justification through the righteousness of Christ, which is proposed to, and received by faith, as Moses himself also hinted." Ibid. Wesley, however, does seem to agree with Guyse that Moses' speech in Deut. 30 "speaks with an ultimate view to gospel-days." Wesley, *Explanatory Notes Upon the Old Testament*, 1:679.

22. Wesley, *ENNT*, 603. Wesley's assessment of the ceremonial law does not always include an emphasis on its pedagogical value. See Wesley, "Upon Our Lord's Sermon on the Mount," *Works* (BE) §I.2, 1:551–52.

out any abatement, was, "Do this and live"; and at the same time purchased for us that better covenant, "Believe and live": "Believe and thou shalt be saved"; now saved both from the guilt and power of sin, and of consequence from the wages of it.[23]

In this brief statement, Wesley notes once again that the law given to Moses is not to be confused with "the first law or covenant"—the covenant of works—given to Adam prior to the fall. Rather, the law given to Moses belongs wholly to "that better covenant," the covenant of grace. There is no mixing of the covenant of works with the covenant of grace.

Wesley substantiates this point by making use of two related but distinct affirmations—one from scripture, "Christ is the *end* of the law" (Rom 10:4); the other from the *Book of Common Prayer*, "that Christ by the oblation of himself once offered . . . had put an *end* to the first law or covenant." [24] His aim appears to be simply to underscore the fact that the covenant of works is no longer in force. For this purpose, he moves on from his passing reference to Romans 10:4 to explain that this end came about by Christ's sacrificial death which also served to effect the inception of the *only* covenant now in effect, the covenant of grace. Again, it must be emphasized that when Wesley speaks of Christ having "put an end to the first law or covenant," his declaration is based upon Christ's mediation as *logos incarnandus* (Christ to be exhibited), for "no man else was ever under [the covenant of works], neither Jew nor Gentile, neither *before* Christ" was manifested in the flesh (*logos incarnates*) "nor since."[25]

That the termination of the covenant of works upon the occasion of the fall is a mainstay of Wesley's theological thought is underscored by its reappearance in the opening of pages of his *Farther Thoughts upon Christian Perfection* published in 1763. Both elements are again present: a) Christ as the end of the law, and b) the specific role of Christ's sacrificial death in bringing about that end. In answering the question of how Christ is the end of the law, Wesley responds,

> In order to understand this you must understand what law is here spoken of; and this, I apprehend, is (1) the Mosaic law, the whole Mosaic dispensation, which Saint Paul continually speaks of as one, though containing three parts—the political, moral, and ceremonial; (2) the Adamic law, that given to Adam in innocence, properly called "the law of works." This is in sub-

---

23. "The Righteousness of Faith," Wesley, *Works* [BE] §3., 1:203. Emphasis mine.

24. "The Communion," *The Book of Common Prayer* (1732), np.

25. Wesley, "The Law Established through Faith: Discourse I," *Works* (BE) §II.3, 2:27.

stance the same with the angelic law, being common to angels and men.... But Adam fell;... consequently, no man is able to perform the service which the Adamic law requires. And no man is obliged to perform it. God does not require it of any man, for Christ is the end of the Adamic, as well as the Mosaic, law. By his death he hath put an end to both; he hath abolished both the one and the other, with regard to man; and the obligation to observe either the one or the other is vanished away. Nor is any man living bound to observe the Adamic any more than the Mosaic law.[26]

What is significant about *this* explanation of Christ as "the end of the law" when compared to his statement in "The Righteousness of Faith," is its expansion of his description of Christ's law-terminating work. Christ is the end not only of the law given to Adam in his innocence but also of the Mosaic Law given subsequent to the fall. Admittedly, Wesley's assertion that Christ, by his death, has put an end to *both* the Adamic and the Mosaic laws, at first glance seems to portray the Mosaic Law as on a par with the covenant of works. After all, upon Christ's death, "the obligation to serve either the one or the other is vanished away." Wesley, however, carefully avoids conflating the covenant of works with the Mosaic Law, and his covenant theology is profoundly shaped by his vigilance on this point—a vigilance stemming from his conception of the perpetuity of the moral law.

The Moral Law in Wesley's Covenant Theology

It is true that Wesley clearly associated the moral law with the Mosaic Law, affirming that God "chose out of mankind a peculiar people, to whom he gave a more perfect knowledge of [the moral law]" and noting that "the heads of this, because they were slow of understanding, he wrote on two tables of stone."[27] In this regard he stands shoulder to shoulder with both Perkins and Ames in acknowledging the Decalogue as the particular historical embodiment of the moral law.

Yet, while the moral law was indeed "contained in the Ten Commandments,"[28] Wesley also insisted that the moral law itself, while thus affixed to the Law given at Sinai, stood in transcendent relation-

---

26. Wesley, *Farther Thoughts Upon Christian Perfection*, 3–4.

27. Wesley, "The Original, Nature, Properties, and Use of the Law," *Works* (BE) §I.5, 2:7–8.

28. Wesley, "Upon Our Lord's Sermon on the Mount, V," *Works* (BE) §I.2, 1:551–52.

ship to it. The moral law, he declares, "is not, as some may possibly have imagined, of so late an institution as the time of Moses."[29] Wesley asserted, "[The moral law] was from the beginning of the world, being 'written not on tables of stone' but on the hearts of all the children of men when they came out of the hands of the Creator."[30] Continuing the previous sentence, he declared, "Every part of this law must remain in force, upon all mankind, and in all ages; as not depending either on time or place, or any other circumstances liable to change, but on the nature of God and the nature of man, and their unchangeable relation to each other."[31] This very point is emphasized in the deliberations of the 1746 Conference as well:

> Q. 24. But do you consider, that we are under the covenant of grace, and that the covenant of works is now abolished?
>
> A. All mankind were under the covenant of grace, from the very hour that the original promise was made. If by the covenant of works you mean, that of unsinning obedience made with Adam before the fall, no man but Adam was ever under that covenant; for it was abolished before Cain was born. Yet it is not so abolished, but that it will stand, in a measure, even to the end of the world; that is, If we "do this," we shall live; if not, we shall die eternally: If we do well, we shall live with God in glory; if evil, we shall die the second death. For every man shall be judged in that day, and rewarded "according to his works."[32]

This conviction is buttressed by Wesley's affirmation of the distinction between the ceremonial law and the moral law[33]—a distinction common to covenant theology. Thus, while the ceremonial law was *abolished* in Christ and the whole Mosaic dispensation itself was concluded upon the appearance of Christ, the moral law remains a vital component of the covenant of grace, having Christ as its *perfecting* end.[34]

---

29. Wesley, "The Original, Nature, Properties, and Use of the Law," *Works* (BE) §I.1, 2:6. This view is not unique to Wesley, as Perkins and Ames, for example, seem to hold a similar understanding on the binding effect of the moral law before the time of Moses.

30. Wesley, "Upon Our Lord's Sermon on the Mount, V," *Works* (BE) §I.2, 1:551–52.

31. Ibid.

32. *Minutes*, 1746 (Jackson), 8:289.

33. See Wesley, "The Original, Nature, Properties, and Use of the Law," *Works* (BE) §II.1, 2:8.

34. See Guyse's exposition of Romans 10:4. Guyse, *The Practical Expositor* (1792), 3:486. Compare Wesley's commentary on Romans 3:20. Wesley, *ENNT*, 469.

But what differentiates Wesley's covenant theology from that of the Puritan divines is what he views as the distinguishing feature of the covenant of works. Ames, like Perkins before him, presents the *moral law itself* as the primary distinguishing feature of the covenant of works. Thus, the moral law and the covenant of works become functionally synonymous on the basis of the requirement common to both: the demand of perfect obedience. Consequently, with this requirement remaining in force even after the fall—on account of the fact of the perpetuity of the moral law as evidenced by its embodiment in the Decalogue—there is necessarily a reinvigoration of the covenant of works *beyond* the fall. A consequence of this view which Wesley found to be unacceptable was the bifurcation of the Mosaic Law: on the one hand, the Mosaic Law represented a re-invigoration of the covenant of works—on account of which the non-elect are ultimately condemned due to their inability to fulfill its terms; while on the other hand, it belonged to the covenant of grace inciting the elect to "flie unto Christ."[35]

Wesley, however, presents *not* the moral law but Adam's *innocence* as the primary distinguishing feature of the covenant of works and the original foundation upon which the moral law was put into effect. *Absent* such innocence, the original foundation of the moral law—"the ability of man himself"[36]—is irrecoverably compromised, rendering the covenant of works obsolete since the covenant of works cannot possibly extend farther than does humanity's state of innocence. So then, for Wesley, the *perpetuity of the moral law* does not signal a *continuation* or re-invigoration of the covenant of works since the *loss of Adam's innocence* signals the *end* of the covenant of works. Therefore, in Wesley's view, the covenant of works does not re-emerge at *any* point after the fall for the simple fact that original innocence is no longer either a characteristic or a possibility of the human condition.

Indeed, the situation is drastically changed on account of the fall. The moral law "not wrote indeed upon tables of stone, or any corruptible substance, but engraven on [Adam's] heart by the finger of God, wrote in the inmost spirit both of men and of angels" is now "wellnigh effaced . . . out of his heart."[37] While the moral law had once stood upon

---

35. Perkins, *The Golden Chaine*, 102.

36. Ames, *The Marrow of Sacred Divinity*, 115. Despite the differences between Wesley and Ames described above, both recognized "the ability of man himself" to be confined to the time of his innocence.

37. Wesley, "The Original, Nature, Properties, and Use of the Law," §I.3–4, *Works* (BE), 2:7.

Adam's *innocence*, now, after the fall and solely on account of the mercies of God, the moral law stands on Jesus Christ, the lamb slain from the foundation of the world. This provision, Wesley declares, is an outcome of the fact that God "did not despise the work of his own hands" but was "reconciled to man through the Son of his love." As a result of this initiative of grace, God "in some measure re-inscribed the law on the heart of his dark, sinful creature."[38] Thus, rather than indicating a continuation or re-emergence of the covenant of *works*, the perpetuation of the moral law is a witness to the triumph of the initiating love of God demonstrated in the covenant of *grace*[39]—the one and only covenant under which *all* of humanity now lives and has *ever* lived *since* the fall.

This point was important to Wesley in serving to clearly underscore that while the moral law, with its continued requirement of perfect obedience, perpetually serves a salvific *purpose*, it holds no salvific *promise* (as the Jews had mistakenly thought). Indeed, under the Mosaic dispensation the endeavor to keep the moral law produces at best only "a bare outward service"[40] and actually "inflames" the "motions of sins," "discovers" sins, and "drags them out into open day."[41] In this way humanity's desperate predicament is set forth by the Mosaic Law. And *purely from the view of this demand of perfect obedience*, Wesley declares in his commentary on Romans 4:15 that grace "though it was in fact mingled with it, is no part of the legal dispensation."[42] In his commentary on Acts 2:1 Wesley makes this same point with a poignant comparison of the legal and evangelical (gospel) dispensations of the covenant of grace: "At the Pentecost of *Sinai* in the Old Testament, and the Pentecost of *Jerusalem* in the New, were the two grand manifestations of God, the legal and the evangelical: the one from the mountain, and the other from heaven; the terrible, and the merciful one."[43] Thus, though the moral law remains incumbent upon all persons, it is at best a schoolmaster by which the standard of "do this and live" is shown as that which is to be *abandoned* (not as a standard of conduct, but as a basis for securing one's justifi-

---

38. Ibid., §I.4. *Works* (BE), 2:7.

39. Of course, classic Puritan covenant theology would also affirm that the perpetuation of the moral law is a demonstration of God's love in the covenant of grace. The difference, however, in Wesley's covenant theology is that, since the fall, all of humanity lives under the covenant of grace.

40. Wesley, "The Original, Nature, Properties, and Use of the Law," *Works* (BE) §2, 2:4–5.

41. Ibid., §2, IV.4, 2:4–5, 17.

42. Wesley, *ENNT*, 472.

43. Ibid., 351.

cation) in order that the better covenant, "believe and live," might be *embraced*. It is in this sense that the Mosaic Law, by pointing to Christ, is unquestionably, even in its terror, "nothing else than a fresh administration of the covenant of grace."[44]

For this reason, Wesley could, on the one hand, assert that the moral law is "holy, just, and good"[45] and, on the other hand, as noted above, declare that "Christ is the end of the Adamic, as well as the Mosaic, law." He is able to make this last declaration on the basis of his conception of Christ's mediation both as *logos incarnandus* (Christ to be exhibited) and as *logos incarnates* (Christ exhibited) introduced earlier. As he explained in the passage from *Farther Thoughts Upon Christian Perfection* referenced above, the Adamic law is "the law of works" (i.e., the covenant of works) and remains restricted to "that given to Adam in his innocence" while the Mosaic Law is identified as "the whole Mosaic dispensation" of the covenant of grace.[46] Christ is first of all the end of the Adamic law (the covenant of works).[47] This follows from the fact that the fall immediately occasioned the *need* of a mediator (there being no such need in the time of Adam's innocence) and God's gracious *provision* of such a mediator: Christ as *logos incarnandus*. As noted earlier, an important result of this mediation of Christ was that God graciously re-inscribed the moral law on the heart of fallen humanity, "although not as in the beginning."[48]

In keeping with the superstructure of covenant theology, Wesley affirmed that the mediatorial work of Christ was brought to *fullness* in his revelation as *logos incarnates*. Thus, whereas the inaugural work of his mediation—as *logos incarnandus*—occasions the end of the Adamic law (i.e., the covenant of works), his mediation as *logos incarnates* occasions the end of "the entire Mosaic dispensation."[49] It is in this sense that Wesley declares, "We are 'dead to the law, by the body of Christ' given for us (Rom 7.4), to the Adamic as well as Mosaic law. We are wholly freed therefrom by his death, that law expiring with him." He further affirms that "In the room of this"—the Adamic law and the

---

44. Leonard Rijssenius cited by Heppe, *Reformed Dogmatics*, 399.

45. The phrase belongs to Rom 7:12, the text of Wesley's sermon, "The Original, Nature, Properties, and Use of the Law," *Works* (BE), 2:4–19.

46. Wesley, *Farther Thoughts Upon Christian Perfection*, 3–4.

47. See also "The Righteousness of Faith," *Works* (BE) §3, 1:203.

48. Wesley, "The Original, Nature, Properties, and Use of the Law," *Works* (BE) §2, 2:4–5.

49. Ibid., IV.4, 2:17.

Mosaic law—"Christ hath established another, namely, the law of faith. Not everyone that doeth but everyone that believeth now receiveth righteousness."[50] Thus Wesley clarifies: "Every believer has done with the law as it means the Jewish ceremonial law, or the entire Mosaic dispensation . . . ; yea, allowing *we have done with the moral law* [only in the sense of our regarding it] *as a means of procuring our justification* (for we are 'justified freely by his grace, through the redemption that is in Jesus')."[51] Therefore, although the moral law is "established" (Rom 3:31) rather than abolished, it is established *not* as the basis of justification but as "an incorruptible picture of the high and holy One that inhabiteth eternity" and is nothing less than "the heart of God disclosed to man."[52]

The achievement of Christ as *logos incarnates* (which occasions the end of the Mosaic dispensation) is what Wesley is referencing when he states that the Apostle Paul has proved "that the Christian had set aside the Jewish dispensation, and that the moral law itself, though it could never pass away," now stands "on a different foundation from what it did before."[53] This different foundation is not faith itself; rather, the "different foundation" is Christ as *logos incarnates* rather than as *logos incarnandus*.[54] That is, it is on the basis of his death *in realiter* that those who believe are "brought . . . under a new dispensation" of the covenant of grace (i.e., the gospel dispensation) and are enabled to "bring forth fruit unto God" on account of their knowing the power of Christ's resurrection.[55]

Wesley and the Idea of Progression within the Covenant of Grace

In speaking of being "brought . . . under a new dispensation" of the covenant of grace, Wesley is reflecting an identifying feature of covenant theology: *the idea of progression within the covenant of grace*. Federal theologians had early on conceived the covenant of grace in terms of three economies or dispensations: before the law, under the law, and upon and

---

50. Wesley, *Farther Thoughts Upon Christian Perfection*, 4.

51. Wesley, "The Original, Nature, Properties, and Use of the Law," *Works* (BE) §2, IV.4, 2:4–5, 17. Bracketed insert and emphasis mine.

52. Ibid., §II.3, 2:9.

53. Ibid., §3, 2:5–6.

54. Wesley, 'The Righteousness of Faith,' *Works* (BE) I. §11–12, 1:208–9.

55. Wesley, 'The Original, Nature, Properties, and Use of the Law,' *Works* (BE) §2, 2:5.

after Christ's coming. This division is evident in Wesley[56] and in covenant theologians more than a century earlier.[57] The various economies (or dispensations) of the covenant of grace represent more than the mere *segmentation* of salvation history; rather, each dispensation represents an *augmentation* in the unfolding story of God's saving purposes. In the gospel or Christian dispensation (sometimes also called the evangelical dispensation), the covenant of grace is *advanced* to its perfection,[58] the fullness of time having come when "God sent forth his Son . . . to redeem those under the law,"[59] i.e., the Mosaic dispensation. A fuller exploration of Wesley's conception and presentation of the idea of progression within the covenant of grace and its import for his soteriology will be undertaken later in this study.

For the moment, however, it is important to note that Wesley was consistent in giving careful attention to the idea of progression and regularly accessed the language of *The Epistle to the Hebrews* from which some of the standard terminology of covenant theology had long been derived. In particular, the terms "type" and "shadow" described the divinely-appointed role of the Mosaic Law as an instrument of the covenant of grace pointing toward the revelation of Christ. This same way of speaking of the Mosaic Law in relation to Christ's appearing is seen with some frequency in Wesley as well.[60]

In order to highlight and preserve distinctions important in conveying the idea of progression, Wesley employed the familiar terminology of covenant theology with a consistent and admirable precision. This is particularly evident in his taking pains to sustain the critical distinction between "covenant" and "dispensation" in order to lessen the confusion of his audience. Whenever he is speaking of any of the economies of the covenant of *grace* he uses the term "dispensation" and adds the appropriate modifier ("legal" or "Christian," for example) when needed. Wesley's resistance to the notion that the covenant of works in any degree continues alongside the covenant of grace motivates him in

56. Wesley, 'The Righteousness of Faith,' *Works* (BE) §1, 1:202–3.

57. See McCoy and Baker, *Fountainhead of Federalism*, 65.

58. See Wesley, *Explanatory Notes upon the Old Testament*, 1:1.

59. Galatians 4:4–5.

60. See, for example, Wesley's sermon, "The Original, Nature, Properties, and Use of the Law," *Works* (BE) §II.2, 2:8–9. Compare Perkins, *A Golden Chaine*, 103; Ames, in *The Marrow of Sacred Divinity*, 193; *The Westminster Confession*, Chap. VII, 21. These words resurface frequently in Wesley's *Notes* on both Testaments. See, for example, Wesley's commentary on Exod 39:1 (Wesley, *Explanatory Notes upon the Old Testament*, 1:337); Heb 8:5; 9:23; 10:1; and Rev 11:19 (Wesley, *ENNT*, 723, 727–28, 859).

taking care to avoid using the word "covenant" as a synonym for, say, the Mosaic dispensation. The precision with which he maintains this distinction requires that he carefully recast for his audience the Pauline antithesis of law and grace in terms that are technically consistent with the language of his covenant theology.[61] By way of example, in his commentary on Romans 6:14 Wesley writes,

> *Sin shall not have dominion over you*—It has neither right nor power. *For ye are not under the law*—A dispensation of terror and bondage, which only shews sin, without enabling you to conquer it; *but under grace*—Under the merciful dispensation of the gospel, which brings compleat Victory over it; to every one who is under the powerful influences of the Spirit of *Christ*. . . . Plainly, "the law" (the Mosaic Law) is *not* the covenant of *works* but is the Jewish dispensation of the covenant of *grace*, "a dispensation of terror and bondage."[62]

To be "under the law" is to not have progressed from the Jewish dispensation into the privileges of the gospel dispensation. Thus, while both bear witness to the covenant of grace exclusively, the witness of the gospel (or, Christian) dispensation was more complete than the witness of the Jewish dispensation.

It is clear enough by now that the place of covenant theology in Wesley's theological thought was neither incidental nor uninspected. He recognized and knowingly subscribed to the superstructure of covenant theology represented in the ideas of the covenant of works and the covenant of grace, convinced that these faithfully portrayed the history of God's redemptive activity. At the same time, he thoughtfully and precisely adapted the presentation of these two covenants to reflect his evangelical Arminianism. At the core of this adaptation lay his unrelenting conviction that the Mosaic Law belonged wholly and only to the covenant of grace, and thus brought all of humanity within reach of the provisions of that covenant. And at the heart this conviction was his understanding that the distinguishing feature of the covenant of works was not the moral law, but was the innocence of "our first parents." Thus, the perpetuity of the moral law from before the fall until the present moment involves no reinvigoration of the covenant of works; rather, the covenant of works was brought to an end coincidentally with the fall

---

61. This is not to say that Wesley always *explicitly* recasts the Pauline antithesis. See, for example, his commentary on Romans 11. Wesley, *ENNT*, 498–501.

62. Wesley, *ENNT*, 478, 604.

and the inception of the covenant of grace. Yet, in concert with classic covenant theology, he centered everything on the mediatorial work of Christ as "the lamb slain from the foundation of the world," and affirmed the Incarnation and outpouring of the Spirit as the culmination of God's saving activity in and for the world.

With this background and a sense of the breadth of the ancestry of Wesley's covenant theology, we are now in a position to examine his exegesis and exposition of Holy Scripture as a further critical resource for learning of the influence of covenant theology on him, particularly as imaged in his use of the servant-son metaphor. As previously noted, the fact that the metaphors of servant and son belonged to the sacred text of the Christian canon was first and foremost to Wesley. This not only legitimized his use of the metaphor, but also created a sense of obligation to employ it as a way of ensuring that he articulated a soteriology that was faithful to divine revelation. For Wesley, the superstructure of covenant theology reflected such faithfulness and, for this reason, also served as a hermeneutic for his interpretation of Scripture.

CHAPTER 4

John Wesley's Covenant Theology and Holy Scripture

DESPITE THE EVIDENCE OF Wesley's thoughtful distillation of the covenant theology mediated to him, we might yet be tempted to conclude that he appreciated its theological value only as a craftsman prizes and uses each tool in his toolbox. But suppose covenant theology was not just a tool in Wesley's hands? Suppose it was a core feature of the infrastructure of his theological thought and consequently influenced the way he used each tool in his toolbox?

There may be no clearer testimony to the veracity of these suppositions than Wesley's approach to the interpretation of Holy Scripture. And the reason this is so is because, for him, covenant theology is derived not from the work of Perkins or Ames, Cocceius or Bengel, or any of their predecessors or successors, but from Holy Scripture. In fact, in Wesley's view, covenant theology witnesses so faithfully to God's redemptive intent and endeavors that it is itself essential to the reading and study of Scripture. This interplay—the scriptural underpinnings of covenant theology and the place of covenant theology in the interpretation of Scripture—is particularly exemplified in the role of the servant-son metaphor as a hermeneutic of Wesley's exegesis and exposition of scripture and, consequently, as a definitive narrative of his vision of the way of salvation.

It is helpful to begin the examination of the influence of covenant theology on Wesley's interpretation of the Scriptures by recalling the high regard in which he held the written Word of God. In the preface to the 1746 edition of *Sermons on Several Occasions*, Wesley concisely stated his purpose in publishing the three volumes as follows: "I have accordingly set down in the following Sermons, what I find in the Bible concerning the Way to Heaven."[1] And for the sake of those readers who

1. Wesley, *Sermons on several occasions* (1746), 1:viii.

believed they saw things more clearly and accurately than he, Wesley offered to yield his position providing they "Shew me it is so, by plain Proof of Scripture."[2]

Without doubt, Wesley perceived Scripture as sufficient in all things necessary to salvation. But his esteem for Holy Writ pushed beyond even this affirmation which stemmed from Protestant opposition to Roman Catholic claims to infallible authority.[3] For Wesley, Scripture was not only the one rule of Christian faith and practice but was also the standard for the articulation of Christian doctrine. The enduring character of the very words of Scripture was, in his view, inextricably bound to and fundamental to its authority. This is a theme consistently and conspicuously present in his theological thought. Responding to John Smith's criticism that his "phraseology"—his practice of using the words of Scripture when speaking to spiritual matters—was "highly improper" due to changing times,[4] Wesley countered,

> But I cannot call those ["]uncommon["] words which are the constant language of Holy Writ. These I purposely use, desiring always to express *Scripture sense* in *Scripture phrase*. . . . And that it is scriptural appears to me a sufficient defence of any way of speaking whatever. For however the propriety of those expressions may vary which occur in the writings of men, I cannot but think those which are found in the Book of God will be equally proper in all ages.[5]

In his commentary on the phrase "let him speak as the oracles of God" (1 Pet 4:11), Wesley declared, "Let all his words be according to this pattern, both as to matter and to manner, more especially in public."[6] He believed he had a fiduciary responsibility to make use of the very words of Scripture in order to perpetuate faithfulness to its soteriological core.

With respect to the servant and son metaphors, the implication of this fiduciary responsibility is twofold. First, the fact that the metaphors themselves are found in the pages of the sacred text proves critical in two ways: on the one hand, this fact *authorizes* Wesley to appropriate

---

2. Ibid., 1:x.

3. See Gilbert Burnet's discussion of Article IV of the Thirty-Nine Articles of Religion and his argument for the sufficiency of Scripture. Burnet, *An Exposition of the Thirty-Nine Articles* (1830), 83–107.

4. Wesley, "'John Smith' to John Wesley (May 1745)," *Works* (BE), 26:143.

5. Wesley, "John Wesley to 'John Smith' (September 28, 1745)," *Works* (BE) II. §6–7, 26:155. Emphasis mine.

6. Wesley, *ENNT*, 769.

the metaphors as an integral component of his soteriology; that is, their mere appearance in Scripture is sufficient as the basis upon which they become legitimately available to him. On the other hand, the contrasting of servant and son in many of those same texts of Scripture *obligates* him—as one endeavoring to "speak as of the oracles of God"—to maintain certain critical distinctions as he articulates his soteriology to his audience. This obligation constitutes a hermeneutical principle to which Wesley seeks to hold his soteriology accountable, despite whatever theological complications may thereby arise.[7]

Second, it is important to note that neither "faith of a servant" nor "faith of a son" is a phrase found in any text of the Old or New Testaments. For Wesley, however, using these phrases is appropriate since they reflect the "Scripture sense" of the soteriological declarations of Scripture. Consequently, he not only includes commentary on the primary components of the metaphor (servant and son) where the terms explicitly appear in the sacred text, but, on occasion, incorporates them into his *Explanatory Notes* even though the text itself would not have required it. This indicates the strength of Wesley's conviction that the servant-son metaphor faithfully expressed essential features of a biblical soteriology.

Wesley's Hermeneutical Premise

As described in the previous chapter, these convictions were shaped by Wesley's appropriation of covenant theology which varied significantly at points from that of Perkins, Ames, and the Westminster Confession (i.e., classic covenant theology). One important variation is seen in the differing conceptions of the representative role of Moses. In the strand of covenant theology propounded by Perkins and other like-minded covenant theologians, Moses stands as representative of the covenant of works while Christ alone stands as representative of the covenant of grace. Ames' position differs somewhat from that of Perkins' but still emphasizes a correspondence between Moses and the covenant of works. Wesley, on the other hand, while affirming with classic covenant theology that the covenant of grace is ever bound up with the revelation of Christ as the lamb slain from the foundation of the world, understands Moses not as representative of the covenant of works but as representative

---

7. Outler observes, "[Wesley] never supposed that the data of revelation could be conceptualized into a single system of coherent thought without ambiguous remainders." Outler, "Introduction," *Works* (BE) 1:66.

solely of the covenant of grace (and this, for *all* of humankind), albeit of the legal dispensation of that covenant.

Wesley consistently and carefully maintains this critical distinction. When discussing law and grace, he clarifies that to be "under the law" is *not* to be under the covenant of works, but is to be situated *within* the covenant of grace, though in "a dispensation of terror and bondage, which only shews sin, without enabling you to conquer it."[8] Similarly, being "under grace" is not a designation contrasting the covenant of grace with the covenant of works but points to the distinction between two divinely-initiated, salvific *moments* within the *one* covenant of grace.[9] Accordingly, as previously noted, Wesley does not equate the new covenant with the covenant of grace but describes it as "the new, evangelical dispensation" of the covenant of grace and the Mosaic Law as "the Mosaic dispensation" of that same covenant.[10] Thus, being under grace is being "under the merciful dispensation of the gospel, which brings compleat victory over [sin], to every one who is under the powerful influences of the spirit of *Christ*."[11]

The law did not make fallen humanity guilty, but revealed to humanity the persistent deception of its thinking itself to be innocent.[12] Thus, in this sense, it is made evident that even the Mosaic Law itself properly belongs to the covenant of grace, bringing terror and bondage *en route* to "compleat victory" in Christ for those responsive to its pedagogical intention. The legal dispensation was not, then, a dead end—though Wesley contends it surely would have been if it actually were nothing more than the covenant of works repackaged and reinstituted. Rather, it was, in fact, "originally intended by God, as a grand means of preserving and increasing spiritual life, and leading to life everlasting."[13] For Wesley, this was the divine intention for all of humankind and not only for the elect.

---

8. Wesley, *ENNT*, 478.

9. Commenting on I John 2:18, Wesley describes the gospel dispensation as "The last"—not the *only*—"dispensation of grace." Ibid., 788.

10. Ibid., 570.

11. Ibid., 478. See also Wesley, "The Spirit of Bondage and of Adoption," *Works* (BE), §5, 1:250.

12. On Romans 7:9 Wesley comments that apart from the "close application" of the Law, "I had much life, wisdom, virtue, strength. *So I thought*." Wesley, *ENNT*, 481. Emphasis mine. Wesley comments similarly on Romans 1:19 and Romans 3:19. Ibid., 461, 468.

13. Ibid., 481.

If there is any association of death with the law it is only that it "seals in death those who *still* cleave to it"; and to them "who *prefer* it to the gospel," the Mosaic dispensation proves to be "the ministration of condemnation."[14] What Wesley clearly implies in his commentary on 2 Corinthians 3 is the genuinely salvific *capacity* of the legal dispensation insofar as it "tended to and terminated in [Christ]."[15] To those not resistant to its intended end, the life-giving Spirit is conveyed.[16]

In his explanation of the phrase "the righteousness of God" (Rom 1:17), Wesley demonstrates the relationship of the two dispensations clearly:

> In this verse the expression means, the whole benefit of God through *Christ* for the salvation of a sinner—Mention is made here, and ver. 18 of a two-fold revelation, of *wrath* and of *righteousness*: the former, little known to nature, is revealed by the law; the latter, wholly unknown to nature, by the gospel. That [i.e., wrath] goes before and prepares the way: this [i.e., righteousness] follow: each, the apostle says, *is revealed*, at the present time, in opposition to the times of ignorance. *From faith to faith*—By a gradual series of still clearer and clearer promises.[17]

This two-fold revelation is the substance of a hermeneutical premise upon which Wesley approaches Holy Writ. Fostered by his covenant theology, this premise exerts marked influence upon him, permeating his exegesis and exposition of Scripture beyond his careful treatment of the law-grace antithesis of the Pauline epistles already noted.

For example, in his commentary on John 1:17, "For the law was given by Moses, *but* grace and truth were by Jesus Christ," Wesley writes, "*The law*—working wrath and containing shadows: *was given*—No Philosopher, poet, or orator ever chose his words so accurately as St. *John. The law*, saith he, was given *by Moses: grace* was by *Jesus Christ.* Observe the reason for placing each word thus: *The law* of *Moses* was not his own. *The grace of Christ was.* His *grace* was opposite to the *wrath*, his *truth* to the *shadowy* ceremonies of the law."[18]

This hermeneutical premise certainly did not originate with Wesley as is plainly evident from the fact that his commentary on this is borrowed from Bengel and reflects an emphasis of Guyse on the passage as

14. Ibid., 570. Emphasis mine.
15. Ibid., 571.
16. Ibid., 570. See Wesley's comment on verse 6.
17. Ibid., 460. Bracketed inserts mine. Compare Bengel, *Gnomon*, 2:17.
18. Wesley, *ENNT*, 269.

well.[19] At a minimum, Wesley's purposeful inclusion of these comments demonstrates the imprint of covenant theology on his thought and witnesses to his commitment to the hermeneutical premise of the two-fold revelation. It is from the vantage point of this hermeneutical premise that the scriptural basis of the servant-son metaphor comes into view.

"Servant" and "Son"

Wesley's correlation of the "two-fold revelation" with Moses and Christ is significant. Not only are the two representative, respectively, of the legal and evangelical dispensations of the covenant of grace, but the movement from lesser to greater inheres in their persons. This correlation is drawn from Hebrews 3 (particularly verses five and six), a passage that supplies for Wesley the "scripture phrase" so integral to the metaphor and to his articulating the "scripture sense" undergirding his soteriology:

> V. 1. . . . He compares *Christ* as an apostle with *Moses*; as a priest with *Aaron*. Both these offices which Moses and Aaron severally bore, he bears together, and far more eminently: . . .
>
> V. 4. *Now* Christ, he *that built* not only this house, but *all things is God*; and so infinitely greater than *Moses* or any creature.
>
> V. 5. *And Moses verily*—Another proof of the pre-eminence of Christ above *Moses*: *was faithful in all his house as a servant, for a testimony of the things which were afterwards to be spoken*—That is, which was a full confirmation of the things which he afterwards spake concerning *Christ*.
>
> V. 6. *But Christ* was faithful *as a son, whose house we are*, while we hold fast, and shall be unto the end, *if we hold fast our confidence* in God, *and glorying* in his promises; our faith and hope.[20]

On the basis of this passage, the biblical authority of the primary terms of the metaphor—"servant" and "son"—is established and their content defined: Moses is the servant *par excellence* while Christ is the son *par excellence*. While it may be argued that this distinction and comparison of these terms is simply the property of the passage itself rather than indicative of any theological affirmation of Wesley's, there are several indicators that this passage is of specific interest and of fundamental importance to him.

---

19. Compare Bengel, *Gnomon* (Fausset), 2:254 and Guyse, *The Practical Expositor*, 2:269, 271–72.

20. Wesley, *ENNT*, 710–11.

First, Wesley's interest in the contrasting of servant and son is clearly evident in his commentary on Hebrews 10:11–12 where neither the passage itself nor the commentary of his sources makes comparative use of the metaphors, servant and son: "V. 11. *Every priest standeth*—As a servant in a humble posture. V. 12. *But he*—The virtue of whose *one sacrifice*—remains *for ever, sat down*—As a son, in majesty and honour."[21]

Second, Wesley seems to look for opportunities to highlight this terminology ("servant" and "son") where possible. Out of Matthew Henry's expansive comment on Deuteronomy 34:12, Wesley makes it a point both to include Henry's own comparison of Moses as "servant" to Christ as "son" (an emphasis not at all demanded by the immediate context of the verse) and to *reposition* Henry's own use of these comparative terms so as to strengthen the focus of the attention of the reader upon the pre-eminence of Christ:

> V. 12. *Moses* was greater than any other of the prophets of the Old Testament. . . . But as far as the other prophets came short of him, our Lord Jesus went beyond him. *Moses was faithful as a servant, but Christ as a son*: his miracles more illustrious, his communion with the father more intimate: for he *is in his bosom* from eternity. *Moses* lies buried: but Christ is *sitting at the right-hand of God*, and *of the increase of his government there shall be no end*.[22]

This is evident yet again in Wesley's commentary on the title "servant of the Lord" given to Moses in Joshua 1:1 where Wesley underscores the pre-eminence of Christ as *son* over Moses as *servant* by his choice to incorporate the words of Matthew Poole in his commentary:

> This title is given to Moses . . . not without cause, to reflect honour upon him, . . . and that the *Israelites* might not think of *Moses* above what was meet, remembering that he was not the Lord himself, but only a servant; and therefore not to be too pertinaciously followed in all his institutions, when the Lord himself should come and abolish part of the Mosaical dispensation; it being but reasonable that he who was only a servant in God's house, should give place to him who was the son, and heir, and lord of it.[23]

---

21. Ibid., 729.

22. Wesley, *Explanatory Notes upon the Old Testament*, 1:701. Compare Henry, *An Exposition of All the Books of the Old and New Testaments*, 1:512.

23. Wesley, *Explanatory Notes upon the Old Testament*, 1:702. Compare Poole, *Annotations Upon the Holy Bible*, np. Notably, Matthew Henry does not develop the thought

The emphasis on "servant" and "son" in relation to Moses and to Christ in his Old Testament *Notes* (produced the decade following the first edition of his New Testament *Notes*) suggests the continued importance of the metaphor in his theological thought. It also summarizes for Wesley the whole sequence of God's redemptive activity comprising the covenant of grace, consummated as it is in the gospel dispensation— "the bringing in of a better hope . . . by which we draw nigh to God."[24]

Continuing in step with the writer of *Hebrews*, Wesley expounds on this "better hope": "The promises of the gospel . . . excel those of the law," that dispensation which, if it "had answered all God's designs and man's wants, if it had not been weak and unprofitable, unable to make anything perfect, *no place would have been for a second* [covenant]."[25] He goes on to specify six aspects unique to the new covenant (that is, the gospel dispensation): "It is new in many respects, (though not as to the substance of it,) 1. Being ratified by the death of Christ; 2. Freed from those burdensome rites and ceremonies; 3. Containing a more full and clear account of spiritual religion; 4. Attended with larger influences of the spirit; 5. Extended to all men, and 6. Never to be abolished."[26]

In his commentary on Hebrews 7:18–19, Wesley emphasizes the soteriological consequences of this better hope, and in weaving together the comments of Bengel, Guyse, and Doddridge on this verse demonstrates the theological application as his own (though not necessarily peculiar to him):

> V. 18. *For there* is implied in this new and everlasting priesthood, and in the new dispensation, connected therewith, *a disannulling of the preceding commandment*—An abrogation of the Mosaic law, *for the weakness and unprofitableness thereof*—For its insufficiency either to justify or to sanctify.
>
> V. 19. *For the law*—Taken by itself, separate from the gospel, *made nothing perfect*—Could not perfect its votaries, either in faith or love, in happiness or holiness; *but the bringing in of a better hope*—Of the gospel dispensation, which gives us a better

---

in this direction. Henry, *An Exposition of All the Books of the Old and New Testaments*, 2:8–10.

24. Wesley, *ENNT*, 721.

25. Hebrews 8:6–7. Ibid., 723.

26. Hebrews 8:8. Ibid. Wesley first expanded his comment on this verse in his second edition of his New Testament *Notes* in 1757, but the most extensive expansion appears only in the 1788 edition.

ground of confidence, does; *by which we draw nigh to God*—Yea so nigh as to be one spirit with him. And this is true perfection.[27]

Clearly, Wesley drew on the scriptural presentation of Moses and Christ as embodying the definitive dispensations of the covenant of grace and on its contrasting them in terms of the metaphors of servant and son.

"Servants" and "Sons"

With the *Scripture phrase* ("servant" and "son") now in hand and the superstructure of covenant theology front and center in his theological thought, the metaphors accomplish more for Wesley than to mark the distinction between each salvation-historical phase. "Servant" and "son" are no longer metaphors joined exclusively to the persons of Moses and Christ as the embodiments of their respective dispensations. Rather, based on the correlation of "servant" as representative of the legal dispensation and "son" as representative of the gospel dispensation, these metaphors also serve as types of the "moments and phases in the subjective experience of faith."[28] Consequently, they serve to identify *both* the historic salvific movements in God's redemptive activity for the sake of all humanity *and* the salvific movements of the Spirit discernible in the lives of all those awakened by and responding to the grace of God. These persons are themselves, then, servants and sons, according to their various circumstances.

The metaphors, then, provided a way of articulating the *Scripture sense* of the experience of those on the way of salvation. The case of Jonathan Reeves reviewed by the 1746 Conference suggests that conceiving of "servant" and "son" as descriptive of the subjective experience of faith was not a novel idea of Wesley's but was likely a matter of some theological familiarity among those attending the Conference. What *can* be confirmed is the strengthened resonance of this extension of the metaphors with Wesley as evidenced in his correspondence from the late 1760s and beyond, and in his 1788 sermons, "On Faith" and "On the Discoveries of Faith." In these letters and publications Wesley sets forth his exegesis of the spiritual realities attending the experience of those who have embarked on the way of salvation. At the heart of this exegesis of experience stands the superiority of the gospel dispensation. The value of the servant-son metaphor was in the assistance it provided him in translating the salvation-historical progress from the Mosaic to

---

27. Ibid., 721.

28. The phrase is borrowed from van Asselt, "The Doctrine of the Abrogations," 104, 109.

the gospel dispensation into the broader notion of the salvific movement "from faith to faith" in the lives of individuals. This movement, too, was also a movement from lesser to greater.

One of the most explicit declarations of the implications of the "better covenant" for the individual is found in his commentary on 1 John 2:8, "For there is no comparison between the state of the Old Testament-believers, and that which ye now enjoy: *the darkness* of that dispensation *is past away; and* Christ *the true light now shineth* in your hearts."[29] While Wesley's comment does not quote any of the sources named in his preface to New Testament *Notes*, it certainly reflects the superstructure of covenant theology shared by them all. On this same verse John Guyse comments, "The darkness of the Old Testament-Dispensation, and of your former State of Ignorance, Error, and Sin is passed away, . . . and in great Measure is over and gone; and the True Light of the Gospel in the Revelation it makes of Christ, who is by way of Eminence *the true Light*, (John i.9) is now display'd in its full glory, and shines in your hearts."[30]

For Wesley, this qualitative development is a faithful presentation of the witness of Holy Scripture. It was evident in John the Baptist's proclamation, "Repent ye, for the kingdom of heaven is at hand."[31] The kingdom of heaven, says Wesley, "properly signifies here, the gospel dispensation" rather than a temporal kingdom as the Jews had supposed.[32] Following the treatment of the messianic text of Psalm 40:7–8, "Lo, I come . . . to do thy will, O God" expounded upon in Hebrews 10:7–9, Wesley again highlights this movement from lesser to greater in his comment on verse nine: Christ came, he writes, "to offer a more acceptable sacrifice; and by this very act, *he taketh away the* legal, *that he may establish* the evangelical dispensation."[33]

At the heart of the matter is the salvific movement of God's redeeming activity in and for the world being replicated in each and every person on the way of salvation. Parallel to the pre-eminence of the gospel over the legal dispensation in the salvation-historical acts of God (exemplified in Christ as Son over Moses as Servant) is the pre-eminence

---

29. Wesley, *ENNT*, 787.

30. Guyse, *A Practical Exposition of the Epistle to the Galatians*, 678. Philip Doddridge writes, "*the Darkness* of heathenism, and Twilight of the Jewish State, *is now passed away, and the true Light now shineth*." Doddridge, *A Family Expositor*, 6:331.

31. Matthew 3:2.

32. Wesley, *ENNT*, 16. Heylyn's influence is evident here. Heylyn, *Theological Lectures*, 13.

33. Wesley, *ENNT*, 729.

of the spiritual state of those who are sons over those who are servants. Wesley makes this point clearly in his commentary on Hebrews 10:1,

> From all that has been said it appears, that *the law*, the *Mosaic* dispensation, being a bare, unsubstantial *shadow of good things to come*—Of the gospel blessings, *and not the* substantial, solid *Image of them, can never with the same* kind of *sacrifices*, though continually repeated, *make the comers thereunto perfect*—Either as to justification or sanctification. How is it possible, that any who consider this, should suppose the attainments of *David*, or any who were under that dispensation, to be the proper measure of gospel-holiness? And that *Christian* experience is to rise no higher than *Jewish*?[34]

Wesley's conviction regarding the transformative reality attending the pre-eminence of the gospel over the legal dispensation is longstanding. On Sunday, November 7, 1742, he recorded the following in his journal:

> I concluded the Epistle to the Hebrews, that strong barrier against the too prevailing imagination that the privileges of Christian believers are to be measured by those of the Jews. Not so: that Christians are under "a better covenant," established upon better promises; that although "the law made nothing perfect," made none perfect either in holiness or happiness, yet "the bringing in of a better hope did, by which we" now "draw nigh unto God"—this is the great truth continually inculcated herein, and running through this whole Epistle.[35]

Elsewhere Wesley describes that salvation which has come by Christ as "So far beyond all that was experienced under the Jewish dispensation."[36]

The Defining Role of Galatians 4

The pre-eminence of the Christian experience reflects the very design of God's redemptive activity: "the whole *Mosaic* dispensation tended to, and terminated in [Christ]."[37] Thus, sonship is the defining reality of the gospel dispensation even as being in "that low, servile state"[38] of a servant

---

34. Ibid., 728. Wesley's rhetorical question at the end of his comment appears to be his own rather than derived from his primary sources.

35. Wesley, *Works* (BE), 19:301.

36. 1 Peter 1:10, Wesley, *ENNT*, 760. This is the argument underlying Wesley's critique of Dialogue XIII of Hervey's *Theron and Aspasio*. See Wesley's extract of Goodwin, *A Treatise on Justification*, 18.

37. 2 Corinthians 3:13. Wesley, *ENNT*, 571.

38. Galatians 4:5. Ibid., 604.

is the defining reality of the legal dispensation. For Wesley, Galatians 4 (particularly the first seven verses) serves as a synopsis of the story-line of this divine design not only in its becoming reality in human history, but also in its outlining the progression of God's saving activity in the hearts and lives of individual persons from generation to generation since the inauguration of the gospel dispensation. The definitive role of this text for Wesley is plainly evident in his commentary on the salutation of the Epistle of Jude. As noted earlier, he takes great pains to demonstrate the varied, distinctive uses of the word "servant" and employs Galatians 4 as the primary interpretive key to discerning its proper meaning. In doing so, he not only highlights the distinctive use of the word in Jude 1 but provides a concise exegesis of the metaphor.

In his commentary on Galatians 4, Wesley begins by highlighting the superiority of the gospel dispensation (restating the assertion of John Guyse[39]): "Now to illustrate by a plain similitude the pre-eminence of the Christian over the legal dispensation."[40] While this emphasis on the surpassing greatness of the grace of God manifested in Christ Jesus is inherent in the larger context of the argument of Galatians itself, Galatians 4:1–7 demonstrated for Wesley the *reason* behind the pre-eminence of the better covenant: the sending of the Son and the work of the Spirit as the spirit of adoption.

Therefore, it is not an exaggeration to say that Galatians 4:1–7 is the theological cynosure of the metaphors "faith of a servant" and "faith of a son," though these exact phrases themselves do not appear in Wesley's commentary on the passage. This passage, however, enables him to articulate the *scripture sense* of the experience of those on the way of salvation. At the heart of the passage is the movement from lesser to greater—from being "under age" to being "adult," from being in bondage to being at liberty, from being a servant to being a son: "*Wherefore thou*—Who believest in *Christ, are no more a servant*—Like those who are under the law, *but a son*—Of mature age, *and if a son then an heir of* all the promises, and of the all-sufficient *God* himself."[41]

In the legal dispensation, the Jewish people are, to use Gordon Fee's phrase, "heirs-in-waiting."[42] The privileges designated are inaccessible apart from believing in Christ. However, in terms of the historical salvific movements of God, the Gentiles were not heirs-in-waiting in

---

39. Guyse, *A Practical Exposition of the Epistle to the Galatians*, 30.
40. Wesley, *ENNT*, 604.
41. Ibid., 604–5.
42. Fee, *Galatians*, 145–46.

quite the same sense and this is evidenced in the distinct nature of their bondage apart from Christ: "*Indeed then when ye knew not God, ye served them that by nature*—that is, in reality, *are no gods*—And so were under a far worse bondage than even that of the *Jews*. For they did serve the true God, though in a low, slavish manner."[43] The point for Wesley is that despite their differing circumstances both Jew and Gentile are, in the first place, deprived the privileges of sons; and, in the second place, are made "adult *sons*" solely on the basis of faith in Christ.[44] The consequence of being made *adult* sons is that both Jew and Gentile come into the inheritance of "all the promises, and of the all-sufficient God himself."[45]

That each person actually would come into this inheritance is, as stated above, the divine intention. The reality of how this comes about is what Galatians 4 describes on three levels: the *historical* ("But when the fullness of the time was come, God sent forth his Son," Gal 4:4), the *soteriological* ("God hath sent the spirit of his Son into your hearts," Gal 4:7) and the *experimental* ("crying, Abba, Father," Gal 4:7).[46] The similitude[47] of the heir-in-waiting becoming the heir-in-possession summarizes not only the unfolding of the provisions of the covenant of grace in human history but the progression of servants becoming sons, the story of those on the way of salvation.

It is increasingly clear that Wesley's deep regard for Holy Scripture combined with his thoroughgoing orientation to the superstructure of covenant theology to formulate his vision of the way of salvation and to shape the way he spoke of the journey experienced by those on that way. Drawing from largely well-established usages and interpretations of Holy Writ, he worked to navigate important nuances of meaning and to preserve critical distinctions and core convictions. The focal point of these efforts was, in conjunction with the prosecution of the revival, the doctrinal integrity and spiritual well-being of the Methodist Societies in the homeland and across the Atlantic. The following assessment of the servant-son metaphor within the context of the Evangelical Revival will yield yet further insight into the place of covenant theology in Wesley's theological thought.

43. Galatians 4:8. Wesley, *ENNT*, 605.
44. See Wesley's comment on Galatians 4:5–6. Ibid., 604.
45. Galatians 4:7. Ibid., 605.
46. These three aspects are explored in Chapter 6.
47. Wesley, *ENNT*, 604.

CHAPTER 5

John Wesley's Covenant Theology in Context

I. The Evangelical Revival and the Conversation on Good Works

As the relationship of the servant-son metaphor to covenant theology comes more into view, its value to Wesley as a definitive narrative of his vision of the way of salvation is more clearly apparent. After all, the biblical foundation of the metaphor was indisputable and its capacity for imaging "the two grand manifestations of God, the legal and the evangelical" had established it from pulpit to pew as a familiar and theologically trustworthy summary of God's saving activity. And yet, the soteriological content of the metaphor is more extensive than its overt relationship to the superstructure of the covenant of grace might suggest on the surface. Indeed, Wesley's exhortation in his 1788 sermon "On the Discoveries of Faith" to "press on . . . from the faith of a *servant* to the faith of a *son*,"[1] involved a whole complex of conclusions on critical soteriological concerns that had long been front and center in the hearts and minds of the heirs of the Reformation.

The bulk of these soteriological concerns revolved around two related issues: first, the question of the role of good works in salvation; and second, the question of the Divine regard toward those who might best be described as "the responsive unregenerate." These two questions occupied Wesley's attention throughout his years as Methodism's leader and even before he found himself in that historic role. They were not, however, questions he *raised* but lively and longstanding conversations he *joined in progress*—conversations the Evangelical Revival had infused with a fresh urgency. For Wesley, a proper understanding with respect

---

1. Wesley, *Works* (BE) §14, 4:35–36.

to these two issues was critical to his exhortation to press on "from faith to faith" and influenced his appropriation of classic covenant theology.

The conversations he joined on these two soteriological concerns had remained lively in part because the various conclusions did not neatly settle out into a Calvinist solution and an Arminian solution. There were, after all, hyper-Calvinists and Calvinist preparationists; Arminians committed to the agenda of latitudinarianism and evangelical Arminians like Wesley. Not surprisingly, then, there were intense discussions on these two soteriological concerns within Calvinism and within Arminianism, and some cross-pollination of those internal discussions.

To better understand these conversations and Wesley's engagement of them, it is helpful to consider them in light of the historical background of the Evangelical Revival in which he labored. A particularly important aspect of the Revival's history is the persistence of the Calvinistic voice in the face of reaction to the excesses of the Commonwealth. This critical contextual concern merits close attention with respect to the two long-standing conversations in which Wesley found himself engaged. For one, the renewal of Reformation doctrine commensurate with the Revival is arguably indebted to this persistent voice. And, for another, its influence on Wesley's soteriology is evident in the fact that he drew from the theological well of his Puritan heritage in responding to the hyper-Calvinism he frequently found on the other end of these conversations as they unfolded over the last fifty years of his life. As a result, Wesley's appropriation of covenant theology influenced—and was deeply influenced by—his engagement in these conversations as reflected in the soteriological affirmations he sought to communicate through the servant-son metaphor.

The Evangelical Revival

While Isabel Rivers places the beginning of the Evangelical Revival in England "in the 1730s,"[2] Rack provides a broader perspective, noting that the Revival in England "was only part of a much more extensive international movement of a similar general character, ..."[3] It was, he suggests, "previewed" in Germany in the rise of Pietism, led most notably by Philipp Jakob Spener (1635–1705) and August Hermann Francke (1663–1727). Continental Pietism was, in part, a reaction to the prevailing "impoverished state of spiritual life" and sought "to create

---

2. Rivers, *Reason, Grace, and Sentiment*, 206. See also Jones, "Calvinistic Methodism," in Haykin and Stewart, *The Emergence of Evangelicalism*, 109.

3. Rack, *Reasonable Enthusiast*, 161.

a more personalized and inward type of piety" that "stressed the importance of good works, a concern which had always been theologically suspect in orthodox Lutheranism."[4]

Rack's summary is generally substantiated in W. R. Ward's *The Protestant Evangelical Awakening*, a detailed account of the evangelical awakening amid the political, cultural, geographical, and religious topography of northern and central Continental Europe. Ward, however, traces the beginnings of revival to a period of time well before Spener's influence gained greater traction with his republication in 1675 of Johann Arndt's sermons under the title *Pia Desideria*. The Revival, Ward proposes, originated with developments in Bohemia and Moravia (and eventually in much of Silesia) in the first half of the seventeenth century. In these regions, organized Protestantism had been essentially obliterated, leaving the population without churches or pastors. One outcome that shaped the notion of revival was a new kind of lay involvement as "Working Protestantism began to be concentrated in the hills and in the farm kitchens of miners and shepherds." In this situation, a form of field-preaching emerged for a period until it, too, was suppressed.[5] While acknowledging the rise of the influence of the Pietistic voice of Halle in furthering the evangelical awakening (particularly from the latter portion of the seventeenth century),[6] Ward specifically identifies the onset of revival with the child camp-meetings which spread across much of Silesia reaching Breslau in 1708. He seems to consider such a role on the part of children to be an indispensable marker of revival so much so that he sees it as *the* validating feature of the revival fire ignited in Zinzendorf's community at Herrnhut in the latter part of August 1727.[7]

In America, the influence of the concern of Continental Pietism for inward religion and the new birth was extended through the likes of T. J.

4. Ibid., 162.

5. Ward, *The Protestant Evangelical Awakening* (Cambridge: Cambridge University Press, 1992), 67.

6. Ward attributes much of the strength of this influence to the endeavours of August Francke whom he describes as "one of the most remarkable organisers in the whole history of Christianity." Ibid., 61.

7. Concerning the revival of Zinzendorf's community, Ward dates the revival from August 23, declaring unequivocally, "It needed only one more sign of the recent revivalist past, an intense spirit of prayer among the children . . ." Ibid., 127. Colin Podmore, on the other hand, places primary emphasis on the "great outpouring of the Holy Spirit on August 13, 1727, when the congregation gathered for Holy Communion in the parish church at Berthelsdorf." Podmore, *The Moravian Church in England*, 6. Ward clearly treats the outpouring at Berthelsdorf as secondary, though not without importance. Ward, *The Protestant Evangelical Awakening*, 126.

Frelinghuysen in the 1720s. And in the early 1730s the Great Awakening took hold in the New England parish of Northampton under the ministry of the Calvinist theologian, Jonathan Edwards. In Wales, in the meantime, Griffith Jones—"the single most important link between the Pietistic spirituality of [1660–1730] and the pioneers of the Methodist revival in Wales"[8]—was holding open air meetings as early as 1714.[9] And in England, Richard Davis in Northamptonshire and Mitchell and Crossley might be identified as forerunners of the Revival in light of their activity in Lancashire and Yorkshire in the late seventeenth and early eighteenth centuries.[10]

A characteristic of the Revival, observes Rack, is that it "developed out of an untidy series of local revivals, eventually consolidating into several distinct bodies and influencing existing churches."[11] The "fundamental common concern" that furthered this consolidation was, he proposes, a conviction of the need for "'inward' Christianity" as opposed to "mere outward observance." And what animated this conviction was "the failure of the attempted Puritan 'revolution' of the seventeenth century, which had been not merely religious, but also political and social."[12] In other words, part of the collateral damage resulting from this failed attempt was to the spiritual state of the established church. Luke Keefer goes so far as to describe the English Arminianism of the Restoration as "a polite religion in an anti-religious age."[13]

Certainly, Arminianism was once again in the favor of the Crown, even as it had been in the years leading up to the Interregnum.[14] In her

8. Jones, *"A Glorious Work in the World,"* 44. Jones states that in the period between 1660 and 1730 "the initiative for the evangelization of the Welsh" arose from "a small group of London-based Welshmen who had been deeply influenced by Pietistic theology." Ibid., 40.

9. Griffith's work in Wales was preceded by the likes of Vavasor Powell (1617–70), "an early exponent of 'heart religion' who championed the use of the cell group" and Morgan Llwyd (1619–59). Their efforts contributed to "an intensely affective experimental Calvinism" which became fertile soil for the later Welsh Methodism. Ibid., 37–38.

10 Rack, *Reasonable Enthusiast*, 164. Rack's overview of the various veins of the revival may be found on pages 158–80.

11. Ibid.

12. Ibid., 178. Rack notes that this concern was widespread and that "all began as movements within established churches."

13. Keefer, "John Wesley and English Arminianism," 20.

14. In the years immediately following the Synod of Dort (and despite the king's declaration to be Calvinist himself), Arminianism was an ally of the political agenda of the Crown with the result that, in England, the outcome for Arminianism was just

overview of developments in the seventeenth century, Rosalie Colie notes that "the Calvinist system did not offer a universally happy solution to separation from the Church of Rome, and 'Arminian' ideas sprang up spontaneously all over the reformed north [of Continental Europe] as a reaction to Genevan strictness of doctrine."[15] A case in point is the "Arminian works" of "one of London's leading Puritan pastors in the mid-seventeenth century," John Goodwin, who defended the tenets of Arminianism against a Presbyterian misrepresentation of them.[16] Such an example illustrates what Colie means when she states that, despite the eventual though brief triumph of Dissent in the mid-seventeenth century, Arminianism "penetrated everywhere in England" and "was not confined to the Church of England."[17]

However, the Arminianism of the Restoration period simply was not, by and large, of the same theological temper as that of its namesake, Arminius. Rather, according to Cragg, it was "a shrunken and attenuated form of Arminianism" that lost its "distinctive note as it merged imperceptibly with Latitudinarianism and Rationalism."[18] Contributing to *this* Arminianism was the influence of the Cambridge Platonists whose message found receptive soil in the new suspicion of enthusiasm that was shared by the general populace following the Interregnum. In the face of the established doctrinal protocols by which the Church of England invoked primitive Christianity as the interpretive key to its creedal statements, the Platonists granted primacy of place to Origen. This emphasis led to a distinctive understanding of the Atonement, "an inordinate emphasis on Divine Love" and an "unwillingness so much as to mention 'original sin.'"[19] In Cambridge Platonism, "'Enthusiasm'

---

the opposite of what occurred in the Netherlands: it was the Arminian prelates of the Church of England who were the persecutors. See Rosalie L. Colie, *Light and Enlightenment*, 21.

15. Ibid., 15.

16. Coffey, "Puritanism," 261.

17. Colie, *Light and Enlightenment*, 21.

18. Cragg, *From Puritanism to the Age of Reason*, 29–30. Cragg observes, "Dutch Arminianism was subsiding into Socinianism even while English Arminianism was drifting toward Desim." Ibid., 29–30.

19. Patrides, *The Cambridge Platonists*, 4–5, 38. Patrides summarizes Benjamin Whichcote's view on the problem of sin as follows: "But sin is then most reversible when man's innate tendency toward goodness is shaped by Christ's example into a thoroughly *rational* awareness of the wisdom inherent in the practice of universal love." Ibid. 39. W. M. Spellman, however, challenges Patrides' representation of the Platonists, noting that the latitudinarians did not oppose the idea of "the essential sinfulness and wilful depravity of man" and remained aligned with Augustinian pessimism. Spellman, *The Latitudi-*

was curbed [and] Protestant scholasticism was discarded. The progress of Calvinism was arrested," Patrides asserts, and "'the highly-esteemed Knowledge called 'Orthodoxness' . . . collapsed under the impact of new ideas forged from old." The result was a "remarkable latitude" and the mantra was, in Whichcote's words, "'Everie Christian must think and believe as hee findes cause.'"[20] This contributed to the rise of what Rivers describes as "the dominant Anglican tradition of moral and rational religion."[21]

The resulting spiritual state of the established church from 1660 has been described in terms of a vacuum created by the reaction against the attempted Puritan revolution. "Having extinguished the blazing flames of Puritanism," writes Keefer, "[the Church of England] was left with no flame of its own to warm the hearth of the nation."[22] G. R. Cragg asserts that "the second half of the seventeenth century saw many changes in English religious thought, but none more striking than the overthrow of Calvinism."[23] John Walsh declares that "the old Puritan Calvinism was virtually extinct" in the Arminian Church of England in which the Revival later arrived.[24] Concerning the state of the Church by the time of Whitefield and Wesley, John Coffey recalls Whitefield's lament: "how sadly are our Church ministers fallen from the doctrines of the Reformation."[25]

At first glance, these summary statements may appear as an obituary both of the spiritual capacities of the Church of England and of the influence of Reformed doctrine. However, David Ceri Jones objects, arguing that, by and large, the spiritual state of the established church has been "unfairly pilloried" by those historians intent on underscoring the Methodist contribution to the Revival. He asserts that the Church was, "In reality, . . . 'far from tepid.'"[26] Nevertheless, it must be noted, says Heitzenrater, that the judgment that "the Church of England did

---

narians, 8–9. See also Spurr, "'Latitudinarianism' and the Restoration Church," 61–82.

20. Patrides, *The Cambridge Platonists*, 40.

21. Rivers, *Reason, Grace, and Sentiment*, 205–6. For an assessment by Wesley of "the candle of the Lord"—the symbol, for the Cambridge Platonists, of Reason and of their confidence in it—see his 1781 sermon, "The Case of Reason Impartially Considered," Wesley, *Works* (BE) §10, 2:598–600.

22. Keefer, "John Wesley and English Arminianism," 20.

23. Cragg, *From Puritanism to the Age of Reason*, 13.

24. Walsh, "'Methodism,'" 22.

25. Coffey, "Puritanism," 271.

26. Jones, *A Glorious Work in the World*, 39. Nevertheless, Jones also states that the Anglican church of that period required 'a root-and-branch reformation'. Ibid. 43.

not rise as a whole to meet the challenge" of "the moral and spiritual lethargy" of the times is the verdict not only of later historians, but was an observation that was prevalent in the early-eighteenth century as well.[27]

Yet, there were signs of spiritual life in the Church. As a case in point, Heitzenrater identifies the religious societies within the Church of England as an "explicit expression" of those clergy and laity "who were increasingly concerned with the revitalization of Christian standards among the people."[28] Walsh describes these societies "peopled with High Church Anglican youths" as "the first reproductive cells of the revival in the metropolitan centers of Bristol and London."[29] Yet, if the appeal of Genevan Calvinism faltered on its strictness of doctrine, the holy living tradition of seventeenth-century Anglicanism (an influential aspect of High Church spirituality and a substantive component of the Oxford Methodists) suffered a similar fate by proving to be too demanding and by arousing aspirations it did not fully satisfy.[30]

With respect to the continued influence of Reformed doctrine, the assessments of both Cragg and Walsh are improved when qualified by Cragg's further observation that the reaction in Restoration England was "more against the temper in which Calvinism had been maintained than against the views which it advanced."[31] Echoing this same qualification, Stephen Hampton has argued that the Anglicanism of the late seventeenth century was not, in fact, completely overrun by Arminianism and that Reformed theology maintained a firm foothold despite the resistance to Calvinism *per se*.[32] Nevertheless, Rivers' evaluation that the diversity of the Revival consolidated as it coalesced around a shared interest in *dissociating* "from the largely ethical preaching typical of the Anglican clergy" and in *returning* "to the Reformation doctrines of justification and regeneration as expounded in the Thirty-Nine Articles"[33] seems amply justified.

27. Heitzenrater, "John Wesley and the Oxford Methodists," 5.
28. Ibid., 8.
29. Walsh, "'Methodism,'" 22.
30. Ibid. 25–26.
31. Cragg, *From Puritanism to the Age of Reason*, 21. Regarding the distinction between traditional and radical Puritanism, see Coffey, "Puritanism," 260.
32. Hampton, *Anti-Arminianism*, 2. Hampton writes of the Anglican Reformed: "'Reformed' was, therefore, an appellation they would have happily embraced. 'Calvinist,' with its seedy foreign overtones, and its hinterland of regicide and Presbyterianism, was not." Ibid., 7.
33. Rivers, *Reason, Grace, and Sentiment*, 205–6.

Others have added weight to the view of a return to these Reformation doctrines. Jones notes that Elie Halévy recognized "significant continuity between Methodism and earlier Protestant traditions" by identifying "the latent Protestant fervor of the English people, a hangover . . . from the Puritan era" as a contributing factor of the Revival in general and of Methodism in particular.[34] And while Walsh credits the Moravians with "the reintroduction of the Reformation doctrine of justification by faith alone, not merely as a creedal proposition but as an experiential reality," he also asserts that "as the great wave of Puritanism receded, it left innumerable rock pools of piety behind it."[35]

Evidence of increased attention to Reformation doctrine lends weight to Gordon Rupp's contention that Puritan Calvinism had remained influential despite the rejection of the Puritan experiment: "It can be no accident that in America, and Wales, and Scotland there was a background of Puritanism, mainly in its Calvinist form, for in the Revival Wesley's Arminianism is the odd one out. . . . In England itself the Anglo-Calvinist tradition [of Bolton, Sibbes, Ambrose, and Marshall] persisted at a depth and to an extent which has probably been underestimated."[36] In a similar vein, Walsh observes that many of those who responded to the preaching of Whitefield and Wesley were Dissenters, and that in this way "the old Nonconformity made its important input to the earliest years of the revival."[37]

Wesley, too, seems to have become convinced of a foundational compatibility between Puritan thought—as a trustworthy custodian of the Reformation doctrine of Justification—and the theological intentions of the Church of England's Thirty-Nine Articles of Religion. This compatibility was, however, a bit awkward. As Keefer notes, the Articles represent Anglicanism's "conflated doctrinal posture"—a result of seeking to hold together the notion of "God's sovereign will in salvation on the one hand and a system of sacramental grace on the other."[38] Wesley managed this awkwardness by appealing to the latitude he perceived the Articles to allow. Thus, he could subscribe to Article XVII ("Of Predestination and Election") on the basis of the affirmations of Article

---

34. Jones, "Calvinistic Methodism," 105–6. Jones argues, too, that the contribution of the Dissenters to the Evangelical Revival has also been understated, and points to the marked growth of Dissenting congregations in Wales in the decades immediately surrounding the turn of the eighteenth century. Jones, *A Glorious Work in the World*, 42–43.

35. Walsh, "'Methodism,'" 27, 29.

36. Rupp, *Religion in England*, 325–26. Bracketed insert mine.

37. Walsh, "'Methodism,'" 29.

38. Keefer, "John Wesley and English Arminianism," 18–19.

XXXI that "the offering of Christ . . . was for all the sins of the whole world, both original and actual."[39] He certainly came to emphasize the continuing influence in Anglicanism of a more Reformed understanding of justification. This is evident in his disavowal of holy living as the condition of justification—along with his former confidence in the sufficiency of his own best efforts to meet that condition—and his severe disappointment in the failure of William Law, his one-time mentor, to point him toward an understanding of justification by faith alone.[40]

It is noteworthy that Wesley was writing *Serious Thoughts upon the Perseverance of the Saints* and *Predestination Calmly Considered* while producing his multi-volume work, *A Christian Library*, in which he includes more selections from the Puritans,[41] whose spiritual vitality he held in high regard, than from any other tradition. For one, he saw no conflict in affirming universal redemption and the Reformation standard of justification by faith alone.[42] And for another, their predestinarian views notwithstanding, he deeply appreciated Puritan practical divinity as an invaluable ally in his effort to bring relief from the scourge of antinomianism.[43] It is not surprising, then, that the minute record of the 1770 Conference draws upon the views of a well-known, albeit controversial, Puritan from the previous century, Richard Baxter.

That Wesley would lean upon Baxter's views as a resource for both the 1745 and the 1770 conferences is significant on two levels. First, it illustrates Wesley's own awareness that he was *joining* and shaping a conversation already in progress rather than initiating a new one. Second, it serves to introduce a conversation that shaped Wesley's use of the servant-son metaphor in articulating his soteriological convictions. This conversation involved and revolved around the two critical soteriological

---

39. For a thorough discussion of Wesley's consideration of these two articles in response to Calvinists, see McGonigle, *Sufficient Saving Grace*, 179–215.

40. Wesley, "To William Law, May 14, 1738," *Letters*, 1:240

41. Coffey's argument that "an image of Puritanism as a solid, cohesive movement of impeccable Reformed orthodoxy" is "rather dated" is convincing. Coffey, "Puritanism," 262. At the same time, it is evident that for Wesley—and, apparently, in his view, for his prospective readers as well—there was, at least, a *perception* of a Puritanism whose praxis and doctrinal core was identifiable, relatively consistent, and fairly widely known. See Wesley's preface in Wesley, *ACL* (1749–1755), 7:np.

42. As Jerry Walls notes, "Wesley is vindicated of the charge of being a confused Calvinist. . . . [He] offers a distinctively different account of God and his saving activity from the Reformed tradition, despite important agreement with them on the disabling nature of sin and the necessity of grace for salvation." Walls, "John Wesley on Predestination and Election," 630.

43. *ACL* (1749–1755), 7:np.

concerns noted above: first, the role of good works in relation to salvation; and second, the question of the Divine regard for the responsive unregenerate.

Wesley and the Question of the Role of Good Works in Salvation

It was the very success of the Evangelical Revival that reinvigorated conversation on the question of the role of good works in relation to salvation—a conversation that had been in progress between Calvinists and Arminians since the early 1600s and that would remain vigorous until the latter years of the nineteenth century.[44] There was overall agreement that good works are certainly the *fruit* of justification. While strict Calvinists resisted attributing any salvific role whatsoever to good works, they stood in agreement with Arminians that good works are typically characteristic of those justified by faith in Christ Jesus. Good works as the fruit of Justification was deeply engrained in Wesley's theological thought, having been articulated so clearly in Article XII of the Thirty-Nine Articles, entitled "Of Good Works": "Albeit that good Works, which are the fruits of Faith, and follow after justification, cannot put away our sins, and endure the severity of God's judgment; yet are they pleasing and acceptable to God in Christ, and do spring out necessarily of a true and lively Faith, insomuch that by them a lively Faith may be as evidently known, as a tree discerned by the fruit."[45]

Just as deeply settled into Wesley's understanding were the declarations of Article XIII, "Of Works before Justification," which served as a further preservative against conceiving of good works as meritorious: "Works done before the Grace of Christ, and the Inspiration of his Spirit, are not pleasant to God, forasmuch as they spring not of Faith in Jesus Christ, neither do they make men meet to receive Grace, or (as the School-Authors say) deserve Grace of Congruity: Yea, rather for that they are not done as God hath willed and commanded them to be done, we doubt not but that they have the nature of sin."[46] Both John Wesley and his brother, Charles, held firmly to this understanding of the relationship of good works to justification.[47]

44. Sell, "Preface," in *The Great Debate*, np.
45. *Book of Common Prayer* (1732), np.
46. Ibid.
47. Wesley's deletion of this Article in its entirety from his abridgement of the Thirty-Nine Articles for the Methodists in America reflects the more practical concern of responding to the American situation than a doctrinal about-face on Wesley's part. See

Wesley echoes the assertions of these Articles in publishing a pamphlet in 1742 occasioning what he identifies as "the first Time I have appear'd in Controversy, properly so called."[48] The pamphlet, *The Principles of a Methodist*, was a response to Josiah Tucker's *A Brief History of the Principles of Methodism* published earlier that year. In his reply, Wesley credited Tucker with being accurate in his presenting Wesley as holding that justification is by faith alone:

> This I allow. For I am firmly persuaded, That every man of the Offspring of *Adam* is very far gone from Original Righteousness, . . . that therefore if ever we receive the Remission of our Sins and are accounted Righteous before God, it must be only for the Merits of Christ, by Faith, and not for our own Works or Deservings of any Kind. Nay, I am persuaded, That all Works done before Justification, have in them the Nature of Sin; and that consequently, 'till he is justified, a Man has no Power, to do any Work which is pleasing and acceptable to God.[49]

Wesley goes on to clarify his position regarding faith and good works in relation to justification:

> But let it be observed, the true Sense of those Words, *We are justified by Faith in* Christ *only*, is not, That this our own Act, *To believe in* Christ, or this our Faith which is within us justifies us . . . But that altho' we have Faith, Hope and Love within us, and do never so many good Works, yet we must renounce the Merit of all, of Faith, Hope, Love, and all other Virtues and Good works, which we either have done, shall do or can do, as far too weak to deserve our Justification: For which therefore we must trust only in God's Mercy, and the Merits of Christ.[50]

At the same time, Wesley also emphasized that while it is true that "St. *Paul* requires nothing on the Part of man" but faith, the faith he requires is to be, nonetheless, "*a True and Living Faith.*" This faith, however, is not wholly passive:

> Yet this Faith does not shut out Repentance, Hope and Love, which are join'd with Faith in every Man that is justified. But it shuts them out from the office of justifying, so that altho' they

---

Blankenship, "The Significance of John Wesley's Abridgement of the Thirty-Nine Articles," 35–47

48. Wesley, "To the Reader," in *The Principles of a Methodist*, np.

49. Wesley, *The Principles of a Methodist*, §2, 3.

50. Ibid., §6, 5.

are all present together in him that is justified, yet they justify not all together. . . . But it should also be observ'd, What that Faith is, whereby we are justified. Now that Faith which brings not forth Good Works, is not a Living Faith, but a dead and devilish one.[51]

This conception of a true and living faith is reminiscent of the distinction made by George Downame (*d.* 1634), bishop of Derry, in *A Treatise of Justification* published in 1633. Downame affirmed, "First, that we are justified by the righteousnesse of Christ alone apprehended by faith, and not by any righteousnesse inherent in us" and "Secondly, that this righeousnesse . . . is apprehended by faith onely."[52] He continued with an important qualification of the meaning of *sola fide*:

> Not that justifying faith is or can bee alone: but because there being many graces in the faithfull, which all have their severall commendations; yet none of them serveth to apprehend Christs righteousnesse, but faith onely, and *yet that faith which is alone, severed from all other inward graces, and outward obedience, doth not justifie either alone or at all; because it is not a true and a lively, but a counterfeit and a dead faith.* . . . So among all the graces of the soule, it is the office of faith alone, as the eye of the soule, to looke upon him that was figured by the brazen Serpent: yet if it should bee severed from the rest, it were dead.[53]

In *A Treatise on Justification* published in 1631, John Davenant (*d.* 1641), bishop of Salisbury, pointed in the same direction but more clearly insisted on the necessity of good works. "Good works are necessary in all the faithful and justified" because, without them, "no one can arrive at a state of justification." This is not because of any "efficacy" in themselves, "but because by the Divine arrangement, they are required either as previous or concurrent conditions" of justification.[54] Good works are also necessary "after justification is obtained; and must be performed with all zeal and diligence throughout the whole course of life."[55]

It is important to appreciate the historical context of Davenant's views on this matter. More a "Calvinist anti-papist than an overt anti-Arminian"[56] Davenant was chosen as one of the British delegation

---

51. Ibid., §4, §8, 4, 6–7. Emphasis mine.
52. Downame, *A Treatise of Justification*, §XII, 15.
53. Ibid. Emphasis mine.
54. Davenant, *A Treatise on Justification*, 1:274–75.
55. Ibid. 1:274.
56. Larminie, "Davenant, John, (*bap.* 1572, *d.* 1641)," *DNB* (http://www.oxforddnb.com).

to the Synod of Dort held in 1618. He joined with his fellow moderate, Samuel Ward, and with ministers from Bremen in arguing for hypothetical universalism, the view that "while Christ died for all men, not just for the elect, not all would receive salvation."[57] The rest of the British delegation was persuaded to this view—a view which, though it did not produce the outcome of the Synod to the degree envisioned by the delegation, secured "a judicious compromise" with the conservative Calvinists nonetheless.[58]

Davenant represented a preparationist view, and the argument of the British delegation to the Synod of Dort gave weight to this point of view. While the orthodox Continental Reformed theologians attending the Synod of Dort insisted that the elect are unwilling to turn to God until their effectual calling, the preparationists believed that God gave the will to convert and thus allowed for a measure of cooperation on the part of the elect. Joseph Hall, another member of the British delegation to the Synod of Dort, describes the preparationist view:

> [F]or the grace of God doth not work upon a man immediately by sudden raptures, but by meet preparations; informing the judgment of his danger, wounding the conscience by the terrors of the law, suppling it by the promises of the gospel. These inward acts tending toward conversion, are, by the power of the word and Spirit of God, wrought in the heart of a man not yet justified.[59]

The continued liveliness of the conversation concerning the relationship of good works to justification is seen in part by the fact that the matter remained a burr in the saddle of conservative Calvinists leading to a dispute among British divines of the late seventeenth century. Herman Witsius was called upon to referee the dispute[60] and responded

---

57. Ibid. A. C. Clifford summarizes this "'double aspect' decree of God" as follows: "the provision of grace is purposed for all conditionally" (*foedus hypotheticum*) "but for the elect absolutely" (*foedus absolutum*). Clifford, *Atonement and Justification*, 154.

58. Larminie, "Davenant, John (*bap.* 1572, *d.* 1641)."

59. Hall, *Via Media*, Art. III. IV. §5, in Wynter, *The Works of the Right Reverend Joseph Hall*, 9:493.

60. According to Gert van den Brink, the dispute arose in the 1690s (the third wave of antinomian controversies in that century) and was occasioned, in part, by the republication of Tobias Crisp's *Christ Alone Exalted*—a work presenting the view of "doctrinal antinomianism" (see the footnote below). Those rejecting the view represented by Crisp were nicknamed *neonomians*. Both camps viewed Witsius as an authority and appealed to him to moderate the controversy. *Irenical Animadversions* is his attempt to reconcile the two parties. See Van den Brink, "Calvin, Witsius, and the English Antinomians," 229–40.

with *Conciliatory, or Irenical Animadversions on the Controversies Agitated in Britain under the Unhappy Names of Antinomians and Neonomians*, published in 1696.[61] However, in his best known work, *The Economy of the Covenants between God and Man*, published in 1693, Witsius had already addressed the central concern and clearly espouses a strict "doctrinal antinomianism."[62] In diplomatic fashion, he identifies the British preparationists as "some among ourselves"[63] and begins by presenting their position in their own words:

> There are *some external works* ordinarily required of men before they are brought to a state of regeneration or conversion, . . . as going to church, hearing the word preached, and the like. 2dly, There are *some internal effects*, previous to conversion, or regeneration, excited by the power of the word and spirit in the hearts of those who are not yet justified; as the knowledge of the will of God, sense of sin, dread of punishment, anxiety about deliverance, some hope of pardon.[64]

He continues by defending the preparationists against the charge of Pelagianism:

> But they differ from the favourers of Pelagianism in this manner. 1st, That they are not for having these things to proceed from nature, but profess them to be the effects of the spirit of bondage, preparing a way to himself for their actual regeneration. 2dly, That they are not for God's bestowing the grace of regeneration from a regard to, and moved by occasion of, these preparations, much less by any merit in them; but they imagine that God, in this manner, levels a way for himself, fills up valleys, depresses mountains and hills, in order the better to smooth the way for his entrance into that soul.[65]

Witsius, however, proceeded to reject the idea that any person may go thus far toward justification, insisting that the preparations described by the British representatives are "not preparations for regeneration, but

---

61. Witsius describes his role in the dispute in his preface. Witsius, *Conciliatory, or Irenical Animadversions*, 5–9.

62. Van den Brink proposes a distinction between "practical antinomianism" (the practice of lawlessness) and "doctrinal antinomianism" which he describes as "the theological system in which good works are radically excluded." Van den Brink, "Calvin, Witsius, and the English Antinomians," 230.

63. Witsius, *The Economy of the Covenants*, 1:366.

64. Ibid. Emphasis mine.

65. Ibid., 1:366–67.

the fruits and effects of the first regeneration" for they necessarily "suppose some life of the soul, which spiritual attends to spiritual things."[66] Thus, according to Witsius, the British delegates are, in actual fact, describing the advance in the life of the elect from "passive justification"[67] to coming to "fiducially lay hold on Christ, and apply himself to the practice of true godliness."[68] If, however, regeneration is meant to denote "the first translation of a man from a state of death to a state of spiritual life" then "none of the orthodox ... can suppose preparatory works to the grace of regeneration." Witsius explains that this would require that either "these works proceed from nature; and so, by the confession of all the orthodox, are but dead and *splendid sins*" or that they would "proceed from the Spirit of God." The latter affirmation would entail affirming that the Spirit works with saving intent not only in the elect but in the reprobate as well; but this is impossible since all the actions of the reprobate are sinful, "let them be ever so much elevated by divine assistance."[69]

Wesley's own participation in the ongoing conversation is evident early on in his encounter with the influence of Philip Molther and others who began to promote the Stillness Doctrine[70] among the Moravians of the Fetter Lane Society in the late 1730s. In the recounting of his severing of ties with the Society in June and July of 1740, Wesley identified the Stillness Doctrine as a development that supplanted the doctrine he had received from the Moravians initially, when he came to know "the old way of salvation by faith only."[71] According to Hindmarsh, in his early encounters with the Moravians Wesley had observed, "a version of

---

66. Ibid., 1:367.

67. By "passive justification" Witsius is speaking of the view that the justification of the elect takes place solely as an act of divine grace exercised *upon* them; that is, at this juncture on the way of salvation, there is no cooperancy whatsoever between divine grace and human response.

68. Ibid., 1:368.

69. Ibid. The acrimonious description of preparatory works as "splendid sins" found its way into the minute record of the Methodist Conference held at Bristol in 1745. While this phrase may not have originated with Witsius, he is at least likely to have popularized it, given his apparent stature among British divines. See van den Brink, "Calvin, Witsius (1636–1708), and the English Antinomians," 5.

70. This is the strict *solafidian* view that one "ought not to pray, or search the Scriptures, or communicate, but to be *still*, ... And then he will surely receive faith, which till he is *still* he cannot have." Wesley, "June 22, 1740," *Works* (BE), 19:154.

71. Ibid., 19:153. Wesley stipulates "about September 1739" as the time during which "certain men crept in among [the Society] unawares." Wesley, *Works* (BE) §8, 18:219.

the Puritan morphology" influenced by Francke and typified by a crisis: "God's grace comes at certain specified moments or 'hours of grace' during which the inward penitential struggle (*Busskampf*) is followed by a sudden breakthrough (*Durchbruch*)."[72] The emergence of the Stillness controversy may well attest to Zinzendorf's steering Moravianism away from *Busskampf*.[73]

In reality, Wesley's efforts to reason from the Scriptures against the Stillness Doctrine and against the rejection of the notion of weak faith which accompanied it, was nothing less than a well-considered argument for the validity of preparation. As part of this argument, Wesley, in a series of four messages from Wednesday, June 25 to Saturday, June 28, 1740 before the Fetter Lane Society, sought to make the case that observing the means of grace was of great value for both believers and unbelievers alike.[74] Yet, he remained firmly within the boundaries of the twelfth and thirteen Articles when he goes on to declare, "We know indeed that the prayer of an unbeliever is full of sin."[75] But in the face of this affirmation he presents what he considers to be incontrovertible proof of God's regard for the unbeliever who, notwithstanding such unbelief, participates in the means of grace: "Yet let him remember that which is written of one who could not then believe, for he had not so much as heard the gospel: 'Cornelius, thy prayers and thine alms are come up for a memorial before God.'"[76]

This was no appeal to works as merit, but only an appeal to acknowledge the irrefutable evidence of divine mercy extended to Cornelius. That just such mercy might be extended to an unbeliever had also been argued by William Ames: "For nothing can be performed by man, since sinne is entred, acceptable to God, . . . Yet these duties are not therefore to be omitted by a man that doth not yet believe; . . . , nay they are often recompensed with divers benefits from God, although not by force of any determined Law, *but by a certaine abundant and secret kindnesse of him*."[77] Wesley's commentary on Acts 10:4 incorporates Ames' recognition of God's "secret kindnesse" and sounds like something Wesley might well have argued before the Fetter Lane Society:

---

72. Hindmarsh, *The Evangelical Conversion Narrative*, 58–59.
73. Ibid., 59.
74. Wesley, "June 25, 1740," *Works* (BE), 19:157.
75. Ibid.
76. Ibid., 19:158.
77. Ames, *Marrow of Sacred Divinity*, 218. Emphasis mine.

> *Thy prayers and thine alms are come up as a memorial before God*—Dare any Man say, These are only *Splendid sins?* Or, that they were an abomination before God? And yet it is certain, [in a *Christian* Sense, that] *Cornelius* was then an Unbeliever. He had not then Faith in *Christ*. So certain it is, that anyone who seeks Faith in *Christ*, should seek it *in* Prayer and doing Good to all Men: Tho' in strictness, what is not exactly according to the Divine Rule, must stand in need of Divine Favour and Indulgence.[78]

The biblical record of God's own response to Cornelius—who was at a far greater disadvantage than those associated with the Society on account of his not having heard the gospel—was, for Wesley, sufficient vindication of his theological judgment against the Stillness Doctrine. If God rewarded Cornelius with such a gracious response, it is inconceivable that there would be any *less* response from God to those having the *advantage* of hearing the gospel!

Biblical accounts such as the story of Cornelius were both compelling and complicating. Though vested with the authority of belonging to the Christian canon, the differences among the various narratives made the theological coherency between them less than self-evident. And yet, this complication was their very attraction in that the variety of biblical accounts provided an authoritative validation of the diversity of religious experience observed in the course of the Revival. Thus, while William Tyndale appealed to the dramatic conversion of the Apostle Paul as normative for the elect, other accounts provided solace for those whose conversions were characterized by faint beginnings and equally undramatic advancement.[79] Richard Baxter's own experience of "being wrought on by . . . Degrees,"[80] exemplified the tension between experiential religion, Reformed dogmatics, and the biblical standards.[81]

---

78. Wesley, *ENNT* (1755), 318. The phrase in brackets is a small but important addition that appears in editions of his New Testament *Notes* subsequent to this first edition. The qualifying phrase does not appear in the *errata* of the 1755 edition. However, the qualification does not reflect a new development in Wesley's thought, for it appears as well in his sermon, "Justification by Faith." See Wesley, *Works* (BE) §III.5, 1:192. This addition is a striking example of distinctions Wesley maintained on the basis of the covenant theology that so permeated his theological thought. The implications of such distinctions are explored more fully in the final chapters of this study.

79. Pettit, *The Heart Prepared*, 6–7.

80. Hindmarsh, *The Evangelical Conversion Narrative*, 52.

81. Pettit notes that this tension tended to be resolved by high Calvinists in the direction of God's majesty but by preparationists in the direction of God's mercy. Pettit, *A Heart Prepared*, 8.

While acknowledging the variety of experience, the mandate to articulate a unifying theological coherency encouraged the discernment of "a discrete spectrum of experience."[82] Those who, like Baxter, could not identify the precise moment of conversion might at least be able to point to evidence of a defined and discernible *process* underway in their lives, and thereby gain some degree of assurance that they themselves were among the elect.[83] Perkins had identified just such a process in some detail at the end of the sixteenth century. In *The Cases of Conscience*, he identified ten divine actions by which a person is brought into God's favor. The first four are those of "first grace" and "are onely *workes of preparation* going before [justifying] grace; the other actions which follow, are effects of [justifying] grace."[84]

Similarly, Richard Sibbes acknowledged the preparatory activity of grace in his sermon, *Lydia's Conversion*, published in 1638. Observing that Lydia "was one that feared God" but "was not ripened in the true religion," Sibbes affirmed: "There is such a distance between the nature and corruption of man and grace, that there must be a great deal of preparation, many degrees to rise by before a man come to that condition he should be in."[85]

It was the case of Cornelius, however, that specially influenced the forging of a Wesleyan Methodist soteriology. At the 1745 Conference the question raised was whether it is possible for a person to be in the favor of God apart from having a sense of God's pardoning love. Consideration of the biblical account of Cornelius raised the possibility that a person may be in the favor of God apart from belief in Christ and, consequently, apart from a sense of God's pardoning love. The Conference acknowledged, on the basis of the biblical witness, that Cornelius was "in some degree"[86] in the favor of God despite his not believing in Christ, and affirmed as well that his works were neither "splendid sins" nor done apart from "the grace of Christ."

The Conference then addressed the question of how it might reconcile this acknowledgement with its allegiance to Articles XII and XIII of the Thirty-Nine Articles.

---

82. Cohen, "Two Biblical Models of Conversion," 195.

83. Pettit, *A Heart Prepared*, 6.

84. Perkins, *The Cases of Conscience*, 46–47.

85. Sibbes, "Lydia's Conversion," *The Complete Works of Richard Sibbes*, 6:522–23.

86. Wesley, *Minutes*, 1745 (Jackson), 8:283. The phrase 'in some degree' does not appear In John Bennet's manuscript minutes of the Conference. *Minutes*, 1745 (Bennet), np.

> Q. 9. How then can we maintain, that all works done before we have a sense of the pardoning love of God are sin? And, as such, an abomination to Him?
>
> A. The works of him who has heard the gospel, and does not believe, are not done as God hath willed and commanded them to be done. And yet we know not how to say that they are an abomination to the Lord in him who feareth God, and, from that principle, does the best he can.[87]

The solution, then, was to introduce a condition upon which the strict theological judgments of the two Articles would be contingent. That condition was simply whether persons whose performance of good works was in question had heard the gospel. If they had *heard* the gospel yet did not believe, their works "were not done as God hath willed or commanded" and they were not in the favor of God. If they had *not* heard the Gospel yet were responding in the fear of the Lord (so far as they might respond in view of the limited amount of light they had received), they were "in some degree" in the favor of God.[88] With this condition in place, the Conference was able to demonstrate adherence to the Thirty-Nine Articles without having to forfeit its judgments concerning Cornelius.

But what, exactly, did this solution entail for a Methodist soteriology? What is the measure and meaning of the favor of God for those who have *not* heard the gospel? And what of those who *have* been privileged with the proclamation of the gospel but who, despite their receptivity and response, are not able bear witness to "the one Christian, saving faith"[89] as their own? These questions weighed heavily on Wesley and necessitated his engagement of the long-running conversation on the question of the Divine regard for the responsive unregenerate to which we now turn.

---

87. Wesley, *Minutes*, 1745 (Jackson), 8:283. In John Bennet's manuscript minutes the words "Therefore they are sinfull" appear after the words "commanded them to be done.' *Minutes*, 1745 (Bennet), np.

88. These same distinctions are emphasized in Wesley's sermon, "On Charity," written in October 1784. Wesley, *Works* (BE) §I.3, 3:295–96.

89. Wesley, "The Scripture Way of Salvation," *Works* (BE) §II.3, 2:161.

CHAPTER 6

John Wesley's Covenant Theology in Context

II. The Conversation on Divine Favor

IT IS INCREASINGLY APPARENT that while there was a strong consensus on many aspects of the theological core of covenant theology and general agreement among Calvinists and Arminians alike on the shape of its superstructure (the covenants of works and of grace), the details were subject to nuancing. And the nuancing was soteriologically critical, as evidenced in the long-running conversations Wesley joined in progress as he sought to stake out the theological foundations of a Methodist morphology of conversion. His regard for the authority of Scripture, his commitment to preserve the Reformation doctrine of justification by faith along with his evangelical Arminianism, and his attentiveness to the testimonies of rank and file Methodists and to the complaints of his critics, conspired to shape his engagement of these conversations.

In moving to the second of the two conversations to which Wesley gave ongoing attention, two factors should be kept in mind with respect to the context of his engagement of them. The first is that the soteriology he was so intent on clarifying and promoting was unsettled in its earliest years. As Rack observes, the rather explosive early growth of Methodism took Wesley and his trusted companions by surprise, resulting in those very doctrines which stood at the heart of that growth being "found" and clarified "only by painful search."[1] This search was an event-filled process to which there really was no well-ordered conclusion, though these doctrines were, indeed, "found" in a manner of speaking.

---

1. Rack, *Reasonable Enthusiast*, 158.

The second factor is Gordon Rupp's astute observation that, in the Evangelical Revival, "Wesley's Arminianism is the odd one out."[2] This is a helpful reminder that Wesley's engagement was forged in response to the prevailing winds of a resurgent Anglo-Calvinist tradition. Consequently, the fact that the servant-son metaphor came to greater prominence over the last quarter century of Wesley's life suggests that even though the constituent elements of his soteriology were more firmly settled by that time,[3] there was yet considerable pressure to define and defend it. This defense took place at the level of soteriological distinctions *within* the framework of covenant theology—a defense that distinguished Wesley's covenant theology.

Wesley and the Question of Divine Regard for the "Responsive Unregenerate"

When the 1745 Conference concluded that Cornelius was "in some degree" in the favor of God, it was participating in a longstanding conversation parallel to that on the preparation of the heart on which the question of the role of good works in salvation had come to center. This parallel conversation concerned the question of divine regard the "responsive unregenerate."[4] What, if any, is the salvific significance of such regard? If Cornelius is in the favor of God to any degree at all, what does this say about his eternal state? And what about one who has *heard* the gospel message and is responsive to it but who does not yet have a sense of the pardoning love of God?

This last question was haunting Wesley's Methodists. The 1745 Conference pondered the situation of John Warr, a member of their own society, who died without a clear sense of pardon: was he not justified, or was he an "exempt case"—someone suffering from some disorder of body or temperament that obscured his experience of such a sense of pardon? That a sense of pardon was the foundation of justification was

---

2. Rupp, *Religion in England*, 325–26.

3. Outler observes that Wesley's sermon, "Justification by Faith," published in 1746, "stands as the earliest full summary of Wesley's soteriology in the basic form in which it will continue." Wesley, *Works* (BE), 1:182.

4. The phrase is offset by quote marks so as to indicate suspended judgment on the question of whether or not a responsive individual should be considered a believer on the basis of evidence of spiritual responsiveness. Without disregard for the debate but for ease of the discussion at hand, the quote marks will not normally appear and the term "unbeliever" is occasionally substituted for "unregenerate."

a position in which Wesley and his fellow conferees were then theologically entrenched:

> [T]hat no works done before justification are done as God hath willed and commanded them to be done, will appear equally plain and undeniable if we only consider God hath willed and commanded that "all our works should be done in charity" (*en agapē*), in love, in that love to God which produces love to all mankind. But none of our works can be done in this love while the love of the Father (of God as our Father) is not in us. And this love cannot be in us till we receive the "Spirit of adoption, crying in our hearts, Abba, Father."[5]

It is not surprising, then, that when the 1746 Conference convened on May 13 at the New-Room in Bristol, the deliberations began with an admonition to rekindle the sort of preaching that will "empty men of their own righteousness" since "till all other foundations are overturned, they cannot build upon Christ."[6] A member of the Conference, Jonathan Reeves, served as an exemplary model of the depth of conviction of sin which such preaching may bring about and how "the stronger the conviction, the speedier is the deliverance."[7]

But it is Reeves' description of experiencing a "degree of peace"—though "not that solid peace of God"[8]—in the midst of the heretofore inconsolable effects of conviction, that brought to center stage the conversation on the question of the salvific import of divine regard for the responsive unbeliever. The Conference concluded that this "trust in the love of God" that had birthed in Reeves a degree of peace (but that was "without a distinct sight of God reconciled" to him), was "an earnest" of "a low degree of justifying faith."[9] It was determined that Reeves himself possessed, at that point, that faith which the Apostles had before Christ's death and the outpouring of the Holy Spirit: "a Jewish faith." Into his heart "God [had] not yet shined, to give him the light of the glorious love of God in the face of Jesus Christ"; yet, he was not a heathen but was "a believer under the Jewish dispensation"—he was "a servant of God: One who sincerely obeys him out of fear."[10]

---

5. Wesley, "Justification by Faith," *Works* (BE) §III.6, 1:193. Wesley reiterates the point in *A Farther Appeal to Men of Reason and Religion*, 2.

6. *Minutes*, 1746 (Jackson), 8:286–87. See Question 2.

7. Ibid., 8:287. See Question 3.

8. Ibid. See Question 7.

9. Ibid. See Question 8.

10. Ibid. See Questions 9–11.

It is important at this juncture to recognize the broader context of the deliberations of the Conference on the question of divine regard for the responsive unregenerate. In Perkins' schema summarized in the previous chapter, the first four stages in the progression of first grace included the *caveat* that these are "onely workes of preparation" and are *antecedent* to justifying grace. On the other hand, the fifth stage—"to stirre up the minde to a serious consideration, of the promise of saluation propounded and published in the Gospel"[11]—is set *in-between*, distinguished both from the preparatory works antecedent to justifying grace and the actual justification of the sinner which occurred at the sixth stage.

This was not a consideration that occupied only the attention of Puritans like Perkins. Jeremy Taylor (*d.* 1667), an influential voice of the Holy Living tradition within Anglicanism, also described just such an in-between place in *The Doctrine and Practice of Repentance*. In his exposition of Romans 7, Taylor first stipulates that "St. Paul speaks not in his own person, as an apostle, or a Christian, a man who is regenerate; but in the person of a Jew, one under the law, one that is not regenerate."[12] Then, in a subsection titled "How far an unregenerate Man may go in the Ways of Piety and Religion," Taylor declares: "To this inquiry it is necessary that this be premised: That between the regenerate and a wicked person, *there is a middle state*: so that it is not presently true, that if the man be not wicked, he is presently regenerate."[13] Taylor develops the concept in some detail:

> Between the two states of so vast a distance, it is impossible but there should be many intermedial degrees; between the carnal and spiritual man there is a moral man; not that this man shall have a different event of things if he does abide there, but that he must pass from extreme to extreme by this middle state of participation.... For a man may have gone many steps from his former baseness and degenerous practices, and yet not arrive at godliness, or the state of pardon; like the children of Israel, who were not presently in Canaan, as soon as they were out of Egypt, but abode long in the wilderness: ....[14]

---

11. Perkins, *The Cases of Conscience* (1604), 47–48.

12. Taylor, *The Doctrine and Practice of Repentance* in *The Whole Works of the Right Rev. Jeremy Taylor,* Sec. IV §24, 9:134.

13. Ibid., Sec. V §28, 9:139. Emphasis mine.

14. Ibid.

These unregenerate are "those whom St. Paul . . . describes to be 'under the law'; convinced of sin, pressed, vexed, troubled with it, complaining of it, desirous to be eased"—ones who are "disposed to life eternal" but are not yet believers.[15] From this "fair disposition" (this intermediate state), Taylor notes, these "became believers upon the preaching of the Apostles."[16]

Within the ranks of Dissent, the matter of divine regard for the responsive unregenerate arose in close relation to concerns over the matter of assurance. While the idea of a "middle state" stands in irreconcilable conflict with Calvinism at one level, the essential features of such a state are evident in the controversy over admission to the church which strained relations between Scottish Presbyterianism and some New England congregations.[17] In those settings where church membership came to be explicitly identified with *external* calling (the calling incumbent upon elect and reprobate alike wherein both are fellow-citizens in the church) rather than *effectual* calling (the calling upon the elect who are alone fellow citizens with Christ), those who relied on church membership as a ground of their assurance of having been effectually called were shorn of that confidence.[18]

Though John Cotton (1585–1652) no longer held a preparationist view,[19] he nonetheless acknowledged that the activity of God's grace may vary in the strength by which it is perceptible by those who must make judgments regarding admission to membership. Accordingly, he allowed that those who "may be *conceived* to be received of God into fellowship with Christ" may be received into church membership.[20] This view seems akin to the idea of "the judgement of charitable Christians" as held by Calvin who acknowledged that since the elect cannot be known "'with the certainty of faith,' all . . . who 'by confession of faith, example of life, and participation in the sacraments' profess God and Christ . . . ought to be taken for elect and members of the church 'by a certain judgment of charity.'"[21]

---

15. Taylor, *The Doctrine of Repentance*, Sec. V §28, 9:140.

16. Ibid., Sec. V §28, 9:140.

17. Samuel Rutherford, a Scottish commissioner to the Wesminster Assembly, wrote *A Peaceable and Temperate Plea for Pauls Presbyterie* in 1642 in critique of New England congregationalism.

18. Tipson, "Invisible Saints," 469.

19. Cotton had initially imbibed his preparationist views from Sibbes. Pettit, *A Heart Prepared*, 132–33.

20. Cotton, *The Way of the Churches*, 56. Emphasis mine.

21. Tipson, "Invisible Saints," 469.

Thus, while Cotton urged a close investigation of those seeking admission into the church, he counseled a generous measure of leniency in the matter: "Wee . . . willingly stretch out our hands to receive *the weak in faith*, such in whose spirits wee can discerne *the least measure of breathing and panting after Christ, in their sensible feeling of a lost estate;* . . . ."[22] Cotton, however, was not quite as generous as his colleague, Thomas Hooker (who had remained strongly preparationist), and criticized him for actually "admitting external covenanters to full church membership on the basis of preparatory 'motions,' or a charitable 'hope.'"[23] Interestingly, the similarity between Hooker's standard and that later applied by Wesley for admission into a Methodist Society is striking: "There is One only Condition previously required, in those who desire Admission into this Society, *A Desire to flee from the Wrath to come, and to be saved from their Sins.*"[24]

The question of the divine regard was not only an ongoing conversation in the broader historical context of the revival but was a matter under consideration by Wesley at least eighteen months before he and his brother, Charles, sailed for Georgia in 1735. John Wesley's diary entry of a meeting with Benjamin Ingham on Sunday, March 17, 1734 is corroborated by an entry in Ingham's own diary and provides additional detail of the theological discussion held: "6.45 Fetched Robson to breakfast with us; he [John Wesley] proposed to us to meet once a week . . . 7 breakfast with them, religious talk of the three different states of men, the natural, [the] Jewish or fearful, and the evangelical, the two last only salvable; . . ."[25] The Wednesday previous, March 13, 1734, Wesley had recorded a discussion on the same topic with Westley Hall.[26] His diary entry for that day records a meeting at ten o'clock in the morning and reads in part, "religious talk, Legal . . . and Evang,"[27] It is of interest that Ingham not only uses the descriptors "Jewish" and "fearful" in reference to the "Legal" state, but also notes an important soteriological conclusion concerning the three states: "the two last only[,] salvable."[28]

The natural state is typified by such a lack of awareness of its desperate spiritual condition that there are as yet no motions toward God

22. Cotton, *The Way of the Churches*, 58.
23. Pettit, *A Heart Prepared*, 133–34.
24. Wesley, *A Plain Account of the People Called Methodists* (1749), 6.
25. Ingham, *Diary of an Oxford Methodist*, 133–34.
26. Ibid., 134.
27. John Wesley, *MS Oxford Diaries IV*, Colman Collection (MARC), 96.
28. Ingham, *Diary of an Oxford Methodist*, 134.

and thus no engagement of proffered grace. The legal state, on the other hand, represents the status of those who are at least cognizant of their alienation from God, who have some desire that this predicament be remedied, and who have, in some sense, set foot on the way of salvation. On this basis, these persons are considered "salvable," along with those in an evangelical state.

This understanding of the legal state is evident in Charles Wesley's soteriological views during his early days serving as an itinerant preacher in the cause of the Revival. On at least twenty-one occasions throughout 1738 and 1739, Charles preached a sermon from 1 John 3:14 entitled, "The Three States of Man."[29] The sermon text is the first half of the verse only: "We know that we have passed from death unto life."[30] The opening of the sermon is comprised of a long quote from John Norris' 1690 work, *Christian Blessedness*. Charles follows Norris' presentation of the three states closely, including basing the distinctions presented on an interpretation of Romans 7 as picturing the unregenerate person.[31] The first state "'is a state of rest and acquiescence in sin; the second is a state of contention; the third is a state of victory.'" Continuing to quote Norris, Charles notes that whereas in the first state the mind is fully and fast asleep, "'in the second she is between sleeping and waking.'"[32]

In Charles' view, the middle state between sleeping and waking was not a state of victory, though persons in this state of contention received "some fore-taste of this happiness" and were "oft refreshed with the dew of heaven, and fed with the fruits of Canaan."[33] These are visitations of the Holy Spirit and favors of God; but to be contented with these—to settle for being "reproved of sin, but not rescued from it"—is to set up "on this side of Jordan" opposite Canaan and thus to forfeit justification.[34] Until the victory so described is realized, those yet in the state of contention are "now spiritually dead" *even though* they are, as he says, "heirs of promise."[35]

By 1740, however, the matter was under review. In the course of a long reply to a letter recently received from Charles Wesley, Benjamin Ingham proposed that those who receive forgiveness (pardon) but then

29. Charles Wesley, *The Sermons of Charles Wesley*, 130.
30. Ibid., 133.
31. Ibid., 133–34. See Norris, *Christian Blessedness*, 73–75.
32. Charles Wesley, *The Sermons of Charles Wesley*, 134.
33. Ibid., 143.
34. Ibid., 140–43.
35. Ibid., 147.

do not progress to the state of victory are, nonetheless, in "the 1st state of the new birth"[36] and are, in fact, "newly justified."[37] Though they are not sealed with the Spirit, "without doubt they are the children of God, they are in a state of Salvation."[38]

This exchange seems to have contributed to a significant revision of the early soteriological views of Charles Wesley and—given their partnership in the prosecution of the Revival in its earliest days—of John Wesley, as well. In John Wesley's preface to his and Charles' 1740 edition of *Hymns and Sacred Poems*, a broader soteriological judgment is evident than what is found in Charles' sermon noted above. While describing those who are partakers of this "great Salvation"[39] in terms of absolute and constant victory similar to Charles Wesley's "state of victory," he nevertheless introduces the essence of Ingham's category of the newly justified. Accordingly, Wesley affirms: "Not that every one is 'a Child of the Devil' . . . till he is, in this full Sense, 'Born of God.'" Rather, he is "a Child of God, and if he abide in Him, an Heir to all the Great and Precious Promises."[40] On this certainty, Wesley offers solace to those whose faith is weak and assures them that "tho 'the Heir, as long as he is a Child, differeth nothing from a Servant, yet is he Lord of all.'"[41] This recognition and accommodation of the state of the "newly justified" is clearly discernible as well in the Wesleys' hymns during this time period.[42]

In his 1741 sermon, "Christian Perfection," John Wesley acknowledges that there are "several stages in the Christian life" and references John the Apostle's distinction between babes, young men, and fathers. While he is unequivocal in stating these as stages in the *Christian* life, he nevertheless declares that "these only"—the fathers, "who have known both the Father and the Son and the Spirit of Christ" and who are "'perfect men, being grown up to the measure of the stature of the fullness

---

36. "A letter from Benjamin Ingham to Charles Wesley (1740)," *London Letters Chiefly Addressed to the Rev. Charles Wesley*, DD/Pr 1 (MARC), 50.

37. Ibid. The term is not Ingham's but Charles' who annotated the letter, "Benj Ingham 1740 of the newly justified."

38. Ibid.

39. Wesley and Wesley, *Sacred Hymns and Poems* (1740) §1, iii.

40. Ibid., §8, viii.

41. Ibid. See the discussion in Chapter 1 regarding the relationship of these references to the metaphors of servant and son.

42. The twenty-two stanzas of "The Just Shall Live by Faith" exemplify this development. Ibid., 161–65.

of Christ'"—"are properly Christians."[43] Those who are justified are, though "born of God," "born again" only "in the lowest sense."[44] Clearly, the Wesleys' understanding of justification was a work-in-progress. As McGonigle notes, John Wesley's early distinction between levels of justification (of being born again in the lower sense or in the higher sense of the word) "anticipated his later distinction between justification and sanctification."[45]

Over the course of the Conferences convened in the mid-1740s there emerged a greater recognition of the spiritual victory secured in justification. In matter of fact, at the 1745 Conference the problem of *downplaying* the rich rewards of justification in order to emphasize those gained by going on to perfection was acknowledged and a corrective direction given.[46] Nevertheless, there seems to have remained a conviction that those "justified but not sealed" belonged to an intermediate state on the way of salvation. The lead question on the second day of the 1745 Conference appears to have challenged this distinction: "Is an assurance of God's love absolutely necessary to our being in his favor?"[47] Though the Conference never recorded an outright answer to this question, an affirmative answer seems to stand as an assumption. The only other discussion regarding the favor of God focused on whether there may be situations where favor is granted *apart* from "an assurance of God's love" (in what the Conference identified as "exempt cases") and where favor may be granted "in some degree" *in spite of* one's not yet having believed in Christ (as in the case of Cornelius who had not yet heard the gospel).

Leaving aside both the question of exempt cases and the situation of Cornelius, the 1746 Conference aimed to clarify exactly what "the proper Christian faith" *is*, in part by clarifying what it is *not*. One distinction that arose in the discussion centered on the faith of those under the Jewish dispensation (such as the Apostles before the outpouring of the Holy Spirit). These persons were determined to have "an earnest" of "a low degree of justifying faith." It is clear that possessing this "earnest" signified a point of spiritual advance but not of arrival, for it "abides for a short time only" presumably on account of the fact that "God hath

---

43. Wesley, *Works* (BE) §II.1–2, 2:105.

44. Ibid., §II.3, 2:106. Yet, even at this stage, they are "in such a sense perfect . . . as . . . , not to commit sin." Ibid.

45. McGonigle, *Sufficient Saving Grace*, 112.

46. *Minutes*, 1745 (Bennet), np. See Questions 19–21.

47. Ibid., np. The version printed by Jackson begins, "Is a sense of God's pardoning love . . ." *Minutes*, 1745 (Jackson), 8:282.

not yet shined in their hearts."[48] At the Conference in 1747 the matter of whether a clear sense of pardon was essential to justification was again taken up. The leading question was very specific as was its answer: "Q. 1. Is justifying faith a divine assurance that Christ loved me, and gave himself for me? A. We believe it is." When the case of the Apostles before the Day of Pentecost was raised, the Conference maintained, "The Apostles themselves had not the proper Christian faith till after the day of Pentecost."[49]

After debating the applicability of a number of scriptures to this question, the conferees considered the question from the point of view of the experience of their own companions in the faith; namely, "J. A., or E. V., who have so much integrity, zeal, and fear of God, and walk so unblamable in all things" and "are continually longing, striveing [sic],—praying for the assurance which they have not." In response to the query of whether these persons might, in fact, be "void of justifying faith," the Conference concluded that such qualities may be found "by nature and habit, with preventing grace" and yet be absent "faith and the love of God." And while acknowledging it to be "scarcely possible [sic]" to render certain judgment on the matter, the Conference concluded, "But this we know, [if] Christ is not revealed in them, they are not yet Christian believers."[50] In the end, however, the Conference determined that the eternal destiny of J. A. and E. V. would ultimately be settled beyond question: "Q. 11. But what becomes of them then, suppose they die in this state? A. That is a supposition not to be made. They cannot die in this state: They must go backward or forward. If they continue to seek, they will surely find, righteousness, and peace, and joy in the Holy Ghost."[51]

It is certain that up to this time the conclusions of the Conference would have been consistent with those of Wesley himself. Over the course of his correspondence with the pseudonymous John Smith, Wesley had clearly articulated the conclusion of the conference that justifying faith is "a divine assurance that Christ loved me, and gave himself for me." In his reply to John Smith on December 30, 1745, Wesley declared

---

48. This is reminiscent of Perkins' scheme describing those who have progressed beyond "onely *workes of preparation*" and who are not, as yet, justified. Perkins, *The Cases of Conscience* (1604), 47–48.

49. Q. 1–4. *Minutes*, 1747 (Bennet), np.

50. Q. 10. *Minutes*, 1747 (Bennet), np. Bracketed insert mine.

51. *Minutes*, 1747 (Bennet), np.

that the "distinguishing doctrines" on which he insists might properly be summed up in what Smith has called "perceptible inspiration":

> But be pleased to observe what we mean thereby. We mean that inspiration of God's Holy Spirit whereby he fills us with righteousness, peace, and joy, with love to him and to all mankind. And we believe it cannot be, in the nature of things, that a man should be filled with this peace and joy and love by the inspiration of the Holy Ghost without perceiving it, as clearly as he does the light of the sun.
>
> This is . . . the main doctrine of the Methodists. This is the *substance* of what we all preach. And I will still believe, none is a *true Christian* till he experiences it; and consequently, that 'people at all hazards must be convinced of this; yea, though that conviction at first "unhinge" them ever so much, though it should in a manner "distract" them for a season. For it is better that they should be "perplexed" and "terrified" now than that they should sleep on and awake in hell.[52]

Wesley further asserted that he "will not move an hair's breadth" from this position and that he takes it "to be the very foundation of Christianity" and necessary to salvation, except for cases of "invincible ignorance."[53]

Yet, within six weeks of the close of the Conference Wesley was willing to move at least "an hair's breadth." On July 31, 1747 he wrote to his brother Charles from Beercrocomb "on a desideratum among us, a *genesis problematica* on Justifying Faith."[54] Wesley now clearly separates what he had so vehemently held together until this time. His conclusion "roughly set down" was clear: "Is justifying faith a sense of pardon? *Negatur*." The question, he notes, is of immense importance, "lest [the preachers] should either make them sad whom God hath not made sad, or encourage them to say peace where there is no peace."[55] He carefully distinguishes the primary terms in question: "By justifying faith I mean that faith which whosoever hath not is under the wrath and curse of God. By a sense of pardon I mean a distinct, explicit assurance that my sins are forgiven."[56] And while he affirms that there *is* such "an explicit

---

52. Wesley, *Works* (BE), 26:181–82. Emphasis mine.

53. Ibid. In *A Farther Appeal*, published earlier that same year, Wesley declared: "And therefore every Man, in order to believe unto Salvation, must receive the Holy Ghost." Wesley, *A Farther Appeal* (1745) §6, 4.

54. Wesley, *Letters*, 2:108.

55. Ibid.

56. Ibid.

assurance," and that such an assurance is "the *common* privilege of *real* Christians" and is "*the proper Christian faith*," he "cannot allow that justifying faith is such an assurance, or necessarily connected therewith."[57]

Substantiating his point, Wesley contested the view that justifying faith "*necessarily* implies such an explicit sense of pardon" on the basis that such a view is contrary to reason, to experience, and to Scripture.[58] He admits that his own church may indeed hold the view which he now disavows, and acknowledges the possibility of this complication. In self-defense Wesley appeals to the Church of England's own acknowledgement of its susceptibility to error[59] and to the higher authority of Scripture: "But to the law and [to the] testimony. All men may err: but the word of the Lord shall stand for ever."[60]

The Soteriological Standard of Scripture: "Fear God and Work Righteousness"

In the July 1747 letter to his brother, Wesley's appeal to Scripture included his specific reference to two passages of scripture: Isaiah 50:10 and Acts 10:34–35.[61] The Isaiah passage had been cited in the deliberations of the 1746 Conference; the passage from Acts, on the other hand, is one to which no appeal had yet been made (at least according to the minute record) during the course of the deliberations of the Conferences held since 1744. Wesley's citation of these particular scripture passages is noteworthy on several counts. First, the 1745 Conference had specifically referred to Acts 10:4, highlighting the divine regard for *Cornelius* who had not yet heard the gospel. In this letter, however, Wesley calls

---

57. Ibid. Emphasis mine. Wesley reiterated the same point decades later in a letter to Joseph Benson on May 21, 1781: "That some consciousness of our being in favour with God is joined with Christian faith I cannot doubt; but it is not the essence of it. A consciousness of pardon cannot be the condition of pardon." Ibid., 7:61.

58. Wesley specifies the case of "J[onathan] R[eeves], etc., etc." Ibid., 2:109.

59. Article XXI of the Thirty-Nine Articles asserts that the General Councils of the church "may err, and sometime have erred, even in things pertaining unto God." *Book of Common Prayer* (1732), np. Wesley described himself as being convinced of this truth as a result of his reading Beveridge's *Pandectae canonum conciliorum*. See Wesley's journal entry for September 13, 1736, *Works* (BE), 18:422.

60. Wesley, *Letters*, 2:109. Bracketed inserts appear in the reproduction of the letter in the Bicentennial Edition of Wesley's *Works*. Wesley, *Works* (BE), 26:255.

61. In Telford's edition of Wesley's letters, only Acts 10:34 is stipulated. See Wesley, *Letters*, 2:109. However, the whole of verse 35 is included both in John Whitehead's reproduction and in the Bicentennial Edition of Wesley's *Works*. See Whitehead, *The Life of the Rev. John Wesley*, 417; and Wesley, *Works* (BE), 26:255.

upon the biblical record of the divine revelation to *Peter*, which revelation is far more general in scope: "Of a truth I perceive that God is no respecter of persons: But in every nation he that feareth him, and worketh righteousness, is accepted of him." Second, Wesley uses this passage to argue the case of those who, *unlike Cornelius*, most certainly *had* heard the Gospel and responded positively to it, but who were yet unable to testify to a sense of the pardoning love of God. Third, it is important to observe that Wesley cites these two scriptures *together* rather than simply one or the other. This raises the question as to what message is common to these scriptures. The answer is plainly evident: fearing God and working righteousness (fearing the Lord and obeying "the voice of his servant").

The Petrine declaration, then, is first and foremost a further confirmation of the broader biblical themes of the fear of the Lord and the attendant obligation of obedience to his commands. This theme was clearly a priority for Wesley in his attempt to rebuff the onslaught of antinomianism. Thus, his *primary* purpose was *not* so much to argue the case of Cornelius as it was to accentuate the truth revealed to the Apostle Peter as a soteriological standard found throughout Scripture. This is indicated by the collection of scriptures which Wesley used interchangeably with Acts 10:35—Isaiah 50:10,[62] Isaiah 1:16–17 ("Cease to do evil; learn to do well"),[63] Deuteronomy 13:4 ("walk after the LORD your God, and fear him, and keep his commandments"), Ecclesiastes 12:13 ("Fear God, and keep his commandments: for this is the whole duty of man"), and Job 2:3 ("feareth God and escheweth evil").[64]

It is certainly the case that Wesley understood the soteriological standard of fearing God and working righteousness to be emblematic of one having the faith of a servant. This is evident in the fact that in one brief paragraph in his 1788 sermon, "On the Discoveries of Faith," Wesley brings into play three of these six scriptures for the specific purpose of explaining what he means when he speaks of those who have the faith of a servant.[65] The point is that one having the faith of a servant would

---

62. See Wesley, "The Wilderness State," *Works* (BE) §8, 2:210–11.

63. See Wesley, "On Working Out Our Own Salvation," *Works* (BE) §4, 3:201–2.

64. This phrase from Job 2:3 also appears in a definition of righteousness by Samuel Hebden in his answer to John Taylor's *Man's Original Righteousness*. Wesley quoted Hebden in his essay "The Doctrine of Original Sin According to Scripture, Reason, and Experience." Wesley, *Works* (Jackson), 9:289.

65. Wesley, *Works* (BE) §13, 4:35. Wesley quotes phrases from Acts 10:35; Isa 1:16–17, and Deut 13:4 (possibly in combination with a portion of 1 John 3:24). In this

certainly evidence intentionality with regard to this soteriological standard. However, it is *not* the case that every reference to this soteriological standard necessarily brings the servant metaphor into play.[66] Thus, though it is true that "fearing God and working righteousness" came to serve as a signature of the servant metaphor, it is important to recognize that the phrase had a history (even in Wesley's thinking) that was broader than, and independent of, the metaphor.

In appealing to Acts 10:34–35 in his 1747 letter to Charles, then, it does not appear that Wesley was arguing the case of Cornelius *per se*; rather, what is more probable is that Wesley was simply applying a widely-recognized soteriological standard to substantiate his point. Thus, in order to understand properly the relationship between "fearing God and working righteousness" and the metaphor, it is important to consider the value of this descriptor to Wesley as yet another declaration of the fundamental soteriological standard revealed throughout Holy Writ.

This standard is evident in Richard Baxter's *Aphorisms of Justification* (first published in 1649) where Baxter applies Acts 10:35 to substantiate his claim that "at the Great Judgment . . . it is beyond Doubt that Christ will then justify Men according to their Works." The context of Baxter's application of the verse is the requirement of the performance *by the justified* of the conditions of the gospel leading to final justification for those who believe in Christ.[67] Wesley himself appears to use the phrase in a similar sense in his reply to John Smith on March 25, 1747, where he defends his deployment of lay preachers by pointing to their "saving so many souls from death, and hiding a multitude of sins" as the ultimate witness to the divine approval of his action. "Many indeed God hath taken to himself," Wesley declared, "but many more remain, both young and old, who now fear God and work righteousness."[68]

This passage is of particular interest because Wesley's use of Acts 10:35 predates both the 1747 Conference and his letter to his brother, Charles, later that summer. It is apparent that the phrase already functioned for Wesley as shorthand identifying those who had been converted. Wesley continued to use the phrase in this broad sense throughout

---

same paragraph, he also quotes a portion of Prov 9:10, which also relates very closely in meaning to the other verses.

66. It should also be noted that Wesley makes no mention of Cornelius in the sermon.

67. Baxter, *An Extract of Mr. Richard Baxter's Aphorisms of Justification*, 33–34.

68. Wesley, *Works* (BE), 26:235.

his life, as evidenced in his sermon, "The Signs of the Times," written in August, 1787:

> All those that experience in their own hearts the power of God unto salvation will readily perceive how the same religion which they enjoy is still spreading from heart to heart. . . . Upon a fair and candid inquiry they find more and more, not only of those who had some form of religion, but of those who had no form at all, who were profligate, abandoned sinners, *now entirely changed*, truly fearing God and working righteousness.[69]

Whereas in the foregoing examples Wesley's use of the phrase leans more toward upholding fearing God and working righteousness as essential features of true godliness, at other times he uses the phrase more broadly as a general recognition and commendation of spiritual *seriousness* (i.e., responsive attentiveness and desire). It is in this sense that Wesley described the "thousands upon thousands" to whom he preached at Birstall in July 1761, the one characteristic common to those joining together in Methodist societies, and the distinguishing mark of those who were no longer merely nominal Christians.[70]

Executing this corporate commitment to spiritual seriousness required, however, a rather bold pastoral initiative on Wesley's part. Describing the evolution of the Methodist work, Wesley outlines the process for admission to a Methodist Society in the early 1740s:

> As the Society increased, I found it required still greater Care to separate the precious from the vile. In order to this, I determined, at least once in three Months, to talk with every Member myself, and to inquire at their own Mouths, as well as of their Leaders and Neighbours, Whether they grew in Grace and in the Knowledge of our Lord Jesus Christ. . . . To each of those, of whose Seriousness and Good Conversation I found no Reason to doubt, I gave a Testimony under my own Hand, by writing their Name on a *Ticket* prepared for that Purpose; every Ticket implying as strong a Recommendation of the Person to whom it was given, as if I had wrote at length, "I believe the Bearer hereof to be one that fears God and works Righteousness."[71]

---

69. Wesley, *Works* (BE) §II.9, 2:530. Emphasis mine. See also Wesley's 1778 sermon "The Late work of God in North America" where he describes the Moravians arriving in the colony of Georgia in 1736 as "men truly fearing God and working righteousness." Wesley, *Works* (BE) §I.1, 3:596.

70. See "July 19, 1761," *Works* (BE), 21:335–36; Wesley, *A Plain Account of the People Called Methodists*, 6; Wesley, "The New Creation," *Works* (BE) §I.1, 3:506.

71. Wesley, *A Plain Account of the People Called Methodists*, 14–15.

This separating "the precious from the vile" is nothing other than Wesley exercising, in his Methodist setting, the "judgment of charity" along lines similar to his Calvinistic counterparts, John Cotton and Thomas Hooker, as earlier described. Indeed, fearing God and working righteousness was the baseline of Christian fellowship to which Wesley held firmly to the very end of his life.[72]

The depth of Wesley's conviction that fearing God and working righteousness is representative of a soteriological standard is also seen in his journal entry for December 1, 1767. Travelling to Norwich on that Tuesday, Wesley writes about thinking deeply "on several points of importance." What appeared to him "as clear as day" as he sat in his chaise was that persons who did not have "clear conceptions" of imputed righteousness or of justification itself—and even those who denied justification altogether—may yet be saved. His concern seems to be that fearing God and working righteousness, the most basic soteriological standard of scripture, was too often obscured either by doctrinal controversy or by the shadows cast by expressions of religious experience that may be, at any given point in time, out-of-step with biblically-sanctioned norms. Wesley seemed to recognize that when all was said and done, separating the precious from the vile had less to do with properly defended or clearly articulated standards of doctrine and more to do with the observable fruit of a person's life. Risking that he may be judged to have set aside the "*articulus stantis vel cadentis ecclesiae,*"[73] Wesley appeals again to the higher authority of Scripture and to the standard of Acts 10:35 in particular, declaring that it is "high time for us . . . to return to the plain word, 'He that feareth God, and worketh righteousness, is accepted with him.'"[74]

It would be careless to conclude, however, that the series of conclusions *en route* to Norwich represent Wesley's relaxing or mollifying his hold upon the doctrine of justification by faith, reducing justification to

---

72. Rack notes Wesley's reference to "fearing God and working righteousness" as the fundamental basis of Christian fellowship as late as October 1790. Rack, *Reasonable Enthusiast*, 530–31.

73. W. Reginald Ward offers the following translation and comment: "'The article of doctrine by which the church stands or falls'. The Protestant Reformers had commonly held that this article was that of justification by grace through faith alone." Wesley, "December 1, 1767," *Works* (BE), 22:114, n. 90.

74. Ibid., 22:114–15. Wesley restates this conclusion in "On Living without God," a sermon written in 1790: "I believe he respects the goodness of the heart rather than the clearness of the head; . . . Without holiness, I own, no man shall see the Lord; but I dare not add, or clear ideas." Wesley, *Works* (BE) §15, 4:175.

nothing more than the divine response to mere sincerity. Wesley's conclusions reflect, instead, his mounting consternation over the ease with which the biblical soteriological standard of the fear of God and obedience to his commands was being set aside. Journal entries for the days immediately *preceding* his travelling to Norwich include several accounts highlighting the increasing prevalence among Wesley's own Methodists of a disturbing disconnection between the faith which justifies and the faith which works. In response to one such report, he declared that "the Methodists that do not fulfil all righteousness will have the hottest place in the lake of fire!"[75]

Wesley is absolutely certain that any claim to being justified by faith is false if the conduct of the life of the person making the claim violates the most fundamental soteriological standard of fearing God and obeying his commands. In fact, in his pondering the issue in the chaise, he concludes that those whose lives meet *this* most basic standard are ones who may be saved, despite their failure to articulate doctrine properly or clearly—and even if they are in outright doctrinal error (such as William Law, who Wesley judged to have denied justification by faith altogether).

The Minutes of the 1770 Conference

In light of Wesley's concern over the steady encroachment of the scourge of antinomianism, it is not surprising that the 1770 Conference took aim at every argument that threatened to marginalize the place of good works. The infamous Minutes of this Conference indicates that the focus of attention was on two categories of persons and their respective relations with God; and, in respect to each of these categories, the salvific role of good works is defended in an effort to deny to antinomianism any foothold whatsoever. First, there is the category of the justified; and secondly, those who have not yet had the gospel proclaimed to them.

The Conference first spoke to the necessity of good works in the lives of the justified. The declaration that "every believer, till he comes to glory, works *for* as well as *from* life"[76] directly reflected the influence of Richard Baxter in his *Aphorisms of Justification* published more than a century earlier:

> It is most clear in the Scripture, and beyond all dispute, that our Actuall, most proper, compleat Justification, at the great

---

75. Wesley, *Works* (BE), 22:111–13.
76. *Minutes*, (WMC, 1770), 59.

> Judgement, will be according to our Works, and to what we have done in flesh, whether Good or Evill: which can be no otherwise then as it was the Condition of that Justification. And so Christ, at that great Assize, will not give his bare Will of Purpose, as the Reason of his proceedings: but as he governed by a Law; so he will judg [sic] by a Law: . . .[77]

In explaining his concluding thesis, Baxter contended that the idea that "we must not work or perform our Duties *for* Life and Salvation, but only *from* Life and Salvation" is "that dangerous Pillar of the Antinomian Doctrine . . . A Doctrine, which, if it were reduced to Practice by all that hold it, (as I hope it is not) would undoubtedly damn them: for he that seeks not, and that striveth not to enter, shall never enter."[78]

It is at this point especially that the minutes suffered, in the words of Wesley's co-laborer, John Fletcher, from "the unguarded and not sufficiently explicit manner in which they were worded":[79] "We have received it as a maxim, that 'a man is to do nothing *in order to* Justification.' Nothing can be more false. Whoever desires to find favour with God, should *cease from evil, and learn to do well*. Whoever repents, should do *Works meet for Repentance*. And if this is not *in order* to find favour, what does he do them for?"[80] Understandably, the broad range of interpretation to which the phrase "to find favour with God" is susceptible without sufficient context (and when coupled with the declaration about repentance involving works "in order to find favour"), easily gave the impression that this paragraph addressed those seeking *initial*[81] justification.

In reality, the minutes were worded in a way that intermingled two theological affirmations that Wesley was adamant in preserving and promoting: first, the necessity of good works to "*retain* the favour of God";[82] and second, the necessity of "works meet for repentance" as "the

---

77. Baxter, *Aphorisms of Justification*, 203. This statement appears as Thesis LXXX in Baxter's *Aphorisms* and as Proposition XLV in Wesley's extract. Compare Baxter, *Aphorisms* (Wesley), 32.

78. Baxter, *Aphorisms of Justification*, 208.

79. Tyerman, *Wesley's Designated Successor*, 185; cited by McGonigle, *Sufficient Saving Grace*, 277, fn 99. For Wesley's own, though defensive, acknowledgement of the problematic wording, see his June 19, 1771 letter to the Countess of Huntingdon. Wesley, *Letters*, 5:258–60.

80. *Minutes* (WMC, 1770), 59.

81. In Wesley's words, "our first acceptance with God." Wesley, *Letters*, 5:264.

82. In a pre-emptive effort to close ranks in response to Walter Shirley's circular beckoning those objecting to the minutes to join in demanding a formal recanting of

appointed way wherein we wait for free salvation."[83] With regard to the former emphasis—how to *retain* the favor of God—Wesley's affirmation echoed that of Baxter's more than a century earlier. Baxter had declared that "the common assertion" that "good works" *follow* but do not *precede* justification must be false unless it is understood in the strict sense of "Actuall obedience." Actual obedience "goeth not before the first moment of Justification" but does "goe before our Justification as continued and confirmed" and "before our compleat and final Justification."[84] Wesley had consistently argued the concept of actual obedience in his adherence to Article XIII.[85] However, his acceptance of the distinction made by bishop George Bull in his *Harmonica Apostolica* between "our first [justification]" and "our final justification" and of the necessity of "both inward and outward good works to be the condition of the latter, though not the former," was, he admits, a significant change of position.[86]

In its review of "the whole affair," the 1770 Conference, for the most part, left aside specific consideration of "the *appointed way*" in which one is to await free salvation (i.e., by doing works meet for repentance) and instead revisited the conclusions of the Conferences of 1745[87] and 1746[88] with respect to the question of finding favor with God:

1. Who of us is *now* accepted of God? He that now believes in Christ, with a loving and obedient heart.

---

them, Wesley emphasized in a letter sent in 1771 to his preachers that "our question, . . . is not, how we *gain*, but how [we] *retain* the favour of God." Wesley, *Letters*, 5:265.

83. This emphasis is evident in advice given by Wesley to Philothea Briggs in a letter dated October 6, 1771 regarding what guidance she might give a friend apparently confused with respect to the role of good works: "You may tell her, 'If you was doing those works, thinking to *merit* salvation thereby, you was quite wrong. But if you was doing them because they are the *appointed way* wherein we wait for free salvation, you was quite right.'" Wesley, *Letters*, 5:280.

84. Baxter, *Aphorisms of Justification*, 213. Compare Baxter, *Aphorisms* (Wesley), 36.

85. "All truly 'good works' (to use the words of our Church) 'follow after justification,' and they are therefore 'good and acceptable to God in Christ,' because they 'spring out of a true and living faith'." Wesley, "Justification by Faith," *Works* (BE) §III.5, 1:192–93.

86. Wesley came to defend Bull's distinction and describes him as "that great light of the Christian Church." Wesley, *Letters*, 264.

87. See Q. 7–9 of the session on Friday, August 2. *Minutes*, 1745 (Bennet), np.

88. See Q. 1–2 of the ten o'clock session on Tuesday, May 13. *Minutes*, 1746 (Jackson), 290.

2. But who [is *now* accepted of God] among those that never heard of Christ? He that feareth God, and worketh righteousness, according to the light he has.[89]

Here, acceptance of those who *have* heard the gospel is conditioned upon their believing *in Christ* "with a loving and obedient heart." Nevertheless, those who have never heard of Christ and thus have not a *loving* heart from which their obedience springs, are likewise "accepted of God" on the basis of their *fearing* God and working righteousness according to the light they have received.[90] These declarations restate the contingency described by the 1745 Conference that conditions the way in which the theological judgments of Articles XII and XIII must be understood; namely, whether or not one has heard of Christ.[91]

The second affirmation of God's favor is *not*, then, to those who *have* heard the gospel but who do not yet believe in Christ "with a loving and obedient heart." This category of persons is not directly addressed by the Conference. This fact has important ramifications for a proper understanding of the servant-son metaphor since it is *precisely* persons in this category whom Wesley identifies as having the faith of a servant.[92] Thus, while Wesley is unrelenting in his conviction that "fearing God and working righteousness" is the one soteriological standard applicable to *all* persons,[93] he does not, on that commonality, equate those who have never heard the gospel (but who are responding in accordance with the light they have been given) with those who have the faith of a servant. This is abundantly clear in every context where Wesley speaks explicitly of the faith of a servant, and is particularly evident in his later sermons that reference the metaphor. This point is critical to a proper

---

89. *Minutes* (WMC, 1770), 59. Bracketed insert mine.

90. Ibid. 60. In his July 10, 1771 letter to his preachers, Wesley restates the revelation to Peter (Acts 10:34–5) and adds to the phrase "accepted with Him" the words, "is in a state of acceptance." Wesley, *Letters*, 5:263.

91. Recall the discussion of this condition earlier in this chapter.

92. See chapter 6 below.

93. In addition to his application to those who have never heard of Christ in Question 2 (see above), note Wesley's response to the objection that "God does in Fact justify those, who by their own Confession, neither feared God nor wrought Righteousness": "His own saying so is not Proof: For we know, how all that are convinced of Sin, undervalue themselves in every Respect." See Question 7, *Minutes* (WMC, 1770), 60. Here only does he reference those who, at one time, had heard the gospel but did not yet believe in Christ with a "loving and obedient heart."

understanding of the servant-son metaphor in Wesley's articulation of his covenant theology.[94]

Real Christians: Distinctions within the Soteriological Standard

While upholding the soteriological standard for all persons, Wesley further distinguished between those who *fear* God and those who *love* him. The distinction itself was not a new development in Wesley's theological thought but was an established element of his soteriological views. In his rebuttal to George Horne's sermon on James 2:24, "Works Wrought through Faith a Condition of our Justification," preached at Oxford on June 7, 1761, Wesley takes up the matter of the role of works prior to "first justification"[95] and makes a critical distinction between fear and love. Horne had accused Whitefield and Wesley of fuelling "the *solafidian*, or *antinomian* heresy"[96] across England and sought to stem the tide by holding forth the necessity of works as a condition of justification. Wesley agreed that while "Repentance and the Fruits thereof are in *some sense* necessary before Justification" they are not necessary "in the *same sense*" as faith: "For in whatever Moment a Man believes (in the Christian sense of the Word), he is justified, his Sins are blotted out, . . . But it is not so, at whatever Moment he repents, ... Faith alone therefore justifies; which Repentance alone does not; . . ."[97]

Wesley substantiates his point by drawing out the difference between one who fears and one who loves God. He begins by restating in his own words what Horne describes as "the particulars" of repentance: "But Repentance comprehends Compunction, Humiliation, Hatred of Sin, Confession of it, Prayer for Mercy, ceasing from Evil, a firm Purpose to do well, Restitution of ill-got Goods, Forgiveness of all who have done us Wrong, and Works of Beneficence."[98] Significantly, excluded from this list is "the *fear* and *love* of God"—a phrase that, in the text of Horne's sermon, appeared between "an earnest *solicitation . . .* of mercy" (in Wesley's restatement of Horne, "Prayer for Mercy") and

---

94. Wesley's understanding of acceptance with God and the matter of the purview of the servant-son metaphor will be investigated in the following chapters.

95. For this terminology, see Wesley's July 10, 1771 letter to his preachers. Wesley, *Letters*, 5:264.

96. Horne, *Works Wrought through Faith*, 5–6.

97. Wesley, *A Letter to the Rev. Mr. George Horne*, 13–14. Seventeen years prior in *A Farther Appeal* Wesley declared the same. Wesley, *Works* (BE) §II.2, 11:110.

98. Wesley, *A Letter to the Rev. Mr. George Horne*, 16.

"a ceasing from Evil."[99] Wesley comments: "I believe [repentance] does comprehend all these, either as Parts or as Fruits of it: *And it comprehends 'the Fear,' but not 'the love of God.'* That [i.e., the love of God] flows from a higher Principle. And he who loves God is not barely in the right Way to Justification: He is actually justified."[100]

In making this distinction, Wesley demonstrates that he at times made use of the Apostle Peter's declaration in a much more specific sense—a sense that distinguished *between* believers. This use of Acts 10:35 is particularly pronounced in his 1786 sermon, "On Divine Providence." There Wesley describes "a threefold circle of that divine . . . superintending providence which regards the children of men." The "outermost circle includes the whole race of mankind." The second circle is comprised of those of whom God "takes more immediate care"; namely, "all that are called Christians, all that profess to believe in Christ"—who "in some degree honour him, at least more than the heathens do." The innermost circle contains "only the real Christians; those that worship God, not in form only, but in spirit and in truth. Herein are comprised all that love God, *or, at least, truly fear God* and work righteousness."[101]

The essence of this distinction between those "real Christians" who love God and those that "at least, truly fear God" comes to light in Wesley's sermon, "On Friendship with the World." Wesley describes an unbeliever as "one that is so far from being a believer *in the gospel sense* . . . that he has not even the faith of a servant: he does not 'fear God and work righteousness.'"[102] This use of Acts 10:35 is evident, too, in his letter of counsel to Ann Foard, "If your mother is willing, I see no objection to your marrying one that fears God and is seeking salvation through Christ. Such an one is not an unbeliever in the sense wherein that word is taken in 2 Corinthians vi. 14."[103]

Clearly, one who *fears* God and works righteousness is distinguished from one who *loves* God and works righteousness; and, furthermore, this distinction stands in direct relationship to the servant-son metaphor.

---

99. Horne, *Works Wrought through Faith*, 11.

100. Wesley, *A Letter to the Rev. Mr. George Horne*, 16. Emphasis and bracketed insert, mine.

101. Wesley, *Works* (BE) §18, 2:543. Emphasis mine.

102. Wesley, "On Friendship with the World," *Works* (BE) §12, 3:132. Emphasis mine.

103. Wesley, *Letters*, 5:45–46. See also Wesley's February 13, 1768 letter to Ann Bolton. Wesley, *Letters*, 5:80–81.

Thus, while in some contexts Wesley applied the standard of "fearing God and working righteousness" in the very broad sense as that which is incumbent upon all believers up until the great Assize, he frequently used that phrase to distinguish *between* those whom he regarded to be among the ranks of "real Christians." This category—"real Christians"—was *not* limited to those having "all the marks of the new birth such as faith, hope, and love,"[104] but was a broad category that, like Thomas Hooker's response to external covenanters, embraced those evidencing "preparatory 'motions,' or a charitable 'hope.'"[105] At the same time, the breadth of Wesley's conception of "real Christians" does not lead him to abandon distinctions that were integral to his appropriation of covenant theology. Instead, he allowed that one may *not* be an *unbeliever* in the sense of 2 Corinthians 6:14 and also may *not* be a *believer* in the gospel sense[106] of *loving* God and working righteousness.

While the Evangelical Revival in England, Wales, Scotland, and Ireland may not have been in full swing until the 1730s, a broader perspective of the emergence of the Revival encourages a balanced assessment of both the influence and the innovation of its principle players, including Wesley. As Rack declares, any biographer of John Wesley must certainly contradict the notion that the Revival *began* with him.[107] Similarly, it is important to acknowledge that, for the most part, rather than generating them, Wesley engaged theological conversations already in progress. Of course, the Evangelical Revival had certainly rejuvenated them, having been precipitated by—and also having precipitated—a return to Reformation doctrines as both Pietistic influences and political and economic hardships converged on eighteenth-century England and her neighbors.[108]

---

104. Collins, "Real Christianity as the Integrating Theme of Wesley's Soteriology," 79. Collins' assertion that Wesley's view of "real Christians" had narrowed in this way and was "the most noteworthy accent during this late interval of Wesley's life" seems to overlook Wesley's emphasis in either of the sermons just noted, both of which are dated in 1786.

105. Pettit, *A Heart Prepared*, 133–34.

106. With respect to such distinctions, see for example Wesley's letters of January 1, 1770 and August 3, 1771. Wesley, *Letters*, 5:170–73, 270–71.

107. Rack, *Reasonable Enthusiast*, 161.

108. Jones has appropriately cautioned that "strictly providentialist interpretations can mask the degree to which the Evangelical Revival began in response to other, more mundane changes in the social, cultural and intellectual milieu of the mid-eighteenth century." Jones, "Calvinistic Methodism," 109–10.

Wesley's substantive and influential participation in the long-standing parallel conversations regarding good works and the divine response to the responsive unregenerate is of particular importance to coming to understand his employment of the servant-son metaphor. As the earlier survey of the chronology of Wesley's use of the metaphor indicates, the metaphor was a valuable theological asset to him. Given his high regard for the Christian scriptures, the metaphor's biblical foundation certainly presents itself as one answer as to why this may be the case. However, this alone does not adequately account for his increasing use of the metaphor during the last twenty-five years of his life. Neither would it explain his determination near the end of his earthly journey to salvage the metaphor from being marginalized by apparent misunderstanding, and to commend it afresh to his audience.[109] These developments suggest a heightened urgency on Wesley's part in helping his people and preachers understand and hold fast to a soteriology that would secure and advance the Methodist message of "universal redemption"[110] and holiness of heart.

Specifically, "fearing God and working righteousness" was, in his view, a scripturally-founded soteriological standard, applicable to *all* persons: the justified, those convinced of sin and conscientiously on the way to justification, and those having never heard of Christ. And while Wesley attached to the servant-son metaphor the Petrine declaration so central to the story of Cornelius, his broad application of this soteriological standard indicates that it is erroneous to assume that every appeal to this standard also invokes the metaphor. Thus, the appeal to the Petrine declaration of acceptance in relation to Cornelius as one who has never heard the gospel is not to be construed as invoking the servant metaphor which Wesley reserved *specifically* for those who *had* heard the gospel. In other words, while the metaphor (particularly, the servant metaphor) does not stand without it, the standard itself has implications and applications beyond those of the metaphor. Having in mind this point and an awareness of the larger historical context in which Wesley labored, it is now of benefit to examine the metaphor in relation to the influence of his covenant theology on his soteriology.

---

109. See, for example, Wesley's sermon, "On the Discoveries of Faith," Wesley, *Works* (BE) §13, 4:35.

110. Wesley used the phrase to contrast his view with the Calvinist notion of "particular redemption." Wesley, *A Short History of Methodism*, 7–8.

CHAPTER 7

The Salvific Sufficiency of the Covenant of Grace

THE ATTENTION GIVEN THUS far to the context of John Wesley's use of the servant-son metaphor has been compelled in part by the need to lay the groundwork for understanding the soteriological affirmations he expected it to convey. But it has also been compelled by the need to account for his apparent confidence that the theological repertoire of his audience was such that he could draw upon the metaphor with little or no introduction. This judgment on Wesley's part suggests that neither the metaphor nor the primary elements of its supporting theology were original to him. Yet, it is hardly the case that his appropriation of covenant theology represented no theological ingenuity on his part or was inconsequential for his soteriology. Discerning Wesley's theological contribution, however, requires attentiveness to a critical theological debate that gained momentum during the century before Wesley and broke upon the emerging Evangelical Revival energized by the countless stories of evangelical conversion. As Hindmarsh observes,

> Increasingly through the seventeenth and eighteenth centuries . . . there was debate about the anthropocentric and theocentric poles of such a gospel. While all agreed that the main existential problem addressed by the gospel was the problem of guilt and the threat of divine judgment, debate centred upon the way in which one could construe the relationship between human and divine agency in salvation. . . . The seventeenth century witnessed a significant anthropocentric turn as theology increasingly concerned itself with the sequencing of salvation and mapped this understanding onto experience as an order of conversion.[1]

---

1. Hindmarsh, *The Evangelical Conversion Narrative*, 15.

In addition, Hindmarsh notes that when speaking of the gospel, "eighteenth-century evangelicals . . . most often equated it more narrowly with the Reformers' teaching about atonement and justification by faith."[2] This important observation serves as a reminder that, in one sense, Wesley did not pick his theological battles. On the one hand, the dominance of Reformed doctrine in shaping the Evangelical Revival exerted relentless theological pressure upon him. This necessitated an ongoing defense of the spiritual well-being of his beloved Methodists against the threats of antinomianism and high Calvinism while remaining firm on the Reformation standards of free grace and salvation by faith. On the other hand, his response was tempered by an equal necessity of fending off the tide of a spiritually insipid moralism which encroached upon the Anglicanism of his day.

Perhaps nothing influenced Wesley's own contribution to the course of the debate over the anthropocentric and theocentric poles of the gospel more than the covenant theology that was foundational to the Reformed orthodoxy promulgated from the time of Heinrich Bullinger. Despite the diversity within covenant theology, its theological superstructure served as the common language for the debate and thereby shaped its very course. While Wesley's theological eclecticism is readily evident, to suggest that, after his middle years, his tempered affinity with Reformed views substantially gave way to a new affinity with Eastern Christianity[3] is somewhat misleading. Such a view fails to adequately account for the fact that, to the end of his life, the superstructure and language of covenant theology oriented the soteriological views of the preponderance of his theological *adversaries* and, therefore, continued to exert influence in his own Societies.

The fact that Wesley's later sermons and correspondence continue to bear the mark of his covenant theology suggests that a more defensible conclusion with respect to the development of Wesley's theological thought is that the influence of Reformed views was particularly intense during his middle years. And while this *intensity* may have waned a bit with a resurgence of his earlier, more Anglican perspective, Wesley's engagement in the debate—and thus his soteriology—continued to be overtly shaped by covenant theology as surely as the rock walls of a canyon dictate the course of the river flowing through it.

With this in mind, we are set to examine the servant-son metaphor in light of its relation to two soteriological pillars of covenant theology:

2. Ibid., 14.
3. Maddox, *Responsible Grace*, 149, 157–58.

the salvific *sufficiency* of the various dispensations of the covenant of grace and, in the following chapter, the salvific *perfection* of the gospel dispensation of the covenant of grace. As previously noted, a component of covenant theology that came to be of increasing importance was the idea of progression within the covenant of grace. More than a mere *segmentation* of salvation history, each dispensation of that covenant represents an *augmentation* in the unfolding story of God's saving deeds. Ultimately, in the gospel (or Christian) dispensation the covenant of grace is *advanced* to its perfection.

Progression as augmentation is clearly described in Stephen Charnock's (1628–80) "A Discourse of the Knowledge of God," an extract of which Wesley included in *A Christian Library*. Charnock casts God's activity "in every dispensation" in terms of the analogy of light ever-increasing:

> As the Light at the Dawn is more obscure than that which is near the Approach of the sun to the Horizon; so there was a more obscure Knowledge of God, and the Redeemer, at the Time of the first Promise. *Adam* might not know well what to think of God, when he saw himself expelled from Paradise, just after a gracious Promise of a Deliverer. It was somewhat brighter at the Giving [of] the Law, when God would give man some dark Shadows and Pictures of *Christ*; and when Himself would be known by his Name Jehovah, and the Conduct of his Angel. It was clearer in the Times of the Prophets, when the Chariot of the Sun of Righteousness was approaching to the World, and the Light broke out before Him; but a more glorious Discovery when this Sun did arise and appear in the Earth; yet from first to last, every Dispensation was made up of some Discovery of God, the Manifestation of his Name, the Declarations and Representations of the Messiah.[4]

This same analogy reappears in Wesley's 1788 sermon "On Faith" where he summarizes the progression as articulated by John Fletcher in his essay, "The Doctrines of Grace and Justice."[5] Wesley, vis-à-vis Fletcher, traces the progression from "the heathen dispensation" which was given "a small degree of light" to the Jewish nation which was given "a far more considerable degree of light," to John the Baptist to whom was given "a still clearer light," and finally to the Christian dispensation in which the Spirit of adoption is received.[6] That this view remained a

---

4. Wesley, "Extracts from the Works of Stephen Charnock," *ACL*, 39:114–15.
5. Fletcher, *The Doctrines of Grace and Justice*, 1–13.
6. Wesley, "On Faith," *Works* (BE) §2–3, 3:492–93.

staple in Wesley's theological thought is seen in its being a virtual echo of the progression described in his sermon, "The Righteousness of Faith," published more than forty years earlier:

> By "the righteousness which is of faith" is meant that condition of justification . . . which was given by God to fallen man through the merits and mediation of his only begotten Son. This was *in part revealed to Adam* soon after his fall, being contained in the original promise made to him and his seed concerning the seed of the woman, who should "bruise the serpent's head." It was *a little more clearly revealed to Abraham* by the angel of God from heaven, saying, "By myself have I sworn, saith the Lord," that "in thy seed shall all the nations of the earth be blessed." It was *yet more fully made known to Moses, to David, and to the prophets* that followed; and through them to many of the people of God in their respective generations. But still the bulk even of these were ignorant of it; and very few understood it clearly. Still *"life and immortality"* were not so *"brought to light"* to the Jews of old as they are now unto us *"by the gospel."*[7]

This progression closely resembles William Ames' description that there "hath beene always a progresse from the more imperfect, to the perfect."[8] Accordingly, he divided the progression along the lines of the advance of God's saving purposes as embodied in the major covenantal events and personages of biblical history: from Adam to Abraham, from Abraham to Moses, from Moses to Christ, and since Christ was exhibited (that is, the gospel dispensation).[9]

Of course, inherent in the idea of *progression* in the covenant of grace is the acknowledgement of the inverse: the relative *deficiency* of each dispensation prior to the gospel dispensation. This observation generates several important questions: What is the significance of the imperfection that Ames acknowledged? What of the salvation of those living before the dawning of the gospel dispensation? In other words, what is the relationship between *augmentation* and *salvific sufficiency* in the unfolding of God's saving purposes?

The short answer is that, from the perspective of covenant theology (including Wesley's), every dispensation of the covenant of grace is salvifically *sufficient*. The essence of this conclusion is captured in Charnock's affirmation that "God doth not save . . . but by the Knowledge

---

7. Wesley, "The Righteousness of Faith," *Works* (BE) I.7, 1:206–7. Emphasis mine.
8. Ames, *The Marrow of Sacred Divinity* (1642), 193.
9. Ibid., 194.

of Himself [in Christ]; though the Discovery of Himself, in divers Ages, hath been various and by Degrees" and that such discovery is "the Design of God in every Age of the World."[10] The basis for this conviction is that sufficiency rests not in the completeness of the revelation of the gospel— which is an attribute belonging only to the gospel dispensation—but in the mediation of Christ who is the lamb "slain from the foundation of the world." Since there is no deficiency in Christ's mediation, his work is complete on behalf of fallen humanity in *all* ages. As William Ames puts it, "Now such a Mediator is given, not for one age onely but for yesterday, to day, and for ever. . . . For this Meditation [*sic*] was equally necessary in all ages: Also, it was sufficient, and effectuall from the beginning, by virtue of God's decree, promises, and acceptation."[11]

Wesley held to this basic tenet of covenant theology as a fundamental aspect of his soteriology. This is evident in "The Mystery of Iniquity," a sermon he had preached four times during the six months immediately prior to its publication in the *Arminian Magazine* in May and June of 1783,[12]

> It is certain that God "made man upright," perfectly holy and perfectly happy. But by rebelling against God he destroyed himself, lost the favour and the image of God, and entailed sin, with its attendant pain, on himself and all his posterity. Yet his merciful Creator did not leave him in this helpless, hopeless state. He immediately appointed his Son, his well-beloved Son . . . to be the Saviour of men, "the propitiation for the sins of the whole world"; the great Physician, who by his almighty Spirit should heal the sickness of their souls, and restore them not only to the favour but to "the image of God wherein they were created." This great "mystery of godliness" *began to work from the very time of the original promise.* Accordingly the Lamb, being (in the purpose of God) "slain from the beginning of the world," from the same period his sanctifying Spirit began to renew the souls of men. We have an undeniable instance of this in Abel, who "obtained a testimony" from God "that he was righteous." *And from that very time all that were partakers of the same faith were partakers of the same salvation; were not only reinstated in the favour, but likewise restored to the image of God.*[13]

---

10. Wesley, "Extracts from the Works of Stephen Charnock," *ACL*, 39:114–15. Bracketed insert mine.

11. Ames, *The Marrow of Sacred Divinity* (1642), §9, 80–81.

12. Outler, "Introductory Comment," *Works* (BE), 2:451.

13. Wesley, *Works* (BE) §2–3, 2:452–53. Emphasis mine.

This allusion to Abel had a long history in Wesley's theological thought and is noteworthy on two counts in particular. First, in Wesley's understanding, Abel's "discovery of God," to use Charnock's phrase, was *salvifically sufficient* despite the inherent *deficiency* of the revelation of God in Christ that characterized his dispensation (and also all those dispensations prior to the gospel dispensation). This affirmation of sufficiency is evident in the second and third stanzas of "Genesis 3:15," a hymn titled after the biblical text so foundational to covenant theology:

> Sin hath poison'd all my soul,
> Sin the serpent's cursed seed:
> No one part in me is whole;
> Yet will I the promise plead,
> . . .
>
> Breathe the breath of simple life,
> Oh! Be Abel born in me
> Previous to the legal strife,
> Innocent simplicity:
> . . .[14]

The hymn clearly contrasts the earliest dispensation (the time of Abel) and the later Mosaic dispensation. Though the time of Abel preceded that during which the law brought sin to light, it nevertheless was a time in which one might "obtain a testimony." What was exemplary of Abel was his obedience to what was required even without the demand of the Law. Abel was a portrait of "innocent simplicity" that yielded to God's terms easily. "Legal strife," on the other hand, characterizes the experience of those under the Law.

Second, it is important to note that Wesley regards this sufficiency as *comprehensive*; that is, it takes in "those two grand branches" of salvation: justification, whereby "we are . . . restored to the favour of God"; and sanctification, whereby we are "restored to the image of God."[15] On November 21, 1759 in a letter to Samuel Furley, Wesley alludes to this comprehensive sufficiency: "I doubt not of Abraham's being perfected in love. . . . And none can doubt but all the Jewish believers were perfected *before* they died. But that many of them were perfected *long before* they died I see no reason to think. The Holy Ghost was not *fully* given before Jesus was glorified."[16] Although Wesley acknowledged in this same letter

   14. Wesley and Wesley, *Hymns and Sacred Poems* (1742), 18–20.
   15. Wesley, "On Working Out Our Own Salvation," *Works* (BE) §II.1, 3:203–4.
   16. The italicized words reflect Wesley's underlining in the text of the original document held at Queens University, Melbourne (Alfred James Derrick Album, Sugden Heritage Collection).

that "the law (unless in a very few exempt cases) made nothing perfect," he was yet convinced "all the Jewish believers were perfected *before* they died" on account of the uncompromising divine standard that "without holiness no man shall see the Lord."[17]

In addition to the general notion of the salvific sufficiency of each dispensation, another foundational element of covenant theology held in common by Wesley and his Calvinistic counterparts was that God's sending his Son, Jesus Christ, "in the fullness of the time" was (and is) the defining act of God in salvation history. It is this act of God that is delineated in covenant theology (including Wesley's) as "Christ revealed" or "Christ exhibited" (i.e., Christ, the lamb "slain from the foundation of the world," now slain *in realiter*). This revelation of Christ inaugurated the gospel dispensation and stood as the crowning moment of God's saving deeds. There was a real progression; an actual augmentation from one dispensation to the next. As Peter Bulkeley (1583–1659) had stated, "Onely this observe, that the further the times were from Christ's coming, the lesse light they had, and the nearer to Christ; the more light sprung up."[18] In his commentary on John 1:14, Wesley describes the Incarnation in terms of this augmentation of the covenant of grace:

> And he did not make us a transient visit, but *tabernacled among us* on earth, displaying his Glory in a more eminent manner, than ever of old in the tabernacle of *Moses*. . . . He was in himself most benevolent and upright; made ample Discoveries of Pardon to Sinners, which the *Mosaic* Dispensation could not do: and really exhibited the most substantial *Blessings*, where as that [i.e., the Mosaic dispensation] was but *a shadow of good things to come*.[19]

---

17. This assertion was a mainstay for Wesley: "I am persuaded, none that has faith can die before he is made ripe for glory. This is the doctrine which I continually teach, . . ." Wesley, "Letter to Miss H— (April 5, 1758)," *Works* (Jackson) 12:230. See also Wesley, "Letter to John Smith (December 30, 1745)." *Works* (BE) §15, 26:182; and his 1790 sermon, 'On the Wedding Garment,' *Works* (BE) §18, 4:148–49.

18. Bulkeley. *The Gospel-Covenant*, 171. Bulkeley, a nonconforming minister who left England for the Massachusetts Bay Colony after being silenced by William Laud, was an exemplary Puritan. His *Gospel-Covenant* evolved from a series of sermons that "defined a salient element of New England's emergent orthodoxy" the effects of which "can be traced in British religious thought, particularly in the development of covenant or federal theology." McGiffert, "Bulkeley, Peter (1583–1659)," *DNB* (http://www.oxforddnb.com).

19. Wesley, *ENNT*, 222. Bracketed insert mine.

This recognition of the *qualitative* differences between the various dispensations of the covenant of grace brought to the fore two important questions: first, what is the nature of this qualitative difference; and second, what are the implications soteriologically? It is precisely at this point that Wesley's intriguing appropriation of covenant theology emerges.

Three Views of the Salvific Sufficiency of the Covenant of Grace

As stated above, critical differences emerge on how the salvific sufficiency of each dispensation of the covenant of grace is to be understood in light of the progression "from the more imperfect, to the perfect."[20] What is significant about these differences is that Wesley's conception of the servant-son metaphor is tethered to his understanding of the salvific sufficiency of the various dispensations. In other words, the metaphor reflects and enforces core elements of the covenant theology that shaped his soteriology.

Wesley's understanding comes into view best when considered in light of these differences, which may be collected into three distinct perspectives: 1) absolute sufficiency; 2) successive, relative sufficiency; and 3) concurrent, relative sufficiency.[21] The first perspective provides something of a benchmark, representing as it does the viewpoint of Reformed orthodoxy. The second viewpoint is represented by the covenant theology of Johannes Cocceius which, though it came into fierce conflict with Reformed orthodoxy, profoundly impacted the development of covenant theology. The significance of this perspective is found not only in its alternative view of salvific sufficiency but in the evidence of its imprint on Wesley's use of the servant-son metaphor. This imprint will be discussed in some detail at the outset of the explanation of the third perspective, which was Wesley's: concurrent, relative sufficiency.

Absolute Sufficiency

On the matter of the salvific sufficiency of the various dispensations, the dominant view from the latter portion of the sixteenth century onward

---

20. Ames, *The Marrow of Sacred Divinity*, §2, 193.

21. While the labels given these three views are not Wesley's, they are descriptive of the critical distinguishing features of those views against which his particular understanding of the salvific sufficiency of the dispensations of the covenant of grace is defined.

was that of Calvinistic covenant theology both on the Continent and in England, and might best be labeled "absolute sufficiency." In short, this understanding is built upon the conviction that the work of Christ in behalf of the elect was complete irrespective of the dispensation in which they lived, from the time of the gospel promise made to Adam and Eve (Gen 3:15) to the present. In this view, "while the New Testament might be more copious in the measure of spiritual blessings, all the benefits thereof were not only attested, but even bestowed in the Old Testament Church." Thus, the distinction between the two Testaments, thus was "quantitative, not qualitative";[22] that is, each dispensation was, in substance, the same although there was "a greater abundance of knowledge discovered to the sons of men, now, in the time of the Gospel." The difference was "onely in the administration of them."[23]

There are two aspects of this view that are of particular importance to the discussion at hand. First, despite the *revelatory* deficiency (or, limits) of the respective dispensations prior to the gospel dispensation, there is no distinction between the elect of the various dispensations in terms of the extent of their enjoyment of the benefits secured by the lamb "slain from the foundation of the world." It is in this sense that the salvific sufficiency of each dispensation is *absolute*. Secondly, and another sense in which this viewpoint might best be termed *absolute*, the participation of the elect in whatever quantitative advantage inheres in the dispensation in which they currently live, is determined *solely* by the properties of the salvation-historical moment *itself*. For example, there are none of the elect now living during the historical time frame of the gospel dispensation who would not also fully participate in the quantitative advantages of the gospel dispensation.

This is clearly evident in the covenant theology of William Ames. Though Ames recognizes the distinctive historical moment of each dispensation, he elucidates the salvific benefits of *each* progression exclusively with respect to the elect and in accordance with the primary components of the Calvinist *ordo salutis*: election, redemption, calling, justification, adoption, sanctification, and glorification.[24] Thus, as described above, the fullness of God's provision in Christ is experienced by the elect *despite* the revelatory limits of the various dispensations prior to Christ's coming in the flesh.

22. Strehle, *Calvinism, Federalism, and Scholasticism* cited by Song, *Theology and Piety*, 28.

23. John Preston, cited by Song, *Theology and Piety*, 215–16.

24. Ames, *The Marrow of Sacred Divinity*, 194–98.

What is of particular significance on this point is that there was, therefore, never a time when the elect were *not* justified, though Christ had not yet appeared *in realiter*. After all, the faith of the elect is only and always faith *in Christ*. As Ames explains: from Adam to Abraham, "the way of justification was set forth by expiatory sacrifices offered and accepted for sins"; from the time of Abraham to Moses, "Justification was illustrated by the express testimony of God, that Faith was imputed to *Abraham* for righteousnesse, as the Father and pattern of all that should believe, and by the Sacrament of circumcision, which was a seale of the same righteousnesse"; and from Moses to Christ "Justification was shewed in many sacrifices, washings, and the Sacrament of the Passeover."[25]

Successive, Relative Sufficiency

In contrast to the foregoing is the view that salvific sufficiency is *relative* to whether or not Christ's work had taken place *in realiter*. That is, salvific sufficiency is not absolute; rather, the salvific sufficiency of those dispensations prior to the gospel dispensation is essentially *distinct*, though no less *sufficient*, from the salvific sufficiency of the gospel dispensation.

At the forefront of this view is the historical orientation that had been relegated to a secondary role in the covenant theology of Perkins.[26] In this view, salvific sufficiency is conceived not only as being *relative* (in the sense just described) but also as being necessarily *successive*. That is, in step with the unfolding, redemptive acts of God in human history, the salvific sufficiency of all those dispensations *prior* to the gospel dispensation is *succeeded* by that of the gospel dispensation. In this succession, the actual though *unperfected*[27] salvific sufficiency of each of the prior dispensations gives way to the actual and *perfected*[28] salvific sufficiency of the gospel dispensation.

---

25. Ibid., §15, 25, 32; 194, 196–97. In contrast to Ames, Wesley generally restricted Justification to the gospel dispensation, thus holding it (Justification) in distinction from the salvific provisions of the earlier dispensations of the covenant of grace. This is consistent with his view that salvific sufficiency is relative, an element common to the second and third views of salvific sufficiency discussed below.

26. Song observes that Perkins' concern was "primarily the redemptive logic, and not redemptive history," and that, consequently, "in all [his] writings there is no evidence that he ever attempted an analysis of the covenants from a historical point of view." Song, *Theology and Piety*, 32, 39.

27. I.e., on account of Christ's death not yet having occurred *in realiter*.

28. I.e., on account of Christ's death *in realiter*.

Cocceius may be said to be the champion of this viewpoint, though elements appearing in his covenant theology are evident in Zwingli and Cloppenburg as well.[29] Cocceius held fast to the fundamental affirmation of covenant theology that "those who believe God's word of promise or the gospel are justified before God at all times."[30] However, he took exception to the notion that there was no essential distinction between the salvific sufficiency of the various dispensations prior to the gospel dispensation and that of the gospel dispensation itself.

The basis for this objection was Cocceius' observation that "salvation works itself out in a history, an *ordo temporum*." As previously noted, Cocceius "depicts five stages (*grades*) through which God leads humanity to eternal life, and in which the consequences of the violation of the covenant of works through sin are gradually nullified."[31] In this, his doctrine of abrogations, Cocceius has in mind the declaration of Hebrews 8:13, "And what is becoming obsolete and growing old is ready to vanish away."[32] In his view, it is the covenant of works that is becoming obsolete as each outcome of its violation at the fall is remedied over the *whole* course of redemptive history.[33]

Several aspects of Cocceius' *schema* are especially important to the present discussion. First, the covenant of works is abrogated only insofar as it has been nullified *as a way of salvation*.[34] Second, the augmentation evident in the progression of the covenant of grace is not only an augmentation of knowledge and clarity regarding the gospel blessings, but entails a greater and greater realization of salvation itself: "The abrogation proceeds (*procedit*) by stages (*gradibus*), through which gradually (*paulatim*) and more and more (*magis magisque*) salvation is realized among believers."[35] And third, Cocceius' doctrine of abrogations recognizes in the religious experience of the elect the lingering but diminishing effects of the covenant of works: "The . . . covenant of works . . . keeps the believers under the Old Testament dispensation in fear and servitude. Not until Christ has really appeared in the flesh is

---

29. Song, *Theology and Piety*, 32. See also van Asselt, *The Federal Theology of Johannes Cocceius*, 28.

30. Van Asselt, *The Federal Theology of Johannes Cocceius*, 239.

31. Ibid., 271.

32. Ibid.

33. Van Asselt, "The Doctrine of the Abrogations," 109.

34. Ibid. 109. The law, "Do this," remains, but the promise "and live: has been abrogated by sin. Therefore, the law is nullified as a way of salvation.

35. Van Asselt, *The Federal Theology of Johannes Cocceius*, 276–77.

there freedom and joy, because what had been promised really happens and now becomes history."[36] Because of the actual inauguration of the gospel dispensation (on account of Christ having come *in realiter*), the elect living within the *historical* "moment" of the gospel dispensation are, for that very reason, partakers of the *soteriological* provisions of the gospel dispensation.

For Cocceius, however, while the gospel dispensation represents a point of perfection in its victory over fear and terror, the struggle against sin persists as a reality for the elect since the obsolescence of the covenant of works is not accomplished until the dawning of the *eschaton*.[37] Nevertheless, the watershed event in the history of salvation is the lamb slain *in realiter*. As a result, there is a fundamental difference between that salvation enjoyed by the elect living during those dispensations *prior* to the gospel dispensation and that enjoyed by those living ever since then. This difference is accentuated by an important distinction Cocceius makes between the nature of the forgiveness granted in the dispensations *before* the revelation of Christ and that which is granted commensurate with the gospel dispensation: "There is a difference in exactly what is secured under the economies. Justification under the Old Testament was only *parēsis*, a passing over of sin, a remission of wrath. In the New Testament, there is justification in the fullest sense: *aphēsis*, full remission of sin and adoption through Christ as sons and heirs."[38]

J. A. Bengel held Cocceius in high regard[39] and appears to have incorporated this distinction into his *Gnomon of the New Testament* on which Wesley relied heavily in producing his *Explanatory Notes Upon the New Testament*. In his commentary on Romans 1:7, for example, Bengel identifies all the believers of the Old Testament as "slaves" and those of the New Testament as "sons," reserving adoption *only* for the elect belonging to the *gospel* dispensation. This is in clear contrast to Ames who, as noted above, confirmed the idea of the progression of the covenant of grace while yet insisting that the elect in *every* dispensation received the adoption as sons. In fact, in his argument for adoption from the earliest

---

36. Van Asselt, "The Doctrine of the Abrogations," 109.

37. Johannes Cocceius, *Summa Doctrinae* (1648) §58 in van Asselt *The Federal Theology of Johannes Cocceius*, 271–72.

38. Van Asselt, "The Doctrine of the Abrogations," 110. To illuminate the distinction, Cocceius contrasts *not demanding payment* of a debt with *cancellation* of a debt altogether. Van Asselt, *The Federal Theology of Johannes Cocceius*, 280 (fn 12).

39. Erb, *Pietists: Selected Writings*, 17. Ernest Stoeffler has traced Bengel's exposure to and interest in Cocceius. See Stoeffler, *German Pietism During the Eighteenth Century*, 96–97.

dispensations of the covenant of grace, Ames specifically *contends* for the term "sons." With respect to the elect living in the time from Adam to Abraham, Ames asserts, "Adoption was declared both by the title of sons at that time common to all the faithfull, and by the translation of *Enoch* into the Heavenly inheritance."[40] Bengel, however, was careful to avoid relating adoption to any dispensation prior to the glorification of Jesus as fully manifested in the outpouring of the Holy Spirit at Pentecost.

Concurrent, Relative Sufficiency

With this background, Wesley's conception of the salvific sufficiency of the dispensations of the covenant of grace now comes into view. As the descriptor indicates, he, too, understood salvific sufficiency to be *relative* to whether or not the Lamb had been slain *in realiter*. That is, in concert with the strain of covenant theology of which Coccejus is the representative if not the progenitor, Wesley understood the gospel dispensation to be not only distinct historically in terms of the unfolding of God's saving deeds (e.g., the incarnation, death, and resurrection of Jesus) but uniquely consequential soteriologically. This is evident in the conversation during the 1746 Conference about what constitutes "the proper Christian faith." The question was asked, "By what faith were the Apostles clean before Christ died?" The answer was unequivocal: "By such a faith as this; by a Jewish faith: for 'the Holy Ghost was not then given.'" Clearly, the outpouring of the Spirit was understood as the watershed event accompanying the death and resurrection of Jesus, inaugurating the gospel dispensation and ushering in the full measure of God's saving purposes.[41] [42]

---

40. Ames, *The Marrow of Sacred Divinity*, 195. Similarly in reference to other dispensations, see 196–97. For Ames, adoption is distinct for the elect of the gospel dispensation not in the sense of its essence but only of its intensity and fullness. Ibid., 199–200.

41. An example of the perpetuation of this understanding among Methodists appears in Ann Bolton's diary entry for Sunday, August 25, 1771: "Before preaching, Br[other] S. read a little of Mr. W[esley]'s journal in which it was observed the apostles receiv'd the grace of purity of Heart when our Lord said [']ye are clean through the word which I have spoke['] but did not feel much of the effects of it or were not confirm'd in it till they received the Holy Ghost." *Ann Bolton Manuscript Journal*, John Banks Research Collection, Item 19 (MARC), Manchester), 33. See also Wesley's November 2, 1759 letter to Samuel Furley, *Letters*, 4:79.

42. The definitive place of the outpouring of the Spirit in conjunction with Christ's death *in realitor* was a constant in covenant theology in general, though its soteriological significance was differently conceived. Here, "full measure" is used in a qualitative sense (this is the central affirmation of the idea of *relative* sufficiency) and as well as in a quantitative sense (i.e. a full*er* measure of the Spirit or—to use the analogy of light

Wesley, however, differed in the way he understood the various dispensations to be successive, although his view was consistent with covenant theology in general in the following three senses.[43] First, with each redemptive intervention in human history, the historical "moment" of the former dispensation is concluded and the historical "moment" of the new dispensation is begun. Second, the revelatory boundaries of the former dispensation are succeeded by the enlarged revelatory boundaries of the newer dispensation. This advancement is discernible both *historically* (e.g. the time of Moses) and *soteriologically* (e.g. the giving of the Law). And third, the progression is successive in the sense that the momentum is always forward. Thus, while redemptive history was initialized in the first redemptive act ('the lamb slain from the foundation of the world'), with each dispensation it gravitates toward and finally concludes with the appearance of Christ.

But it is here that Wesley headed in a different direction. In the Cocciean scheme, it was the *historical* "moment" that dictated the *soteriological* benefits actually accruing to the elect. Therefore, as described above, the elect living within the historical "moment" of the gospel dispensation were, *for that very reason*, presently partakers of the *soteriological* provisions of that dispensation. For Wesley, however, there is a difference between the *availability* of the soteriological benefits and the actual *accrual* of those benefits.[44] Thus, while the historical "moment" of the gospel dispensation is determinative of what is now *available* soteriologically, there is a variety as to what actually *accrues* in any given person's life at any given point in their personal history (though the divine aim and intention as to what accrues is singular and fully calibrated to the perfection of the gospel dispensation). In Wesley's view, this variety is attributable to the fact that the various dispensations remain "live" in terms of being salvifically active; that is, they are *concurrent* with one another despite the onset of the historical "moment" of the gospel dispensation. The implications of this are highly significant for Wesley's understanding of the way of salvation, and to understand them we must explore his distinctive conception of the covenant of grace as multidimensional: historical, soteriological, and existential.

---

so common at that time to the discussions on this matter—a great*er* display of light).

43. These three senses would be true of even of covenant theologians subscribing to the view of salvific sufficiency described above as "absolute sufficiency".

44. This distinction is rooted, ultimately, in his evangelical Arminianism with its attending convictions both of the availability of salvation to all persons and of the element of divine-human cooperancy in salvation.

Historical Dimension. The historical dimension is linear and, humanly speaking,[45] can only be successive. For example, Christ cannot be concurrently slain *in realiter* and not slain *in realiter*. Ames organized his consideration of the covenant of grace along the lines of this historical dimension, writing one chapter on the administration of the covenant before Christ's coming and titling the next, "From Christ exhibited to the end of the World."[46] At times, Wesley, too, spoke of the dispensations of the covenant of grace in the strict sense of their respective *historical* moments. That is, the historical dimension always exhibits the furthest advance of the covenant of grace within the redemptive purposes of God *up to that point in time*. A clear example of this may be found his sermon "On Faith" where he describes Jewish faith in terms of the *historical* parameters of the Jewish dispensation: "By *Jewish* faith I mean the faith of those who lived between the giving of the law and the coming of Christ."[47] What is important to understand on this point is that it is only in terms of this *historical* dimension that Wesley would confirm that all persons now living do in fact live within the historical moment of the gospel dispensation. Limiting the historical dimension to this narrow sense not only signifies a critical departure from the two conceptions of the salvific sufficiency of the covenant of grace just presented, but also represents a soteriological point of reference that is of fundamental importance to Wesley.[48]

Soteriological Dimension. This dimension is not as easily defined. On the one hand, it is calibrated to the historical advancement of the covenant of grace to the gospel dispensation. Thus, none of humankind need await the appearance of the Messiah for the Messiah has already come and was crucified, buried, and raised to life. *Soteriologically*, this has import for all of humanity whether or not all of humanity recognizes or even knows of the fact. However, the soteriological dimension is, in a sense, *indifferent* to the realities of the historical advancement of the covenant of grace.

This indifference is itself multi-faceted. For one, while all of humankind now living is "soteriologically privileged"—seeing as all are living within the *historical* moment of the gospel dispensation and

---

45. This is an important qualifier to this statement. In Wesley's understanding, God is one "to whom all things are present at once, who sees all eternity at one view." Wesley, *Predestination Calmly Considered*, 12.

46. Ames, *The Marrow of Sacred Divinity*, 193, 198.

47. Wesley, *Works* (BE) §I.5, 3:495.

48. This soteriological point of reference will be discussed further in chapter 9 and in the Epilogue.

participate (at least provisionally) in its soteriological benefits, not all who are living are "kerygmatically privileged"; that is, not all have benefited from being under the sound of the gospel.[49] This obvious fact was acknowledged at the 1770 Conference when the matter of what it means to be accepted with God was reviewed. Consideration of the question was oriented to the juxtaposition of who *was* and who was *not* "kerygmatically privileged": "Who *of us* is accepted of God?" and, by contrast, "But who *among those who never heard* of Christ?"[50] The same point is recognized by Wesley in his sermon "On Living Without God" written in the summer of 1790. In this sermon, he specifically uses the term "Christian dispensation" not in the sense of the *historical* dimension described above but in the sense of the *soteriological* dimension:

> [A]ll morality, all the justice, mercy, and truth which can possibly exist without Christianity, profiteth nothing at all, is of no value in the sight of God, *to those that are under the Christian dispensation. Let it be observed, I purposely add, "to those that are under the Christian dispensation," because I have no authority from the Word of God "to judge those that are without."* Nor do I conceive that any man living has a right to sentence all the heathen and Mahometan world to damnation.[51]

Understanding that all of humankind now lives in the historical moment of the gospel (Christian) dispensation, Wesley's choice of words is deliberate and precise. By purposefully adding the qualifying phrase, "to those that are under the Christian dispensation," he is acknowledging that while *all* persons live *in* (the historical moment of) the gospel dispensation, *not* all persons live (soteriologically-speaking) *under* the gospel dispensation.

Another facet of the indifference of the soteriological dimension to the historical is found in a letter expressing Wesley's assurances to Ann Bolton on the occasion of the passing of a child:

> There can be no possible reason to doubt concerning the happiness of that child. He did fear God, and according to his circumstances work righteousness. This is the essence of religion,

---

49. In a letter to Thomas Whitehead (possibly) on February 10, 1748, Wesley declared: "'The benefit of the death of Christ is not only extended to such as have the distinct knowledge of his death and sufferings, but even unto those who are inevitably excluded from this knowledge.'" Wesley, *Letters*, §6, 2:118.

50. *Minutes* (WMC, 1770), 59. Emphasis mine.

51. Wesley, *Works* (BE) §14, 4:174–75. Emphasis mine.

according to St. Peter. His soul, therefore, was "darkly safe with God," although he was only under the Jewish Dispensation.[52]

Again, this child lived *in* the gospel dispensation but, Wesley judged, "*under* the Jewish Dispensation." As indicated by the concluding phrase of the above quote, the descriptor seems to have commended itself to Wesley in light of its affinity to the standard description by covenant theologians in general of the Mosaic dispensation as an "imperfect and shadowy dispensation."[53] Judging from the apparently close association of the child with Ann Bolton, an exemplary leader among the Methodists by this time, it is likely that this child *was* kerygmatically-privileged; and furthermore, there seems to have been a level of response by which Wesley judged the child to belong to the Jewish dispensation. This aligns with the judgment of the 1746 Conference (forty years before Wesley penned the letter to Ann Bolton) regarding the spiritual experience of Jonathan Reeves who, though living in the *historical* moment of the gospel dispensation nevertheless lived under the Jewish dispensation *soteriologically*.[54]

Of particular significance with respect to Wesley's multi-dimensional conception of the dispensations of the covenant of grace is that not only is there a sense in which the various dispensations may be considered as being *concurrent* in a *soteriological* sense, but also that the salvific sufficiency of each dispensation is judged to be *ongoing*; that is, their respective and *relative* sufficiency persists into the historical moment of the gospel dispensation. For this reason, those *not* living "under the Christian dispensation" are not judged to be eternally lost simply by reason of their living, at present, under some *other* dispensation *soteriologically*. So, the child having died while "under the Jewish dispensation" is, nonetheless, "safe with God."

Wesley's confidence that the salvific sufficiency of each dispensation is *ongoing* (though at the same time, as regards those dispensations prior to the gospel dispensation, *surpassed* by the gospel dispensation) is evident in Wesley's letter to George Horne in 1762. In his sermon

---

52. Wesley, "John Wesley to Ann Bolton (December 15, 1786)," *Letters*, 7:358. The phrase "darkly safe with God" appears in a poem entitled "On Clemens Alexandrinus's Description of a Perfect Christian." See John Wesley and Charles Wesley, *Hymns and Sacred Poems* (1739), 37–38. See also Wesley, "The Wilderness State," *Works* (BE) §III.8, 2:217–18.

53. Wesley, "The Original, Nature, Properties, and Use of the Law," *Works* (BE) §II.2, 2:8–9.

54. See Question 10 of the minute record. *Minutes*, 1746 (Jackson), 8:287.

at St. Mary's, Horne contested the notion that faith alone is sufficient for salvation and called upon a number of scriptures to substantiate his point, including Acts 10:35. Wesley restated Horne's contention: "'St. Peter also declares, 'In every nation, he that feareth God and worketh righteousness is accepted of him.' He is," Wesley responded, revealing a conviction that is fundamental to his soteriology, "but none can either fear God, or work righteousness, *till he believes according to the dispensation he is under.*"[55]

It is not, then, that Wesley's confidence in the eternal well-being of one *not* living under the Christian dispensation stems from a generic appeal to the mercies of God, or from conceiving of previous dispensations as salvifically sufficient for that person merely as a result of that dispensation's place in the history of God's saving deeds. Rather, such confidence stems from Wesley's conviction regarding both *the necessity and efficacy of faith no matter the dispensational reach of that faith.*[56] In a letter to Theophilus Lessey written in early 1787, Wesley not only restates this conviction but speaks specifically to the matter of the dispensational reach of faith, establishing that God himself is not only the giver of faith but also as the one who determines exactly *what* faith shall be given:

> There is no one point in all the Bible concerning which I have said more or written more for almost these fifty years than faith. I can say no more than I have said. To believe the being and attributes of God is the faith of an heathen. To believe the Old Testament and trust in Him that was to come was the faith of a Jew. To believe Christ gave Himself for me is the faith of a Christian. This faith He did give to you, and I hope does still; hold it fast without any philosophical refinement. *When we urge any to believe, we mean, "Accept that faith which God is now ready to give."* Indeed, believing is the act of man, but it is the gift of God.[57]

---

55. Wesley, *A Letter to the Rev. Mr. Horne*, 15. Emphasis mine.

56. The idea of faith having a "dispensational reach" was not altogether new. Bulkeley had proposed the following: "There was lesse power of faith in the Saints before Christ, then since. When the doctrine of faith was more fully revealed, then was faith it selfe more revealed in the hearts and lives of the people of God, *Gal.* 3.23. *Before faith came*, (saith the Apostle) implying there was a time when there was less faithe in Gods people. According to the measure of the *manifestation* of the doctrine of faith, such is the *apprehension* of faith." Bulkeley, *The Gospel-Covenant*, 174–75. While this view seems to surface in Wesley's conception, whether or how it may have been mediated to Wesley is uncertain.

57. Wesley, *Letters*, 7:361. Emphasis mine.

Thus, for Wesley it was *not* the historical moment of the dispensation in which persons actually lived that alone determined the extent of the soteriological benefits that would accrue to them; rather, what was determinative was their accepting the *faith* which God himself was "ready to give."

For Wesley, this is a real situation *soteriologically* and not simply an *existential* conundrum for the believer. Comparatively, in Calvinistic strains of covenant theology, the situation would be *only* (though not insignificantly) an *existential* matter since the only faith that God gives to the elect living in the present time (the gospel dispensation) is "the faith of a Christian"; that is, the effectual calling of the elect ushers them immediately into the salvific completeness of the gospel dispensation without any intervening habitation under some lesser dispensation. For Wesley, however, the various dispensations of the covenant of grace are *soteriologically* concurrent, and persons inhabit, as it were, the dispensation that is within the reach of the faith they have been given.

To this feature of Wesley's soteriology we must add yet another; namely, that in actual fact, "the faith of a Christian" is rarely if ever that faith which is given *initially*—though *ultimately* the enjoyment of such faith is the divine intention for the believer. The wide distance there often is between the starting point of the faith initially given and its designed finishing point coincides with Wesley's understanding of the desperate condition of the heart. Progress, then, on the way of faith requires that "the Holy Spirit prepares us for his inward kingdom by removing the veil from our heart" thereby "enabling us to know ourselves as we are known of him" so that we are convinced of "the desert of our sins, so that our mouth is stopped, and we are constrained to plead guilty before God."[58] Such progress, Wesley goes on to assert, "implies a species of faith"; and yet, "this faith is only the faith of a servant, and not the faith of a son."[59]

Existential Dimension. This last dimension of Wesley's conception of the concurrence of the various dispensations of the covenant of grace is best understood by way of example. While to *be* "altogether sinful, altogether guilty, and altogether helpless" is the *soteriological* reality, to be "*constrained* to plead guilty" and to "*feel* [our]selves at once altogether sinful,

---

58. Wesley, "On the Discoveries of Faith," *Works* (BE) §12, 4:34–35.
59. Ibid., §12–13, 4:34–35.

altogether guilty, and altogether helpless"[60] is the reflection *existentially* of this soteriological reality.

For Wesley, the dilemma facing fallen human beings is their lack—indeed, their *inability* in and of themselves—to know themselves and thus to know accurately their own situation soteriologically. Consequently, *existentially* they are completely out of alignment with the soteriological reality of their lives. Restoring alignment requires the preparatory work of the Holy Spirit in "removing the veil," "enabling us to know ourselves," and "'convincing us of sin.'"[61] The end result of this work of the Holy Spirit is that the individual is brought into the experience of bondage and servile fear. These are the *existential* accompaniments of those situated, *soteriologically*, in the legal (Mosaic) dispensation.

At this point, one other aspect of the *existential* dimension should be noted. In a letter to Thomas Rutherford, Wesley briefly delineates his understanding of assurance and concludes by commenting on the matter of "exempt cases":[62]

> Yet I do not affirm there are no exceptions to this general rule. Possibly some may be in the favour of God, and yet go mourning all the day long. But I believe this is usually owing either to disorder of body or ignorance of the gospel promises. Therefore I have not for many years thought a consciousness of acceptance to be essential to justifying faith.[63]

Wesley's comment serves as an informative illustration of his distinction between the soteriological and existential dimensions. While he believed it was the common privilege of the child of God to know the witness of the Spirit to the pardoning grace of God, Wesley was willing—and even compelled—to distinguish the soteriological from the existential and to allow for the possibility of an occasional anomaly (i.e., an exempt case). He recognized that there are cases in which a

---

60. Wesley, "On the Discoveries of Faith,," *Works* (BE) §12, 4:34–35. Emphasis mine.

61. Ibid.

62. This descriptor appears in a number of places, always with the basic idea of something which has the characteristic of being an anomaly. Examples include Wesley, "The Law Established through Faith, Discourse I *Works* (BE) §I.3, 2:22–23; and Wesley, "The Cure of Evil-Speaking," *Works* (BE) §III.4, 2:261–62. See also Wesley's letter to Ann Loxdale on March 9, 1782. Wesley, *Letters*, 7:113–14.

63. Wesley, *Letters*, 5:358–59. Wesley was not alone in his attentiveness to such complicating factors. See Burk, *A Memoir of the Life and Writings of John Albert Bengel*, 157–58.

person may be under the Christian dispensation *soteriologically* while *existentially* remaining in the throes of the fear characteristic of the legal (Mosaic) dispensation—a fear which results in "mourning all the day long." This, too, is indicative of a misalignment of the existential with the soteriological. However, *this* misalignment is due *not* to sinful self-deception as in the case of the deluded self-assessment of fallen, unawakened human beings, but is "owing either to disorder of body or ignorance of the gospel promises."[64]

Wesley's carefully crafted appropriation of covenant theology is now beginning to come into view. There can be little doubt that the lineage of his covenant theology is broader than the Puritan influence mediated by Perkins, Ames, and the Westminster Confession. We might reasonably speculate, based on the foregoing, that while the classic covenant theology of Puritan descent was mediated to Wesley and deeply embedded in his theological thought, he seems to have consciously adapted structural elements derived from a Cocceian strand of covenant theology. The end result is hugely significant for his soteriology. But we have explored only one of the pillars of covenant theology, the salvific *sufficiency* of the various dispensations of the covenant of grace. The other pillar, and the one which brings Wesley's covenant theology into full view, is the salvific *perfection* of the Christian or gospel dispensation of the covenant of grace.

64. Wesley, *Letters*, 5:358.

CHAPTER 8

The Holy Spirit and the Salvific Perfection of the Covenant of Grace

THE SALVIFIC SUFFICIENCY OF the various dispensations of the covenant of grace, though variously conceived, is one of the primary soteriological affirmations of covenant theology. The sufficiency of each dispensation rests on the promise of Genesis 3:15, a promise for which the warranty is "the lamb slain from the foundation of the world." Wesley's vision of the way of salvation is profoundly shaped by his understanding that this promise and warranty are extended to all of fallen humanity rather than to the elect only, and by his conceiving the salvific sufficiency of the covenant of grace to be concurrent and relative.[1]

As is true of covenant theology in general, Wesley's vision of the way of salvation does not stand apart from the second pillar upon which the soteriological affirmations of covenant theology rest: the salvific *perfection* of the covenant of grace. Without this, the construct of covenant theology is gutted and its soteriological affirmations rendered meaningless. The hope lodged in the lamb slain from the foundation of the world is vanquished if the lamb is not slain *in realitor*. But this, of course, is not the case. The message of Christianity is that the lamb was slain *in realitor*, and this is the ground upon which Wesley exhorts his listeners and readers to press on "from the faith of a servant, to the faith of a son."

As noted earlier, one attribute of the progression of the covenant of grace is that the momentum is always forward; that is, all that has gone before both *points* to and, so to speak, *gravitates* toward the present dispensation. The metaphor of increasing light was drawn upon frequently to convey the properties of this attribute, perhaps because it

---

1. Wesley's understanding of the salvific sufficiency of each dispensation of the covenant of grace is presented in the previous chapter.

most adequately accentuated a kind of movement forward that is certain and unquestionable; even, in a sense, inevitable. With the inauguration of the Christian dispensation, the divine design that the Jewish dispensation (and, for that matter, *every* dispensation of the covenant of grace previous to the Christian dispensation) should be succeeded by the salvific perfection of the Christian dispensation, is manifested.[2]

Without any suggestion of disregard for either the fact or the significance of the earlier dispensations, it is the Jewish (Mosaic) dispensation and the Christian (gospel) dispensation that received the most attention by covenant theologians in general, and certainly by Wesley. The impetus for this narrowing of focus is the soteriological agenda that lies at the heart of covenant theology. The central event is the revelation of Christ *in realiter* and the outpouring of the Holy Spirit the attending focal point, both of which together signal the advance of the covenant of grace from salvific *sufficiency* to salvific *perfection*. And further, the divinely-ordained course of such advance was not only paradigmatic of the *progress* of those on the way of salvation but the law-gospel sequence served as the equally divinely-ordained pattern for the *proclamation* of God's saving deeds.

The Indwelling Spirit: "The Blessing of the Gospel"

In concert with covenant theology in general, Wesley fixes the climactic triumph of Christ's death and resurrection in inextricable relationship to the outpouring of the Holy Spirit. This relationship is underscored in his sermon, "Christian Perfection." Here Wesley emphasized that it is the outpouring of the Holy Spirit that distinguishes the historical moment of the Christian dispensation from the Jewish:

> It is of great importance to observe, and that more carefully than is commonly done, the wide difference there is between the Jewish and the Christian dispensation, and *that ground of it* which the same Apostle [John] assigns in the seventh chapter of his Gospel, verse thirty-eight, etc. After he had there related those words of our blessed Lord, "He that believeth on me, as the Scripture hath said, out of his belly shall flow rivers of living water," he immediately subjoins, "This spake he of the Spirit," *emellon lambanein oi pisteuontes eis auton* "which they who should believe on him were afterwards to receive. For the

---

2. This point is captured by Fletcher in his amplification of John 5:46, "For had ye believed Moses, and submitted to his dispensation, ye would have believed me, and submitted to my gospel." Fletcher, *Essay on Truth*, 149.

Holy Ghost was not yet given, because that Jesus was not yet glorified."[3]

For Wesley, the distinction between the Jewish and Christian dispensations rested upon the matter of being made "more than conquerors over sin"—a victory which came only by the Holy Spirit when Jesus was glorified.[4] Wesley clarified, however, that it was not the "miracle gifts" which were given in conjunction with the outpouring of the Holy Spirit but was, rather, the "sanctifying graces."[5] Yet, the purpose of this clarification was not to contrast justification with sanctification. Instead, his intent was to underscore the contrast between what the Law could *not* do and what only the Spirit *can* and *will* do. This is evident, in part, in Wesley's understanding of Romans 7, as indicated by his including "An Exposition of the Seventh Chapter of the Epistle to the Romans; extracted from a late author" in the December, 1780 issue of the *Arminian Magazine*. The author expends a significant amount of effort establishing the fact that the person described in Romans 7 "is not only, not an Apostle, but not a *regenerate* man."[6] Instead, the writer argues, "it should be considered that the Apostle was here representing the sinful condition of those persons, who had no other help against their lusts than the law of *Moses*."[7]

In 1742, a year after Wesley's sermon "Christian Perfection," Charles Wesley echoed this same declaration regarding the difference between the Jewish and the Christian dispensation in his sermon, "Awake, Thou That Sleepest." There he describes the Holy Spirit as "the blessing of the gospel"—"that great gift" which God "hath fully bestowed since the time that Christ was glorified."[8] He goes on to assert that "the indwelling Spirit of God is the common privilege of all believers" and "the criterion of a real Christian," declaring unequivocally that "He is a Christian who hath received the Spirit of Christ. He is not a Christian who hath not received him."[9]

---

3. Wesley, *Works* (BE) §II.11, 2:110. Emphasis and transliteration mine.

4. Ibid.

5. Ibid.

6. Wesley, *AM* (Dec 1780), 628. See below for a further discussion of Wesley's understanding of Romans 7.

7. Ibid., 626.

8. Wesley, *Works* (BE) III.3–4, 7, 1:153, 155. Wesley included his sermon in each edition of his *Sermons on Several Occasions*.

9. Charles Wesley, "Awake, Thou That Sleepest," *Works* (BE) §III.7, 1.155. Compare this instance of a narrow use of the phrase "real Christian" with the broader sense

The emphasis here is heavily colored by the technical terminology of covenant theology, where the term "Christian" means not so much "believer" (as opposed to nonbeliever) but rather means "a believer under the Christian dispensation" as opposed to being "a believer under the Jewish dispensation."[10] This is the sense in which Wesley is responding to John Smith in his dialogue with Smith on the perceptible inspiration of the Holy Spirit: "The sum of what I offered before concerning *perceptible inspiration* was this. 'Every *Christian* believer has a perceptible testimony of God's Spirit that he is a child of God.'"[11] While the inherently inclusive nature of the term "every" is hardly disputable, the context of his dialogue with Smith indicates that Wesley is not arguing the point that *all* versus *some* Christian believers have this perceptible inspiration, but is contending for the validity of perceptible inspiration itself as concomitant with those who are under the Christian dispensation soteriologically.[12] The basis for his confidence is that it is this privilege that distinguishes the Christian dispensation from every other dispensation. This is the foundation for his appeal in the same paragraph to Romans 8:16 (the immediate context of which is the declaration concerning adoption).[13] There is no indication that Wesley ever shifted from the conviction regarding the indwelling of the Holy Spirit as the particular and specific "blessing of the gospel."

The Witnessing Spirit and the Law

It would be incorrect, however, to conclude from the foregoing that Wesley viewed the work of the Spirit as reserved for those who are under the Christian dispensation in the soteriological and existential sense described in the previous chapter. Quite the reverse is true: it is the Spirit who brings fallen human beings under the Jewish dispensation (again, in the soteriological and existential sense). While this is not a *receiving* of the Spirit in the sense spoken of by Wesley in his sermon "Christian Perfection," it is a discernible *operation* of the Spirit by which that "first

---

used by John Wesley in his 1786 sermon, "On Divine Providence." Wesley, *Works* (BE) §18, 2:543.

10. This technical aspect of the language of covenant theology is important to keep in mind when reading such passages.

11. Wesley, "To John Smith, July 10, 1747," *Works* (BE) §6, 26:246. Emphasis mine.

12. Overlooking Wesley's use of the terminology of covenant theology, Collins argues a point he is making by emphasizing the word "every" when citing this quote. Collins, *The Theology of John Wesley*, 133.

13. Wesley, "To John Smith, July 10, 1747." *Works* (BE) §6, 26:246.

slight, transient conviction of having sinned against [God]" progresses toward that "larger measure of self-knowledge, and a farther deliverance from the heart of stone" (i.e., repentance, the fruit of "convincing grace" properly stewarded).[14] This "farther deliverance" is neither "slight" nor "transient" but is, rather, intense and sustained.

This work of the Spirit, Wesley observes, is accomplished ordinarily (though not exclusively) by the Law "which, being set home on the conscience, generally breaketh the rocks in pieces."[15] Preaching only the gospel—"speaking of nothing but the sufferings and merits of Christ"—fails to convince of sin and to awaken "those who are still asleep on the brink of hell." Wesley is willing to allow that under such preaching "one in a thousand may have been awakened by the gospel" but warns that "this is no general rule" as "the ordinary method of God is to convict sinners by the law, and that only."[16] Wesley continues, "It is absurd therefore to offer a physician to them that are whole, or that at least imagine themselves so to be. You are first to convince them that they are sick; otherwise they will not thank you for your labour. It is equally absurd to offer Christ to them whose heart is whole, having never yet been broken."[17]

The priority of the preaching of the Law was a well-established conviction of Wesley's. A roster of significant contributors to this conviction appears in the form of the extracts of their works which Wesley chose to include in his *A Christian Library*. One such contributor is Robert Bolton (1571–1631) whose sermon, "Instructions for a Right Comforting Afflicted Consciences,"[18] supplies a significant example and demonstrates the relationship between the preaching of the Law and the work of the Spirit. In the course of presenting his argument for the necessity of the preaching of the Law, Bolton highlights an important distinction: "'The heart is prepared *for* faith . . . and not *by* faith.' Justification, being

---

14. Wesley, "On Working Out Our Own Salvation," *Works* (BE) §II.1, 3:203–5.

15. Wesley, "The Original, Nature, Properties, and Use of the Law," *Works* (BE) §IV.1, 2:15. Wesley describes this as the "first use" of the Law.

16. Wesley, "The Law Established Through Faith, Discourse I," *Works* (BE) §I.3, 2:22–23.

17. Ibid.

18. Wesley, *ACL*, 8:129–292. The influence of Bolton on Wesley is evidenced not only by his including an extract of the sermon but in his reading and explaining Bolton's "General Directions for a Comfortable Walking with God" to the congregation at the Foundery. See Wesley, "May 13, 1754," *Works* (BE), 20:486. See also his recommendation of the same sermon in a letter to Joseph Atlay on May 26, 1781. Wesley, *Letters*, 7:63–64.

the work of God, is perfect in itself: but our hearts are not fit to apply it, until God have humbled us, brought us to despair in ourselves."[19] Wesley states the same in the first of his thirteen discourses on the Sermon on the Mount: "Who then are the 'poor in spirit'? Without question, the humble; they who know themselves, who are convinced of sin; those to whom God hath given that first repentance which is *previous* to faith in Christ."[20] Similarly, in his response to George Horne's sermon, Wesley described those who are thus humbled as ones who are "in the right *way* to justification" though not "actually justified."[21]

Bolton goes on to specify the role of the Holy Spirit: "The Holy Ghost . . . puts an Efficacy into the Law, and makes that powerful to work on the Heart; to make a Man poor in Spirit; so that he may be fit to receive the Gospel. The Spirit of Bondage must make the Law effectual; as the Spirit of Adoption does the Gospel."[22] This same understanding appears in Richard Sibbes' "The Witness of Salvation":

> The first work then of the Comforter is to put a man in fear. Further, hence is shewed, that until this Spirit doth work this fear, a man doth not fear. . . . No man must think this strange, that God deals with men at first in this harsh manner, as it were to kill them, ere he make them alive; nor be discouraged, as if God had cast them off for ever as none of his; for this bondage and spirit of fear is a work of God's Spirit, and a preparative to the rest.[23]

Though Wesley did not include an extract of this sermon in his *A Christian Library*, his view is consistent with that of Sibbes'. This work of the Spirit is preparative; that is, the Spirit is active in behalf of those who are not yet justified, escorting them, as it were, toward "the proper Christian salvation."[24] In his commentary on Romans 8:15, Wesley remarks extensively on the role of the Holy Spirit in this preparatory work:

> *The spirit of bondage* here seems directly to mean, those operations of the Holy Spirit, by which the soul, on its first conviction, feels itself in bondage to sin, to the world, to Satan, and

---

19. Wesley, *ACL*, 8:152. Emphasis mine.
20. Wesley, *Works* (BE) §I.4, 1:477–78. Emphasis mine.
21. Wesley, *A Letter to the Rev. Mr. Horne*, 16. Emphasis mine.
22. Wesley, *ACL*, 8:152. Bolton is quoting George Throgmorton.
23. Sibbes, "The Witness of Salvation," in *The Complete Works of Richard Sibbes*, 7:370.
24. Wesley, "On Working Out Our Own Salvation," *Works* (BE) §II.1, 3:203–4.

obnoxious to the wrath of God. This therefore and *the spirit of adoption* are one and the same spirit, only manifesting itself in various operations, according to the various circumstances of the persons.[25]

This conception was quite broadly accepted. It was, for example, apparent in William Burkitt's *Expository Notes*[26] and largely reproduced by Matthew Henry (1662–1714) in his commentary on the verse.[27] Wesley's closing phrase—"according to the various circumstances of the persons"—may coincide in meaning with Henry's view that the spirit of bondage is not only "that Spirit of Bondage, which the Old Testament Church was under, by reason of the Darkness and Terror of that Dispensation" but also is to be understood as "that Spirit of Bondage, which the Saints were many of them themselves under at their Conversion, under the Convictions of Sin and Wrath set home by the Spirit." By way of example Henry then lists persons living in the *historical* moment of the gospel dispensation, including those baptized at Pentecost, the jailor, and the Apostle Paul.[28] Thus, the Spirit who witnesses to the pardoned that they are the children of God did also *beforehand* witness to their spirits that they were children of sin and thus children of wrath.[29]

Thomas Boston details this work of the Spirit in *Human Nature in Its Fourfold State* in a section belonging to his discussion of the State of Grace entitled "How the Branches are Taken Out of the Natural Stock, and Ingrafted into the Supernatural Stock." Using the imagery of "the pruning knife of the *Law*, in the Hand of the *Spirit* of God," Boston traces the journey of sinners from their being completely oblivious with respect to their depraved estate to their experience of overwhelming fear and helplessness once they have come to see the gravity of their predicament spiritually. In Boston's description, it takes twelve strokes with "the Ax of the Law" before, finally, the last fiber of self-righteousness is severed and all hope of self-remedy in any of its forms is forsaken.[30]

---

25. Wesley, *ENNT*, 484. Emphasis mine.

26. Burkitt, *Expository Notes*, np.

27. Henry, *An Exposition of All the Books of the Old and New Testaments*, 6:31. In the preface, Henry acknowledges Burkitt's work as one of his primary sources.

28. Ibid. Henry describes the operations of the Spirit as follows: "God, as a Judge, says Dr. *Manton*, by the *Spirit of Bondage*, sends us to Christ as Mediator, and Christ as Mediator, by the *spirit of Adoption*, sends us back again to God as a Father." Ibid.

29. Boston, *Human Nature in its Fourfold State*, 122.

30. Ibid., 222–24. For the slight shift in imagery, compare page 222 with page 232.

Wesley, too, acknowledges just such a journey. In his response to William Law's *Spirit of Prayer*, Wesley objects to Law's assertion that "The painful *Sense* of what you are, *kindled into a working State of Sensibility* by the Light of God, is the Light and Fire from whence the *Spirit of Prayer* proceeds" and that "its first Prayer is *all Humility*."[31] Wesley countered that "[i]n its first kindling nothing is found, but Pain, Wrath, and Darkness" and that while "during the first Convictions" there is "very often" found "sweet Gleams of *Light*, Touches of *Joy*, of *Hope*, and of *Love*, mixt with Sorrow and Fear . . . much less is it true, that the *first Prayer* of an awakening Sinner is *all Humility*." Rather, "a Sinner newly awakened, has always more or less Confidence in himself, in what he *is*, or *has*, or *does*, and *will do*; which is not *Humility*, but downright *Pride*. And this mingles itself with all his Prayer, till the Day-star is just rising in his Heart."[32]

The fruit of the tenacious labors of the Spirit is described in detail by Wesley in "On the Discoveries of Faith," a sermon written, it is important to recall, late in his life:

> The Holy Spirit prepares us for his inward kingdom by removing the veil from our heart, and enabling us to know ourselves as we are known of him; by "convincing us of sin," of our evil nature, our evil tempers, and our evil words and actions; all of which cannot but partake of the corruption of the heart from which they spring. He then convinces us of the desert of our sins, so that our mouth is stopped, and we are constrained to plead guilty before God. At the same time we "receive the spirit of bondage unto fear," fear of the wrath of God, fear of the punishment which we have deserved, and above all fear of death, lest it should consign us over to eternal death. Souls that are thus convinced feel they are so fast in prison that they cannot get forth. They feel themselves at once altogether sinful, altogether guilty, and altogether helpless.[33]

Wesley's description is instructive in many regards. This preparatory work of the Holy Spirit results in the awakening of the sinner by removing the veil, enabling self-knowledge, and convincing of sin. It also brings a strong sense of desperation and grave concern with regard to this condition. This activates a plea from within the one so convicted

---

31. Law, *The Second Part of the Spirit of Prayer*, 172.
32. Wesley, *A Letter to the Reverend Mr. Law*, 74–75.
33. Wesley, *Works* (BE) §12, 4:34–35.

that is expressed in the poem, "Moriar ut Te Videam!" which appeared in the 1742 edition of the Wesleys' *Hymns and Sacred Poems*:

> O Thou, who know'st what is in Man
> Who searchest out the Reins and Heart,
> Me, Jesu, to Myself explain,
> A Ray of Heavenly Light impart;
> Impart Thyself, Thou Real Light,
> And manifest my Nature's Night.[34]

It is also important to observe that Wesley's description involves an *ordering* of the various aspects, affective and otherwise, of this work of the Spirit: "The Holy Spirit prepares us . . . by removing the veil" and "enabling us to know ourselves. . . . *He then* convinces us of the desert of our sins. . . . *At the same time* we 'receive the spirit of bondage unto fear.'"[35] The end result is an intense and extended experience of fear of the wrath of God and of the punishment of eternal death. Forty years earlier in his sermon, "The Spirit of Bondage and Adoption," Wesley provided a more thorough outline of the progression of this work of the Spirit. First, "terribly shaken out of his sleep" "God touches the heart of him that lay asleep in darkness" "and awakes into a consciousness of his danger. Perhaps in a moment, perhaps by degrees, the eyes of his understanding are opened, and now first (the veil being in part removed) discern the real state he is in."

The work of the Spirit intensifies as "the inward, spiritual meaning of the law of God now begins to glare upon him" and "pierces 'even to the dividing asunder of his soul and spirit, his joints and marrow.'" Soon, "he is stripped of all, and wanders to and fro seeking rest, but finding none"; instead, "the more he strives, wishes, labours to be free, the more does he feel his chains." "Thus he toils without end, repenting and sinning, and repenting and sinning again, *till at length* the poor sinful, helpless wretch is even at his wit's end, and can barely groan, 'O wretched man that I am, who shall deliver me from the body of this death?'"[36] In this regard, then, the work of the Spirit is to restore the alignment of the existential with the soteriological, so that the person who *is* soteriologically "at once altogether sinful, altogether guilty,

---

34. Wesley and Wesley, *Hymns and Sacred Poems* (1742), 20–21. The hymnbook includes the translation of the title as "Let me die that I may see Thee!" Compare John Wesley, "Hymn II. A prayer for one convinced of sin," *Hymns and Spiritual Songs, Intended for the Use of Real Christians*, 6–7.

35. Wesley, *Works* (BE) §12, 4:34–35. Emphasis mine.

36. Wesley, *Works* (BE) §II.1–10, 1:255–60.

and altogether helpless"[37] comes to also *feel* this reality (the existential dimension).

The idea of progression with respect to the work of the Spirit as the spirit of bondage is indicated in Wesley's commentary on Romans 7:14, "In answering two objections (*Is then the law sin?* ver. 7. and *Is the law death?* ver. 13.) [the Apostle Paul] interweaves the whole process of a man reasoning, groaning, striving, and escaping from the legal to the evangelical state. This he does from ver. 7. to the end of this chapter."[38] That this remained Wesley's view of Romans 7 from early on[39] is suggested by the exposition of the chapter reprinted in the December 1780 issue of the *Arminian Magazine*, as previously mentioned. In that article, the process—and the dilemma—of the man "escaping from the legal to the evangelical state" is evaluated as follows:

> Not that [the Apostle Paul] speaks of one who is wholly dead in sin; but of one who is *struggling* with sin; yet not *conquering*. The person here described is one whose conscience is awakened; for he *delights in the law of God, after the inner man*, . . . yet his practice is enslaved: for what he hates, that he doth; . . . He is in the rank of *unwilling sinners*; but he is a *lost sinner* still. . . . So that as for all the *ineffectual striving*, and *sinning with regret*, which is so often mentioned in this chapter, it belongs not to any *regenerate* person, but only to a sinner who is something changed, but not enough; and who is in the way to become a Child of Grace, though for the present he be a son of Death and Hell.[40]

Illustrative of this groaning and striving is the case of Thomas Davenport, a correspondent of Wesley's. In a letter to Davenport on December 2, 1781, Wesley identified that Davenport was, in fact, a beneficiary of the work of the operation of the Holy Spirit as the spirit of bondage:

> Your case is plain. You are in the hands of a wise Physician, who is lancing your sores in order to heal them. He has *given* you now *the spirit of fear*. But it is in order to *the spirit of love and of a sound mind*. You have now *received the spirit of bondage*. Is it not the forerunner of the Spirit of adoption?[41]

---

37. Wesley, *Works* (BE) §12, 4:34–35.
38. Wesley, *ENNT*, 481–82. Bracketed insert mine.
39. See "The Spirit of Bondage and of Adoption," *Works* (BE), §II.9, 1:259–60.
40. Wesley, *AM* 3 (December 1780), 630–31.
41. Wesley, *Letters*, 7:95. Note that Wesley finds in 2 Tim 1:7 the primary constituent attributes of those in the legal state (fear) and those having escaped to the evangelical state (love).

Wesley, having reminded Davenport that this operation of the Spirit is indicative of a further work of the Spirit that is certain to come, gives a further word of encouragement: "He is not afar off. Look up! And expect Him to cry in your heart, Abba, Father!"[42]

It is what Wesley says to Davenport *next* that is of particular interest and that coincides with the assertion of the exposition of Romans 7: the person so described is "in the way to become a Child of Grace" though at present is yet "a son of Death and Hell."[43] Wesley proceeds with an encouraging reminder: "He is nigh that justifieth! that justifieth the ungodly and him that worketh not! If you are fit for hell, you are just fit for Him! If you are a mere sinner, He cannot cast you out!"[44]

The Spirit's work of applying the Law came to be summarized in the term "legal." Yet, the term meant more than "having to do with the Law." It served as shorthand for the whole complex of soteriological and existential progressions typifying the unregenerate under the frightful torrent of fear and condemnation released by the Spirit's application of the law—from their first "reasoning" and "groaning" to the moment when, "tired of [their] legal terror,"[45] they take "recourse to Jesus Christ for refreshing"[46] and escape "from the legal to the evangelical state."

One of the most famous poems in which the term is found is that which was engraved upon the headstone marking the grave of Wesley's mother, Susanna, who passed away in London on Sunday, August 1, 1742:

> In sure and stedfast hope to rise,
> And claim her mansions in the skies,
> A Christian here her flesh laid down,
> The cross exchanging for a crown.
>
> True daughter of affliction she,
> Inured to pain and misery,
> Mourned a long night of griefs and fears,
> *A legal night of seventy years.*

---

42. Ibid.

43. Wesley, *AM* 3 (Dec 1780), 630.

44. Wesley, *Letters*, 7:95.

45. Wesley, "Instructions from a Right Comforting Afflicted Consciences," *ACL*, 8:157.

46. Ibid.

The Father then revealed his Son,
Him in the broken bread made known;
She knew and felt her sins forgiven,
And found the earnest of her heaven.

Meet for the fellowship above,
She heard the call, "Arise my love":
I come, her dying looks replied,
And lamb-like, as her Lord, she died.[47]

The Witnessing Spirit and the Revelation of Christ

The verse appearing on Susanna Wesley's headstone introduces the relationship between the two operations of the Spirit noted by Wesley. The Spirit witnesses not only to enslavement to sin but also to adoption as children of God. While the well-documented hardships of Susanna's life are noted in the description of her as a "true daughter of affliction . . . inured to pain and misery," the next two lines signal a shift from the difficult circumstances that accompanied the course of her life as a wife and mother to commentary on her spiritual journey over the years. The last line of the stanza—"a legal night of seventy years"—is written as an appositive to the line previous, "mourned a long night of griefs and fears."

The term "mourned" belongs to the technical terminology associated with the morphology of conversion common to the Evangelical Revival. In this use, the term routinely denoted the mourning experienced by one under the awakening influences of the spirit of bondage. Such persons were identified as "mourners" and were also classified according to the current status of their escape from the legal state to the evangelical. This is exemplified in the table of contents of John and Charles Wesley's 1780 edition of *A Collection of Hymns*. Part II of the collection is titled simply "Convincing"—emphasizing the initial effect of God's arresting grace. Part III is untitled but contains five sections; including Section II entitled "For Mourners Convinced of Sin" and Section III entitled "For Mourners Brought to the Birth."[48] This last section is a collection

---

47. Wesley, "A Short Account of Mrs. Susannah Wesley," *AM* (June, 1781), 312–16. Emphasis mine. Wesley includes the poem in his journal entries related to his mother's passing, beginning Tuesday, July 18, 1742 and continuing through Sunday, August 1, 1742, the day of her death and the date of the poem itself. Wesley, *Works* (BE), 19:283–84.

48. This analogy of being brought to the moment of birth appears also in Boston. See Boston, *Human Nature in its Fourfold State*, 60.

of hymns for those who longingly wait upon God who alone is able to bring them from the legal to the evangelical state. Hymn CXXVI, from the section "For Mourners Brought to the Birth," includes the same elements (night/darkness and the revealing of Christ) evident in the verse found on Susanna's headstone:

> Send forth one ray of heavenly light,
> Of gospel hope, of humble fear,
> To *guide me through the gulf of night*,
> My poor desponding soul to cheer;
> Till thou my unbelief remove,
> And show me all thy glorious love.
> . . .
> My Saviour thou, *not yet revealed*,
> Yet will I thee my Saviour call,
> Adore thy hand, from sin withheld;
> Thy hand shall save me from my fall;
> Now, Lord, throughout my darkness shine,
> And show thyself for ever mine![49]

The case of John Wesley's mother, Susanna, is of particular note. First, there is the matter of the chronological reference: "seventy . . . years," This is not a reference to her life span. She was mid-way through her seventy-*second* year at her passing. Rather, the seventy year time frame mentioned coincides with two key events: the first is her birth, January 20, 1669; the second, it appears, is an experience Susanna had sometime in August, 1739 when she was lodging with her daughter and son-in-law, Martha and Westley Hall. In his journal entry for September 3, 1739, Wesley recorded the gist of a long conversation with his mother:

> She had scarce heard such a thing mentioned as the having forgiveness of sins now, or God's Spirit bearing witness with our spirit; much less did she imagine that this was the common privilege of all true believers. "Therefore" (said she) "I never durst ask for it myself. But two or three weeks ago, while my son Hall was pronouncing those words, in delivering the cup to me, 'The blood of our Lord Jesus Christ, which was given for thee,' the words struck through my heart, and I knew God for Christ's sake had forgiven me all my sins."[50]

---

49. Wesley, *A Collection of Hymns* (1780), 128. Emphasis mine. Note also in Stanza 2 the longing for a ray of "gospel" hope.

50. Wesley, "September 3, 1739," *Works* (BE), 19:93–94.

The Holy Spirit and the Salvific Perfection of the Covenant of Grace

This experience certainly is reflected in the third stanza of the epitaph:

> The Father then revealed his Son,
> Him in the broken bread made known;
> She knew and felt her sins forgiven,
> And found the earnest of her heaven.[51]

For John Wesley and his brother, Charles, it appears that this signaled the moment of Susanna's "escape" from the legal to the evangelical state; that is, though Susanna had lived to the fullness of the faith God had given her, she had lived under the limits of the Jewish dispensation until, in that moment during communion, "one ray of heavenly light, of *gospel* hope" was sent forth.[52]

The relationship between the concluding of the "legal years" and Christ being revealed is firmly rooted in Wesley's covenant theology and is understood by him to be intricately related to the operations of the Holy Spirit. It is vital to recall that in covenant theology, the history of God's saving deeds was divided into "before Christ was exhibited" and "Christ exhibited," the moment of such division having been *"when the fulness of the time—Appointed by the father . . . was come."*[53] This moment in the history of God's saving deeds signified not only the demarcation between the *historical* "moments" of the Jewish and Christian dispensations of the covenant of grace, but also served to identify the status of the individual *soteriologically* as being either "under" the Jewish or "under" the Christian dispensation. That is, whether Christ has been revealed is a watershed event in an individual's life in a way that *parallels* what the revelation of Christ meant (and means) for salvation history.

By Wesley's time, this parallelism was already well-accepted as a way in which individual believers might conceptualize and evaluate their progress on the way of salvation. In his sermon "Looking Unto Jesus," extracted by Wesley for publication in *A Christian Library*, Isaac Ambrose provides an example of this in the questions by which he pressed his hearers to consider their respective spiritual states: "Is Christ manifested *in* thee? Surely this is more than Christ manifested *to* thee. The bare history is a manifestation of Christ unto thee, but there is a mystery

---

51. Wesley, "A Short Account of Mrs. Susannah Wesley," *AM* 4 (June, 1781), 312–13. The epitaph also appears in Charles Wesley's *Hymns and Sacred Poems, in two volumes* (1749), 1:282.

52. Wesley, *AM* (June, 1781), 312–13. Emphasis mine. Charles Wallace claims that John and Charles inflated the significance of the event to fit their conception of a Methodist morphology of conversion. Wallace, *Susanna Wesley*, 16.

53. Galatians 4:4. Wesley, *ENNT*, 604.

in the inward manifestation. . . . [B]ut has he revealed Christ in thee? has he let thee see into the wonders of his glory? has he given thee the light of his glory within?"[54]

Ambrose clearly understood the revelation of Christ as being the work of the Spirit and unequivocally declared, "If Christ be not manifest in thy Heart by his blessed Spirit, thou are no Son of God."[55] It is important to observe, on the one hand, the distinction between the revelation of Christ and the witness of the Spirit, and, on the other, the indivisibility of the two.[56] Bolton spoke of the two acts of the Holy Spirit which follow the Spirit's work as the spirit of bondage. These are 1) "to reveal Christ," thus making known to the prepared heart "the unsearchable riches of Christ" and "what is the hope of his calling"; and 2) to testify to the spirit of one whose heart is so prepared "that Christ is thine . . . and God is thy Father."[57]

For Wesley, too, the revelation of Christ was indeed a critical soteriological marker both in the "bare history" of God's saving deeds and in the life of the individual; and, while the revelation of Christ in the heart must necessarily precede the witness of the Spirit, such revelation was itself a work of the Spirit. It is noteworthy that in preparing his sermon "The Circumcision of the Heart" for publication in his second volume of *Sermons on Several Occasions* in 1748, Wesley footnoted the following addition to the sermon which otherwise remained largely in the form in which it was originally preached at St. Mary's, Oxford in 1733:

> ["This is the victory which overcometh the world, even our faith": that faith which is not only an unshaken assent to all that God hath revealed in Scripture, . . .] but likewise the *revelation of Christ in our hearts*: a divine evidence or conviction of his love, his free, unmerited love to me a sinner; a sure confidence in his pardoning mercy, *wrought in us by the Holy Ghost*—a confidence whereby every true believer is enabled to bear witness, "I know that my Redeemer liveth"; that I "have an advocate with the Father," that "Jesus Christ the righteous is" my Lord, and "the propitiation for my sins." I know he "hath loved me, and given himself for me". He "hath reconciled me, even me to God"; and

---

54. Wesley, *ACL*, 14:253.

55. Ibid.

56. See Q. 1 and 2, *Minutes*, 1746 (Jackson), 8:290.

57. Wesley, "Instructions for a Right Comforting Afflicted Consciences," *ACL*, 8:153.

I "have redemption through his blood, even the forgiveness of sins."⁵⁸

This understanding may be seen in his commentary on the sixteenth verse of Galatians 1: "*To reveal his Son in me*—by the powerful Operation of his Spirit . . . as well as *to* me, by the Heavenly Vision."⁵⁹ In "The Nature of Enthusiasm" (written three years *after* his 1747 letter regarding whether a sense of pardon was a condition of justifying faith), Wesley warned his listeners, "You may have much joy; you may have a measure of love, and yet not have living faith. Cry unto God that he would not suffer you, blind as you are, to go out of the way; that you may *never fancy yourself a believer in Christ till Christ is revealed in you,* and till his Spirit witnesses with your spirit that you are a child of God."⁶⁰

That this was of paramount importance in his theological thought throughout his life is overwhelmingly evident throughout the Wesley corpus.⁶¹ In speaking directly to the subject of the metaphor in his sermon "On the Discoveries of Faith," Wesley clearly identifies "Christ revealed" as a distinguishing element between those who have the faith of a servant and those who have the faith of a son:

> Exhort him to press on by all possible means, till he passes "from faith to faith"; from the faith of a *servant* to the faith of a *son*; from the spirit of bondage unto fear, to the spirit of childlike love. He will then have "Christ revealed in his heart," enabling him to testify, "The life that I now live in the flesh I live by faith in the Son of God, who loved *me*, and gave himself for *me*"—the proper voice of a child of God.⁶²

The testimony of those who press on to the faith of a son is so consistent in its substance that it is recognizable as "the proper voice of a child of God." Such testimony is completely dependent upon the

---

58. Wesley, *Works* (BE) §I.7, 1:405. Emphasis mine. Text from the original sermon appears in brackets, after which Wesley inserted the following footnote: "N.B. The following part of this paragraph is now added to the sermon formerly preached." Repeatedly and at least as late as 1778, Wesley identified this sermon as representative of his teaching concerning salvation from all sin. See Outler's introductory comment to the sermon, *Works* (BE), 1:398–400.

59. Wesley, *ENNT*, 596.

60. Wesley, *Works* (BE) §35, 2:58–59. Emphasis mine.

61. Examples among his sermons include: "Scriptural Christianity," Wesley, *Works* (BE) §IV.8, 1:177; "The Witness of Our Own Spirit," *Works* (BE) §8, 1:304; "The Imperfection of Human Knowledge," *Works* (BE) §III.3, 2:583–84.

62. Ibid., §14, 4:35–36.

revelation of Christ in the heart—a discernible reality in which the individual's cooperation is necessary and yet, by definition, ultimately (and notably) passive. In addition, such revelation, together with the testimony that accompanies it, signals a fundamental transformation: the person is "born of God" and "inwardly changed." This speaks of a *new* reality *soteriologically*, not just a new *feeling* about or sensitivity to an *existing* reality.

In short, until Christ is revealed, a person's faith, though invested with all sincerity, is at best aspirational and produces "outward" righteousness, to use Wesley's word. Such faith—the faith of a servant—is faith bound within the dispensational reach of the legal dispensation (the habitation of the awakened) so that while it leans as far as possible into the promise[63] ("'We have an advocate with the Father, . . . he is the propitiation for our sins'"), it nevertheless groans under a sense of the wrath of God[64] as described in Romans 7. On the one hand, this faith is neither to be disregarded nor downplayed as it is itself a gift of God by the work of the Holy Spirit. On the other hand, such faith is not to be *confused* with the faith of a son by which a person is truly and radically transformed, "changed by the mighty power of God from 'an earthly, sensual, devilish' mind to 'the mind which was in Christ Jesus.'"[65]

A further outcome of the revelation of Christ is the *confirmation* of having been "inwardly changed." This "consciousness of being in the favour of God"[66] is the operation of the Spirit as the spirit of adoption: "'Ye are the sons of God by faith'; and *because ye are sons*, God hath sent forth the Spirit of his Son into your hearts, crying, Abba, Father.'"[67] There is a significant distinction here; namely, it is not the witness of the Spirit that *confers* sonship.[68] Rather, the Spirit witnesses to sonship *already conferred*. However, Wesley affirmed that in witnessing to sonship, the Holy Spirit works as well to "'evince the reality of our sonship.'"[69]

---

63. Wesley observed that the evangelical state was "frequently . . . mixed with the legal" with the result that "few of those who have the spirit of bondage and fear remain always without hope." Wesley, "The Spirit of Bondage and of Adoption," *Works* (BE) §IV.2, 1:264–65.

64. Wesley, "Scriptural Christianity," *Works* (BE) §II.4, 1:166–67.

65. Wesley, "On the Discoveries of Faith," *Works* (BE) §14, 4:35–36.

66. Wesley, "To Thomas Rutherford, March 28, 1768," *Letters*, 5:337.

67. Galatians 4:6. Wesley, *ENNT*, 604. Emphasis mine.

68. The notion that the witness of the Spirit confers sonship was precisely what Wesley objected to in his letter to his brother Charles written on July 31, soon after the 1747 Conference.

69. Wesley, "The Witness of the Spirit, Discourse I," *Works* (BE) §I.11, 1:275–76.

Wesley is consistent in his distinguishing between sonship *itself* and the witness of the Spirit to sonship. In his commentary on Galatians 4:4, he states, "*God sent forth*—from his own bosom, *his son*,"[70] reflecting Bengel's emphasis on the Apostle Paul's reflexive use of the pronoun *autou*. This was a point of particular importance to Bengel who observed that its meaning "appears from the train of thought of this passage, for we have received first *adoption*, then the *Spirit of adoption*. Therefore Christ himself is not the Son of God, merely because he was sent and anointed by the Father."[71] In other words, Jesus was not the Son because he was anointed; rather, he was anointed because he was the Son. Extending this emphasis, Bengel commented on Galatians 4:6, "The indwelling of the Holy Spirit is the consequence of *the condition of sons*, the latter does not follow the former."[72]

Bengel was certainly not Wesley's only source with respect to this distinction; and it may well be that Wesley's attentiveness to Bengel on this point arose from the fact that he was already firmly convinced of the distinction. There is no doubt that the concept was theologically proximate to Wesley, as it appears in "*Vindiciæ Pietatis*," a sermon by Richard Alleine, an extract of which Wesley included in *A Christian Library*. In the sermon, Alleine discusses the distinction between sonship and the witness to that sonship in terms of the *grace* of adoption—"whereby the Lord has given us the Relation of Children, and a right to all those Privileges and Blessings that flow from that Relation"—and the *spirit* of adoption "that witnesses to our sonship."[73]

In his own commentary on John 1:12, Wesley incorporates Galatians 4:6 in order to accentuate the distinction and to mark the connection between sonship and the witness of the Spirit to that sonship: "*But as many as received him* . . . The moment they believe, they are sons; and because they are sons, God *sendeth forth the spirit of his Son into their hearts, crying, Abba, Father*."[74] In his sermon, "On the Witness of the Spirit, Discourse I," Wesley underscores the point: "Again, the

---

In using the term "evince," Wesley avoids the notion of conferring sonship and instead echoes the assertion Richard Alleine that the Spirit "works in us the Dispositions and dutiful Affections of Sons." Richard Alleine, "*Vindiciæ Pietatis, ACL*, 30:204.

70. Wesley, *ENNT*, 604.
71. Bengel, *Gnomon*, 2:362.
72. Ibid. 2:362.
73. *ACL*, 30:203–4.
74. Wesley, *ENNT*, 268.

Scriptures describe the being born of God, which must precede the witness that we are his children."[75]

Another outcome of the revelation of Christ is "the love of God shed abroad in the heart by the Holy Spirit." The new soteriological reality of being "inwardly changed by the mighty power of God" is reflected existentially in relief from that *servile* fear ("fear of the wrath of God") that had characterized life under the spirit of bondage. In its place there is now a *filial* fear, "an awful reverence toward [God], and an earnest care not to give place to any disposition, not to admit an action, word, or thought, which might in any degree displease that indulgent Power to whom [we owe our] life, breath, and all things."[76]

Wesley's conception of the relationship of fear and love is summarized in his commentary on 1 John 4:18, "*There is no fear in love*—No slavish fear can be where love reigns," for "*perfect*, adult *love casteth out* slavish *fear*, because such *fear hath torment*, and so is inconsistent with the happiness of love."[77] In commenting on this passage, he includes the distinctions he had highlighted in Galatians 4; namely, that "the adoption" signifies we are "adult sons" having lifted us from "that low, servile state."[78] What typifies the awakened person is "fear without love"[79]—and this state, which is the fruit of the work of the spirit of bondage, is what characterizes the one having the faith of a servant: one who is inadmissible to the rights and privileges of the awaiting inheritance (on account of not yet being an "adult"), and therefore "in a kind of servile state" and thus "under the legal dispensation."[80] All of these elements are present in a brief recollection by Ann Bolton in a letter to Wesley, dated at Finstock on July 7, 1775 in which she describes her own journey "from faith to faith":

> O happy choice! What reason have I to praise and adore God, that he ever caused the joyful sound of salvation by faith, to reach my ears, and affect my heart! glory be to him that he imparted to me the spirit of bondage, whereby I feared because I had sinned! and thanks be to him that he left me not without

---

75. Wesley, *Works* (BE) §II.5, 1:279. Emphasis mine.
76. Wesley, *A letter to the Reverend Dr. Conyers Middleton*, 199.
77. Wesley, *ENNT*, 794.
78. Wesley, *ENNT*, 604. In his commentary on 1 John 4:18 Wesley also incorporates aspects of 1 Cor 3:1 and 1 John 2:12–13.
79. Ibid. 794–95.
80. Ibid. 604. See especially Wesley's commentary on Galatians 4:1–5.

hope; but revealed in me the Son of his love, and enabled me by the Spirit of adoption, to cry Abba, Father.[81]

The foregoing emphasis on the distinction between sonship and the Spirit's witness to sonship is not to suggest that the existential confirmation of the soteriological reality of sonship is in any way inconsequential. Wesley's insistence that "explicit assurance . . . is the common privilege of real Christians"[82] was a foundational element of a Methodist morphology of conversion and, for that very reason, was frequently a topic of controversy.[83] But far be it from Wesley to relegate the witness of the Spirit to being nothing more than an existential enhancement! Wesley understood the witness of the Spirit to be of continuing and profound soteriological consequence as well. As he declared in his sermon, "Satan's Devices": "[U]nless we love God it is not possible that we should love our neighbour as ourselves; nor, consequently, that we should have any right affections either toward God or toward man. It evidently follows that whatever weakens our faith must in the same degree obstruct our holiness."[84] For Wesley, then, the witness of the Spirit stood as a signpost on the way of salvation, a definitive attribute of the gospel (Christian) dispensation that was both existentially accessible and soteriologically indispensable.

The Witnessing Spirit and the Consciousness of God's Favor

The revelation of Christ is the work of the Spirit—specifically, a work of the spirit of adoption who witnesses to "the adoption of sons." Such adoption is evidenced by the love of God being shed abroad in the heart so that the believer "obeys out of love" (rather than fear). This obedience from love is "the privilege of all the *children of God*."[85] Wesley clarifies that these markers are descriptive of those who have passed from the faith of a servant to the faith of a son. He specifies, "'He that believeth' *as a son* (as St. John observes) 'hath the witness in himself.'"[86] And by this

---

81. A. B., "Letter CCCCXXXV," *AM* (September 1787), 499–500.

82. Wesley, "To the Revd. Charles Wesley, July 31, 1747." *Works* (BE), 26:254–55.

83. See, for example, Wesley's exchanges with John Smith, Richard Tompson, and Thomas Rutherford.

84. Wesley, *Works* (BE) §I.8, 1:143–44.

85. Wesley, "On the Discoveries of Faith," *Works* (BE) §13–14, 4:35–36.

86. Ibid., §14, 4:35–36. Emphasis mine. The first half of 1 John 5:10 reads, "He that believeth *on the Son of God* hath the witness in himself." Emphasis mine. Wesley's

witnessing work of the Spirit, the child of God comes into a *consciousness* of the favor of God.

Not infrequently, Wesley found himself having to defend his understanding of the work of the Spirit as the spirit of adoption, ministering to the child of God a consciousness of the divine favor. In responding on March 28, 1768 to Thomas Rutherford's charge against the Methodists, Wesley provides an overview of his doctrine of assurance:

> I believe a few, but very few, Christians have an assurance from God of everlasting salvation; and that is the thing which the Apostle terms the plerophory or full assurance of hope. I believe more have such an assurance of being now in the favour of God as excludes all doubt and fear. And this, if I do not mistake, the Apostle means by the plerophory or full assurance of faith. I believe a consciousness of being in the favour of God (which I do not term plerophory, or full assurance, since it is frequently weakened, nay perhaps interrupted, by returns of doubt or fear) is the common privilege of Christians fearing God and working righteousness.[87]

It is evident from this brief paragraph that Wesley conceives of degrees of assurance. The question is, who is Wesley including in his final assertion that "a consciousness of being in the favour of God . . . is the common privilege of Christians fearing God and working righteousness"? Is the association of "a consciousness of being in the favour of God" with "fearing God and working righteousness" sufficient reason to conclude that Wesley is including those who have the faith of a servant to be among those who have a consciousness of the favor of God? This possibility seems to gain support in the fact that the 1745 Conference regarded Cornelius—one who feared God and worked righteousness—to be in the favor of God even before he believed on Christ explicitly, seeing that his prayers and alms had come up as a memorial before God.[88]

However, the argument that those having the faith of a servant enjoy "a consciousness of being in the favour of God" does *not* find support in the distinctions between the faith of a servant and the faith of a son drawn by Wesley in his sermon, "On the Discoveries of Faith." Indeed, such a consciousness was most definitely *not* a property of that faith

---

adaptation of the text is significant and underscores the fact that the focus at this point in the sermon is the matter of *sonship*.

87. Wesley, *Letters*, 5:358.

88. *Minutes*, 1745 (Bennet), np. See Q. 7 of the minute record for Friday, August 2, 1745.

which typifies the faith of servant. As Wesley observed in that sermon, those having the faith of a servant keenly feel the *absence* of God's favor and, in fact, fear the wrath of God and feel "altogether helpless" in the face of that wrath, convinced as they are that they are "so fast in prison that they cannot get forth."[89]

Wesley did affirm that those having the faith of a servant possessed "a species of faith."[90] And yet, such faith was evidence *not* of their enjoyment of a consciousness of being in the favor of God; rather, such faith was identified as the basis from which they are able to fear God and work righteousness *despite* lacking a consciousness of being in the favor of God. Thus, the textual evidence (and this, significantly, from Wesley's late sermon on the metaphor) suggests that Wesley employed the phrase "fearing God and working righteousness" in his response to Rutherford as descriptive of the standard of conduct typical of *all* who have a proper Christian faith. And, in clarifying to Rutherford his doctrine of assurance, it would not be uncharacteristic for Wesley to have applied the term "Christian" in order to distinguish such consciousness of being in the favor of God as "the common" existential "privilege" "of *Christians*" "fearing God and working righteousness" as opposed to those under other dispensations.[91]

In reality, it appears that Wesley understood divine favor in both a narrow sense and in a broad sense. This distinction is evident and, in fact, comes to light in his two 1788 sermons that deal specifically with the metaphor: "On Faith" and "On the Discoveries of Faith."[92][93] In its broad sense, the divine favor is the result of a merciful *suspension* of "the divine rule" rather than the actual *recovery* of favor (the narrow, "proper" sense).[94] Although Wesley affirmed the salvific sufficiency of each dispensation of the covenant of grace—and, remaining in step with the view of covenant theology in general, asserted that Abel and Abraham enjoyed the actual recovery of the favor and image of God—the fact that the historical moment of the gospel dispensation had dawned upon the world established a new criterion with respect to such recovery: explicit

---

89. Wesley, "On the Discoveries of Faith," *Works* (BE) §12–13, 4:34–35.

90. Ibid., §12, 4:35.

91. Wesley, *Letters*, 5:337. Emphasis mine.

92. See Wesley's commentary on Acts 10:4. Wesley, *ENNT*, 384.

93. The affirmations of these two sermons with respect to the metaphor will be evaluated in the following chapter.

94. See "The Righteousness of Faith," *Works* (BE) §I.11; II.9; III, 1:208–9, 213–19.

belief *in Christ*.⁹⁵ Thus, a feature of the story of Cornelius that was of particular importance to the 1745 Conference was that Cornelius belonged to those who had *not* yet heard the gospel. Accordingly, the question regarding favor largely turned on this distinction.⁹⁶ The same is true with respect to the infamous *Minutes* of the 1770 Conference.⁹⁷

To be sure, Wesley made allowance for those without benefit of the proclamation of the gospel, choosing to commend them to the mercies of God rather than to condemn them out of hand. Yet, the story of Cornelius is not a story aimed at establishing the adequacy of "Jewish faith." Rather, the primary emphasis of the biblical account of Cornelius was the demonstration of the divine acceptance of the Gentiles on the basis of *faith in Christ* rather than on the basis of racial privilege and the moral (and spiritual) advantage accruing to "Jewish faith."⁹⁸ The gospel dispensation (as the perfection of the covenant of grace) called for all to move *beyond* that faith which typified the Jewish dispensation.

This emphasis of the passage, that God is "not a respecter of persons" was not lost on Wesley.⁹⁹ Nevertheless, rather than argue Cornelius' being in the favor of God in the narrow sense of the word, he took pains to carefully distinguish the god-fearing Cornelius from those who have a proper Christian faith, noting that Cornelius "had not then faith in Christ" though he was "in some measure accepted."¹⁰⁰ This is evident, too, in Wesley's commentary on Peter's message to Cornelius and his household. Wesley gave special attention to highlighting belief in Christ ("whoever believeth *in him*") and making special note that remission of sins came by way of such *belief* "though he [i.e., whoever believes] had not before either feared God, or worked righteousness."¹⁰¹ Likewise,

---

95. Wesley, *ENNT*, 383–84.

96. See *Minutes*, 1745 (Bennet) Q. 9, np.

97. See *Minutes*, (WMC, 1770), Q. 1–2, 59. Note: Question numbering represents the listing of questions under the section of the minute record in response to "Review the whole affair." As noted previously, though Wesley does indeed associate the descriptor "fearing God and working righteousness" with the faith of a servant, he never describes Cornelius himself as one having the faith of a servant, despite multiple opportunities to do so.

98. See his commentary on Acts 10:36. Wesley, *ENNT*, 386.

99. Ibid.

100. Acts 10:4 and 10:35, and commentary. Ibid., 384, 386. Wesley stipulated that Cornelius was "in the favour of God" and accepted "through *Christ*," the lamb slain from the foundation of the world, "though he knew him not."

101. Acts 10:43 and commentary. Ibid., 387. Emphasis mine. See the prior discussion of the minute record of the 1770 Conference.

despite its emphasis on good works, the priority of faith is not set aside by the declarations of the 1770 Conference. As Wesley confirmed in a letter to Mrs. Bennis on March 1, 1774:

> None of us talk of being accepted for our works: That is the Calvinist slander. But we all maintain, we are not saved without works; that works are a condition (though not the meritorious cause) of final salvation. It is by faith in the righteousness and blood of Christ that we are enabled to do all good works; and it is for the sake of these that all who fear God and work righteousness are accepted of Him.[102]

A consciousness of being in the favor of God is, without doubt, the existential compliment to one who has gone on from the faith of a servant to the faith of a son. Wesley clearly associates the developmental imagery of the First Epistle of John *not* with the one having the faith of a servant, but with the one having the faith of a son. This is plainly evident not only in his 1788 sermon, "On the Discoveries of Faith," but also in several other of his sermons[103] and in his correspondence. When Wesley adapted Bengel's commentary on 1 John 4:18—"Men's condition is varied: without fear and love; with fear without love; with fear and love; without fear with love"[104]—he was much more specific: "A natural man has neither fear, nor love; one that is awakened, fear without love; a babe in *Christ*, love and fear; a father in *Christ*, love without fear."[105]

In a letter to Mary Bosanquet on January 2, 1770, Wesley stipulated that the degrees of assurance correlated with the advancement of faith: "The moment any are justified, they are babes in Christ, little children. When they have the *abiding* witness of pardon, they are young men."[106] Writing to Joseph Benson on March 16, 1771, Wesley outlined the relationship as follows: "A *babe* in Christ (of whom I know thousands) has the witness *sometimes*. A young man (in St. John's sense) has it continually. I believe one that is *perfected in love*, or *filled with the Holy Ghost*, may be properly termed a *father*. This we must press both babes and young men to aspire after—yea, to expect."[107]

---

102. Wesley, *Letters*, 6:76–77. The phrase in the last line, "it is for the sake of these" is a reference not to good works but to "the righteousness and blood of Christ."

103. Wesley, *Works* (BE) §15, 4:36–37. See also "The First-Fruits of the Spirit," *Works* (BE) §II.5, 1:239; "On Sin in Believers," *Works* (BE) §IV.12, 1:331–32;

104. Bengel, *Gnomon*, 2:802–3.

105. Wesley, *ENNT*, 794–95.

106. Wesley, *Letters*, 5:175. Emphasis mine.

107. Wesley, *Letters*, 5:229.

In his March 22, 1775 letter to John Fletcher, Wesley confirms this understanding as part of his expressing a point at which his conception differs from that of Fletcher's:

> It seems our views of Christian Perfection are a little different, though not opposite. It is certain every babe in Christ has received the Holy Spirit, and the Spirit witnesses with his spirit that he is a child of God. But he has not obtained Christian perfection. Perhaps you have not considered St. John's threefold distinction of Christian believers: little children, young men, and fathers. All of these had received the Holy Ghost; but only the fathers were perfected in love.[108]

This very point is underscored in his sermon "On Patience," written in 1783 and published in the *Arminian Magazine* in 1784. Here Wesley makes the further point that the fear of the babe in Christ is not the servile fear of one having the faith of a servant but is the fear of not enduring to the end.[109]

Finally, it is important to resist assuming a direct correlation between "young men" and "fathers," on the one hand, and, on the other, "adult" sons as spoken of by Wesley in his commentary on Galatians 4:1–6. Such a correlation has led some to equate the descriptor "babe" with the one having the faith of a servant and the "young men" and "fathers" as having the faith of a son.[110] However, when Wesley speaks of "adult" sons in the Galatians passage, he is contrasting states of *privilege* (child-heir as servant vs. adult-heir as son) rather than states of *maturity* or degrees of assurance. As he indicates at the outset of his commentary on the passage, this contrast of privilege reflects the profound difference between the legal and the Christian dispensation—between those under the legal dispensation who are altogether *denied* the rights and privileges of sons (and, thus, are servants), and those under the Christian dispensation who are *granted* such rights and privileges in full (that is, are sons). It is not, essentially, a question of maturity. In Wesley's view, no one, after all, simply matures into sonship any more than the legal dispensation can be said to have simply matured into the Christian dispensation. The text itself is quite clear on this very point: the child-

---

108. Ibid., 6:146.
109. Wesley, *Works* (BE) §10, 3:175.
110. Heitzenrater appears to arrive at this conclusion. Heitzenrater, *Mirror and Memory*, 148. Cubie goes so far as to say that "a servant may cry, 'Abba, Father!'," but one would be hard-pressed to find any such assertion by Wesley. Cubie, "Placing Aldersgate in John Wesley's Order of Salvation," 47.

heir "is under tutors and stewards" not until some point of maturity is reached but "till the time appointed by the father."[111] The demarcating event was nothing *other* than and nothing *less* than the revelation of the Son—sent by the Father "in the fulness of the time."[112] The parallelism of this demarcating event in the history of God's saving deeds and in the lives of the awakened is central to Wesley's understanding and use of the servant-son metaphor.

Foundational to Wesley's soteriology is his understanding of the divinely-ordered progression throughout the history of God's redemptive activity. This progression—the blessings of which, in Wesley's adaptation, are extended to *all* of mankind—is marked not merely by key developments plotted on a chronological timeline, but by the soteriological progression of the various dispensations of the covenant of grace from lesser to greater. The idea of such a progression is not peculiar to Wesley, and neither is his view that the covenant of grace is salvifically sufficient within each of its several dispensations. However, he moves beyond the norms of covenant theology in envisioning the salvific sufficiency of each dispensation as concurrent (though not equivalent, given that there really is a progression from lesser to greater) with the present historical "moment" of the gospel dispensation. This allows Wesley to think of the *totality* of the covenant of grace as soteriologically active even in the present time. Thus, though there is only one dispensation (the present gospel dispensation) that is "live" in a strict *historical* sense, past dispensations are not mere relics of God's redemptive activity; rather, they, too, like the gospel dispensation, are *soteriologically* and *existentially* "live," as evidenced in the spiritual journeys of those on the way of salvation.

With respect to the gospel or Christian dispensation, Wesley (in concert with covenant theology in general) understands it to be the salvific perfection of the covenant of grace. This perfection is centered upon the revelation of Christ in human history, as declared by the Apostle Paul in Galatians 4:4 ("God sent forth his son . . .") and inaugurated by the outpouring of the Holy Spirit at Pentecost. However, the witnessing work of the Spirit is active not only in the *historical* moment of the present dispensation but also in awakening and stewarding sin-deadened human beings to the *soteriological* and *existential* realities of the covenant of grace. The witnessing work of the Spirit is first as the spirit of bondage, and then as the spirit of adoption. The former involves

---

111. See Gal 4:2. Wesley, *ENNT*, 604.
112. See Gal 4:4. Ibid.

the excruciating experience of coming to know the darkness of our own hearts—evidence of a faith which, for the moment, can reach no further than the legal (Mosaic) dispensation; the latter involves the revelation of Christ, the conferment of sonship, and the consciousness of God's favor experienced in the Spirit's giving witness to that sonship—all of which are outcomes of a faith brought current with the provisions of the gospel dispensation.

Wesley's soteriology is profoundly shaped by his covenant theology and the servant-son metaphor testifies to this fact. Indeed, the metaphor serves as a strategic articulation of his covenant theology and its application to the experience of those on the way of salvation. It is this pastoral application that is the primary agenda of the servant-son metaphor.

CHAPTER 9

"From Faith to Faith"

John Wesley's Pastoral Application of Covenant Theology

WHEN WESLEY SPOKE OF "the whole process of a man reasoning, groaning, striving, and escaping from the legal to the evangelical state,"[1] he was bearing witness that there is "a definite teleology to divine grace."[2] The centerpiece of this testimony was that the revelation of Christ was (and is) the salvation-historical event that demarcates the legal from the evangelical (gospel, Christian) dispensation of the covenant of grace. This was more than a theological affirmation, for even as the revelation of Christ in the course of the history of God's saving deeds ushered all of humanity into the Christian dispensation (historically speaking), so also the revelation of Christ in the course of one's spiritual history ushers that individual into the soteriological privileges and existential benedictions of the Christian dispensation.

This parallelism, and the idea of progression associated with it, is of fundamental importance in Wesley's theological thought. Even as all of God's saving deeds before the revelation of Christ pointed *to* Christ and are finally and fully realized *in* Christ, so also do all God's saving initiatives in each person's life point *to* and intend progress toward the actual revelation of Christ within. The momentum is always forward, gravitating toward the Christian dispensation and the fullest privileges available thereunder.[3] For Wesley, the servant-son metaphor captures the essence of this forward momentum not simply in its capacity to chronicle critical dynamics of participating in the divine reconciling

---

1. Wesley, *ENNT*, 482.
2. Hindmarsh, *The Evangelical Conversion Narrative*, 37.
3. This is not to suggest that this momentum is irresistible, but only that the Divine intention is steadfast and predictable in the lives of the responsive.

initiative, but particularly in its ability to define the trajectory of that participation. The servant-son metaphor accomplished *this* through its capacity to enunciate the pre-eminence of sonship. Accordingly, Wesley consistently employs the metaphor to *emphasize* the contrast between servant and son rather than to *minimize* the distinction.

It is important, then, to grasp Wesley's unshakable regard for and understanding of the standard of sonship. At the same time, and as a consequence of his conviction of the pre-eminence of sonship, attention must be given to his understanding of the spiritual status of one having the faith of a servant. On this point, Wesley's defense of the faith of a servant (particularly in his later sermons on the matter) is of particular importance. And finally, some soteriological affirmations abiding at the core of Wesley's theological thought warrant consideration in light of the pastoral aims and achievements of the metaphor. But first, it is paramount to consider more fully the purview of the metaphor in its relation to Wesley's vision of the *via salutis* as this is a crucial element in gaining a proper understanding of the place of covenant theology in his theological thought.

The Purview of the Metaphor in Wesley's Theological Thought

As noted above, in Wesley's view the revelation of Christ in the history of God's saving deeds is replicated in the lives of those on the way of salvation, signaling their escape "from the legal to the evangelical state." This outcome was not the result of the individual having successfully strung together a series of co-operant incidents but was, rather, "pneumatologically determined," to use Robert Del Colle's description of the schema of "the Wesleyan gospel."[4] The "Pentecost of Sinai" and the "Pentecost of Jerusalem"[5] represented for Wesley the respective soteriological realities accompanying the work of the Spirit; first, as the spirit of bondage and fear, and then, consequent with the revelation of Christ, as the spirit of adoption. It is significant that when Wesley makes use of the

---

4. Del Colle, "John Wesley's Doctrine of Grace," 175. Maddox asserts, "But if one continued to respond to God in this beginning sense, it would develop into the confident faith of a 'son,'" Maddox, *Responsible Grace*, 127. The emphasis of both is on the initiative of the Holy Spirit. Maddox's assertion, however, minimizes the distinction between servant and son, framing it as merely a matter of the levels of confidence before God. This is consistent with Maddox's view that Wesley's distinction between servant and son belongs primarily to his doctrine of assurance.

5. Wesley, *ENNT*, 351.

metaphor he consistently does so specifically in relation to persons who are situated *soteriologically* within either the Jewish dispensation or the Christian dispensation. In both of the late sermons in which he makes extensive use of the metaphor, Wesley describes those having the faith of a servant in terms of attributes of the Jewish or legal dispensation.[6]

This fact raises the question of what might properly be inferred from the association of the descriptor—"fearing God and working righteousness"—both with the metaphor and, in Acts 10, with the person of Cornelius as representative of a heathen living to the level of light given. As previously discussed, "fearing God and workinat righteousness" is a phrase used with a variety of applications. And certainly, although the phrase is resident to the Cornelius story, it has a utility value for Wesley that transcends the story. Consequently, while every explicit appearance of the metaphor does, implicitly or explicitly, actuate the descriptor ("fearing God and working righteousness"), the appearance of the descriptor does not necessarily actuate the metaphor. Neither does Wesley's use of scripture require that the appearance of this descriptor constitute a re-presentation of the Cornelius story at *all* much less every theological element of the story.

Further, it does not appear that Wesley is seeking to uphold Cornelius as the epitome of one having the faith of a servant. Interestingly, in his *Explanatory Notes* he makes no comment at all on the biblical description of Cornelius as a man "fearing God with all his house" and as "a just man, and fearing God."[7] It might also be observed that there is nothing in the story itself or in other references by Wesley that identify Cornelius' experience in terms that typify those whom Wesley most clearly described as having the faith of a servant (specifically, those terms reminiscent of Romans 7 which Wesley understood to be typically descriptive of those who were under the legal dispensation *soteriologically*). In fact, though Wesley references aspects of the account of the Gentile Pentecost in relation to the servant-son metaphor, he explicitly presents Cornelius as exemplary of the responsive heathen and passes up multiple opportunities to present Cornelius as representative of one who is under the Jewish dispensation. For Wesley, Cornelius' relationship with the Jewish community and his having adopted Jewish prac-

---

6. See Wesley, "On the Discoveries of Faith," *Works* (BE) §12–15, 4:34–35. In "On Faith," Wesley describes the one who has the faith of a servant in terms of the *absence* of those attributes of the Christian or gospel dispensation. See Wesley, *Works* (BE) §I.12, 3:497–98.

7. See Acts 10:2, 22. Wesley, *ENNT*, 383, 385.

tices (prayer and the giving of alms) do not equate with his being under the legal dispensation, *soteriologically* or *existentially*, though it certainly did illustrate a heathen living according to the light received.[8] Although Wesley was not hesitant to extend certain theological affirmations to the heathen like Cornelius[9] or to those having "only the faith of a servant,"[10] he restricted his use of the servant-son metaphor to those who were, *soteriologically*, clearly under the Jewish dispensation or under the Christian dispensation.

Thus, those in whose behalf Wesley employs the metaphor are persons who have no recourse to "the footing of honest heathens"[11] (i.e., invincible ignorance) upon which they might be granted an exceptional extension of divine mercy given the limited amount of light available to them. They have, after all, come under the sound of the gospel. And, those whom Wesley deems to have the faith of a servant are persons who are experiencing the excruciating and escalating intensity of awakening to the realities of their spiritual condition. In Wesley's view, these persons have received that measure of faith by virtue of which they are now experiencing the law as the schoolmaster leading them to Christ (Gal 3:24). That is, they are positioned within the bounds of the legal dispensation of the covenant of grace and are, at this point, ones who have "only the faith of a servant, and not the faith of a son."[12]

Without doubt, those in such a state would not yet enjoy assurance. However, Wesley's concern in employing the metaphor was not to creatively label those who were or were not in the enjoyment of assurance. Indeed, the *absence* of direct, explicit discussion of assurance in those contexts where Wesley employs the metaphor is conspicuous. And equally conspicuous is the fact that he does not invoke the metaphor in those contexts where he addresses challenges to his doctrine of assurance.[13] His concern was to identify for them the *soteriological basis*

---

8. The view that Cornelius is representative of the heathen had its own long interpretive history. See, for example, the explanation of the views of the Remonstrants in *The Athenian Gazette* (February 16, 1695), np.

9. While Wesley asserted that Cornelius was "in a *Christian* sense . . . an unbeliever," he nevertheless rejected the idea that Cornelius' good works were "an abomination before God" and affirmed him as a model for "every one who seeks faith in *Christ*." Wesley, *ENNT*, 383–84.

10. See the discussion below on Wesley's understanding of acceptance with God.

11. For this description see "On the Trinity," *Works* (BE) §18, 2:385–86.

12. Wesley, "On the Discoveries of Faith," *Works* (BE) §13, 4:35.

13. When Wesley spoke of his understanding of assurance, he did so in a straightforward manner as may be seen in his response to two of his adversaries, Richard Tompson

for the presence or absence of assurance. That is, when speaking of those who have "only the faith of a servant," Wesley was calling attention to a state of affairs *soteriologically* that, in light of the advance of the covenant of grace to the perfection of the gospel dispensation, fell short of the over-arching divine intention and promise.

His concern was to move his hearers "from faith to faith."[14] When he used this phrase in conjunction with the metaphor he was specifically focusing his attention on those having the faith of a *servant*. Strictly speaking, the *formal* purview of the metaphor encompassed both those who, having been awakened, were desirous of reconciled relationship with God (i.e., those having the faith of a servant) *and* those who had received the spirit of adoption (i.e., those having the faith of a son), though they may yet be babes in Christ plagued with doubts and fears. However, aside from the sermons "On Faith" and "On the Discoveries of Faith" where both metaphors (servant and son) are drawn out, the emphasis most often falls upon the "faith of a servant." This consistent focus on those who are situated soteriologically within the legal dispensation—and experiencing the realities of being so situated—might be best described as the *operative purview* of the metaphor.

The advance "from faith to faith," accompanied as it was by a clear (though perhaps initially intermittent) sense of pardon, was absolutely essential in Wesley's view since "inward and outward holiness flow from a consciousness of the favour of God."[15] Thus, at the heart of the servant-son metaphor stood a conviction that was fundamental to his theological thought: *the pre-eminence of sonship*.

The Standard of Sonship: "Till Christ is Revealed in You"

The strength of Wesley's conviction regarding the pre-eminence of sonship is recognized in his maintaining sonship as the soteriological baseline of the gospel dispensation and as that to which all persons are not only invited but called. Rather than indicating a new development in his theological thought, Wesley's more frequent use of the metaphor in his mature years suggests he found the servant-son metaphor to be *increasingly* helpful as a way of highlighting the divine provisions of the gospel

---

and Thomas Rutherford. See respectively, Wesley, *Works* (BE), 26:569, 575; Wesley, *Letters*, 5:337.

14. Wesley, "On the Discoveries of Faith," *Works* (BE) §14, 35.
15. Wesley, *Letters*, 7:101–2.

dispensation. And, as evidenced in his continued firm insistence on the revelation of Christ in the heart, the influence of his covenant theology certainly did not dissipate in his later years.

In a letter to James Creighton written at Enniskillen on May 24, 1773 (notably, the thirty-fifth anniversary of Wesley's Aldersgate experience), Wesley very briefly answered the questions Creighton had posed to him. To the ninth question, he responded, "Revelation is complete: yet we cannot be saved unless Christ be *revealed* in our hearts."[16] In a letter written four years later on August 29, 1777 to Alexander Knox, Wesley emphasized this important point and drew a clear connection between the revelation of Christ and the witnessing work of the Spirit as the spirit of adoption, an indication that the two were more theologically than experimentally distinct: "You are not yet a son, but you are a servant; and you are waiting for the Spirit of adoption, which will cry in your heart, 'Abba, Father.' . . . you have cause to bless God for what you have, and to wait patiently till He gives the rest by revealing His Son in your heart."[17]

Wesley wrote along similar lines to Thomas Davenport just over four years later on December 2, 1781: "You have now *received the spirit of bondage*. Is it not the forerunner of the Spirit of adoption? He is not afar off. Look up! And expect Him to cry in your heart, Abba, Father!"[18] And in his 1788 sermon, "On the Discoveries of Faith," Wesley addressed those in Davenport's situation, urging each person "not to rest till he attains the adoption of sons; till he obeys out of love, which is the privilege of all the *children* of God." He assured them that the person who passes "from the faith of a *servant* to the faith of a *son*; from the spirit of bondage unto fear, to the spirit of childlike love . . . will then have 'Christ revealed in his heart' enabling him to testify, 'The life that I now live in the flesh I live by faith in the Son of God, who loved *me*, and gave himself for *me*'—the proper voice of a child of God."[19]

It is clear that Wesley understood the revelation of Christ in the heart to be the incontrovertible evidence of escape from the legal to the evangelical state, and that the witness of the Spirit as the spirit of adoption was consequent with that revelation. Until the revelation of Christ in the heart, being under the Jewish (legal) dispensation was characterized by "reasoning, groaning, [and] striving." This appears to be true of

---

16. Ibid., 6:38.
17. Wesley, *Letters*, 6:272–73.
18. Ibid. 7:95.
19. Wesley, *Works* (BE) §13–14, 4:35–36.

persons who, like Davenport, seem to have advanced to the brink of escape.[20] Others may not have felt themselves to be on the very threshold of escape but were, nonetheless, in the throes of the agony described in Romans 7. This state of affairs is exemplified in the letter previously referenced that Wesley received in 1779 from one of his preachers in Ireland: "When I told you my state in Sligo, you observed, it was that of a servant, and not of a son. It is no better with me since. I feel my bondage great through unbelief, and such deadness of soul that I cannot mourn with those that mourn, nor rejoice with those that rejoice."[21]

The process of coming into the privileges of the evangelical dispensation is commemorated in the context of communal worship. The hymnody of the Wesleys identifies, instructs, and encourages those awaiting the revelation of Christ in the heart and the accompanying witness of the Spirit. One striking example is Hymn XXV appropriately titled, "Groaning for the Spirit of Adoption." The groaning is felt in questions raised, promises recollected, and pleas lifted. And the longing for sonship appears unmistakably from the opening stanza of the hymn:

> Father, if Thou my Father art,
> Send forth the Spirit of Thy Son,
> Breathe Him into my panting heart,
> And make me know as I am known:
> Make me Thy conscious child, that I
> May, Father, Abba, Father, cry.[22]

Though Wesley remained steadfast in his conviction that a clear sense of pardon was not a *condition* of pardon, he continued to uphold it as a signal attribute of "the proper Christian faith,"[23] and to affirm that "a clear sense of God's pardoning love" was the means by which "mourners . . . are comforted."[24] In a letter to his niece on July 17, 1781, Sarah

---

20. Recall that Wesley distinguished between "mourners convinced of sin" and "mourners brought to the birth." Wesley, *A Collection of Hymns*, np.

21. "Letter CCCCLXXXVII From Mr. A. B. to the Rev. J. Wesley," *AM* (March, 1789), 162.

22. Wesley, *Hymns and Spiritual Songs*, 37–38.

23. Wesley responded to Richard Tompson, "I agree with you that justifying faith cannot be a conviction that I am justified. . . . But still I believe, the proper Christian faith which purifies the heart implies such a conviction." Wesley, *Works* (BE), 26:575.

24. These phrases appear in Ann Bolton's reports to John Wesley on the progress of the Society at Witney, Oxfordshire. See *AM* (May 1785), 277 and *AM* (March 1786), 173.

Wesley, Wesley clearly asserts that the favor of God cannot be attained "till we have the Spirit of adoption."[25]

The person having the faith of a servant—and who thus lives under the spirit of bondage—is discomfited, at times even tormented, by the prospect of *not* being in the favor of God. Nonetheless, Wesley was not inclined to alleviate such discomfort by substituting something less than sonship. For Wesley, this is a matter which must be settled in each person's life, and finally *is* settled only by the revelation of Christ in the heart and the witness of the Spirit as the spirit of adoption. While always the encourager to those feeling some despair with regard to their spiritual state, Wesley's steadfastness on this point is confirmed in his letter to Mary Cooke on October 30, 1785: "I blame no one for not believing he is in the favour of God till he is in a manner constrained to believe it."[26]

This affirmation is consistent with Wesley's response to James Morgan on this very subject seventeen years earlier. Morgan had created a stir at the Conference in the summer of 1768 when he had reportedly argued, "'All penitents are in the favour of God,' or 'All who mourn after God are in the favour of God.'" Wesley responded in a letter to Morgan on September 3, 1768, that many at the Conference felt this view was "unscriptural and unsafe" and contrary to what had always been taught.[27] Wesley strongly concurred with that critique. In his response he underscored the relationship of the favor of God with the conjunction of the revelation of Christ and the work of the Spirit as the spirit of adoption, evidence of the strength with which he held these convictions:

> That this [i.e., that all who mourn are in the favour of God] is contrary to what we have always taught is certain, as all our hymns as well as other writings testify. . . . We have always taught that a penitent mourned or was pained on this very account, because he felt he was "not in the favour of God," having a sense of guilt upon his conscience and a sense of the divine displeasure at the same time. Hence we supposed the language of his heart was, "Lost and undone for aid I cry." And we believed he was really lost and undone till God did
>
> *Peace, righteousness, and joy impart,*
> *And speak forgiveness to his heart.*

---

25. Wesley, *Letters*, 7:74–75.
26. Ibid., 7:298.
27. Ibid., 5:103–5.

> I still apprehend this to be scriptural doctrine, confirmed not by a few detached texts, but by the whole tenor of Scripture, and more particularly by the Epistle to the Romans. But if so, the contrary to it must be unsafe, for the general reason, because it is unscriptural. To which one might add this particular reason,— it naturally tends to lull mourners to sleep; to make them cry, "Peace, peace," to their souls, "when there is no peace." It directly tends to damp and still their convictions, and to encourage them to sit down contented before Christ is revealed to them and before the Spirit witnesses with their spirits that they are the children of God.[28]

Wesley anticipated the pastoral objection that such a view offered no relief to those who groaned for the revelation of Christ and the confirming witness of the Spirit. Intent on honoring rather than subverting the work of the Spirit, Wesley responded: "But it may be asked, 'Will not this discourage mourners?' Yes, it will discourage them from stopping where they are; it will discourage them from resting before they have the witness in themselves, before Christ is revealed in them. But it will encourage them to seek Him in the gospel way—to ask till they receive pardon and peace."[29]

For Wesley, the salvific perfection of the Christian dispensation was the standard for what is to be anticipated and experienced in the life of the individual believer. This firm conviction certainly played itself out in Wesley's correspondence. This is of particular significance because Wesley explicitly related the metaphor to the affirmations expressed in his letter to James Morgan. At this point, a pair of case studies is helpful: first, the story of one of Wesley's most beloved correspondents, Ann Bolton, of Witney, Oxfordshire; and second, his correspondence with Alexander Knox.

The Case of Ann Bolton

As noted previously, Wesley had written to Ann Bolton as early as April 7, 1768, describing her spiritual condition in terms of the metaphor: "He has already given you the faith of a servant. You want only the faith of a child." He continues with a word of encouragement:

---

28. Ibid. Bracketed insert mine.
29. Ibid.

> And is it not nigh? What is it you feel *now*? That spark just kindling in your heart which enables you to say:
>
> *Lord, I am Thine by sacred ties,*
> *Thy child, Thy servant bought with blood!*
>
> Look up, my sister, my friend! Jesus is there! He is ever now interceding for *you*! Doubt not of it! Doubt not His love! Forget yourself, a poor, vile, worthless sinner. But look unto Jesus! See the Friend of Sinners! *Your* Friend; your ready and strong Saviour![30]

It is helpful to see these admonitions against the backdrop of Bolton's own account of her spiritual journey. In his study of Ann Bolton, Banks equates her conversion with the occasion of her joining the Methodist Society in 1763. However, rather than describing conversion, Bolton indicates that it was her awakening to her spiritual need that occasioned her joining the Society. She had, she wrote, until recently "remained ignorant of [her]self and of [her] want of a redeemer," but now found herself to be in a new, but disconcerting spiritual state: "the true light began to shine upon my dark soul, I felt with all my former doings I was not safe, I was but a whited wall[, a] white painted sepulchre which might appear beautifull without, but [was] full of uncleanness . . . my soul longed for his salvation & panted for him as the hart for the water Brook."[31]

This is clearly the language of one under the legal dispensation, of one in bondage and fear who has embarked on "the whole process . . . of reasoning, groaning, and striving."[32] During this time she described her spiritual battle as intensifying "for that great adversary the devil, finding he was likely to lose me, strove much to prevent it."[33] In January 1767, she records that she was "stired [sic] up to cry to the Lord that he would remove sin the sting of death" but that, though "incouraged [sic] to trust in the Lord in reading the 27 Psalm, . . . unbelief still kept me from casting my soul upon him for life and salvation."[34]

---

30. Ibid., 5:86.

31. See Ann Bolton's "Some Memorandums of the Lord's Dealings with My Soul" in Banks, *Nancy Nancy*, 11–13. This self-assessment is corroborated by her journal entry on her twenty-sixth birthday, June 3, 1769. *Ann Bolton Manuscript Journal*, John Banks Research Collection, Item 16 (MARC).

32. Wesley, *ENNT*, 482.

33. Bolton, "Some Memorandums of the Lord's Dealings with My Soul" in Banks, *Nancy Nancy*, 11–13.

34. *Ann Bolton Manuscript Journal*, Item 16 (MARC). Bracketed inserts mine.

The first extant letter from Wesley (quoted above) in which he applies the metaphor to Bolton was written the following year (1768). He alludes to the metaphor again two years later in a letter dated August 12, 1770:

> My Dear Sister,—"He that feareth God," says the Apostle, "and worketh righteousness," though but in a low degree, is accepted of Him; more especially when such an one trusts not in his own righteousness but in the atoning blood. I cannot doubt at all but this is your case; though you have not that joy in the Holy Ghost to which you are called, because your faith is weak and only as a grain of mustard seed.[35]

Clearly Wesley identifies her as one having been "brought to the birth." His assessment comes to light all the more clearly against the backdrop of Bolton's own journal entries that same summer:

> Augst 2d. . . . *I cannot come to him in that assurance of Faith as to call him my Reconciled Father* . . .
>
> Friday 3d. . . . I could appeal to God that I desired nothing so much as to forsake every evil way and as he had given me this desire I was encouraged to expect the accomplishment of his promise and was led to expect it thro Jesus alone . . . I do see in order to increase we must hold fast that degree of confidence we have [received]. For want of this I afterward yeilded [*sic*] to a reasoning spirit. O Lord do thou give me Faith and Faith's increase.
>
> Wend [*sic*] 8. . . . O Jesus shed abroad thy Love in my heart, that I may love and obey Thee.[36]

The following month the chronicle of Bolton's longing and turmoil continues. The opening sentence for Sunday, September 2, is particularly revealing regarding her own understanding of her spiritual state: "This morning it was good for me to wait upon God, especially in singing the Hymn, which was 'Father of Light[s] from whom proceeds'. It spoke the language of my heart."[37] Subtitled "A Prayer for one convinced of Sin," the lyrics of the hymn read,

> Since by thy Light myself I see
> Naked, and poor, and void of thee,

---

35. Wesley, *Letters*, 5:197.

36. *Ann Bolton Manuscript Journal*, Item 16. Emphasis is Bolton's; bracketed inserts mine.

37. *Ann Bolton Manuscript Journal*, Item 19 Bracketed inserts mine.

> Thine Eyes must all my Thoughts survey,
> Preventing what my Lips would say;
> Thou seest my Wants, for Help they call,
> And ere I speak, Thou know'st them all.
>
> . . .
>
> Ah, give me, Lord, myself to feel,
> My total Misery reveal;
> Ah, give me, Lord, (I still would say),
> A Heart to mourn, a Heart to pray;
> My Business this, my total Care,
> My Life, my every Breath be Prayer![38]

The journal entries of September 1770 continue with further insight to her self-assessment:

> Sund 2d. . . . At the Lord's supper my soul long'd to feed on him in my heart by Faith. I cou'd in some degree behold his dying Love but still had not the witness of the spirit in my soul to testify I was his child.
>
> Monday 10. . . . I feel the need of the sprinkleing of the Blood of Jesus, to cleanse from the guilt, power, and being of sin, but still I do not venture upon his merits alone so as to rejoice in the Liberty of his Children.
>
> Friday 28. I awoke this morning oppress'd with guilt. . . . He incouraged [me] to come unto him with these words "Being justified freely by his grace." He shewed me I cou'd in no wise clear myself or get any relief, but by comeing unto him and humbly confess my sin, and lay hold on his merits for pardon and power to live to his glory in thought and word.[39]

Bolton apparently wrote again to Wesley describing her spiritual state, as evidenced by Wesley's response dated from London on November 16, 1770: "I am glad you are still waiting for the kingdom of God: although as yet you are rather in the state of a servant than of a child. But it is a blessed thing to be even a servant of God! You shall never have cause to be ashamed of His service."[40] As noted, this letter comes to Ann Bolton with essentially the same message it bore two and a half years earlier: she has the faith of a servant, but not that of a child. Certainly, it

---

38. John Wesley, "Hymn II," *Hymns and Spiritual Songs* (1753), 2–3. The hymn clearly pictures the painful awareness of one under the spirit of bondage.

39. *Ann Bolton Manuscript Journal*, Item 19.

40. Wesley, *Letters*, 5:207.

was no question of desire or even of readiness on her part. Nonetheless, it does appear to be a question of *sonship*—of whether Christ has been revealed and whether there has been the witness of the spirit of adoption.

Sometime after mid-October[41] and perhaps after having received the November letter from Wesley, Ann Bolton apparently came to have the faith of a child. This period of time corresponds with the chronology identified in a letter from Bolton to Wesley dated at Witney on October 30, 1778, where she reminisces concerning her experiences described in the journal entries cited above: "After a long delay, I once more take up my pen to acquaint you with the Lord's gracious dealings with me. It is now near eight years since my soul experienced that depth of distress, and afterward that joy and consolation inexpressible."[42] Wesley's own assessment of Bolton's spiritual state changed from this point forward and extant correspondence indicates no further appropriation of the metaphor in her regard. Instead, his letters and Bolton's own journal entries take up the matter of going on to perfection.[43]

The Case of Alexander Knox

The case of Alexander Knox, another of Wesley's correspondents, is similar in its application of the metaphor. One of the earlier letters addressing Knox's spiritual state is that of May 28, 1776 where Wesley suggests that the health complications experienced by Knox might possibly be "the ministry of angels, to balance the natural petulance of youth" and to keep him "steady in the pursuit of that better part" which can never be taken from him.[44] In a letter the following spring, Wesley observes, "It is a blessing that He has given you that fear which is the beginning of wisdom; and it is a pledge of greater things to come. How soon? Perhaps today . . ."[45] On August 29, 1777, Wesley employs the metaphor to aid Knox in understanding his situation spiritually:

41. The John Banks Research Collection does not include photocopies of Ann Bolton's manuscript journal from about mid-October, 1770 to May of the following year. Originals remain in possession of the Bolton family.

42. Wesley, "Letter CCCCLXXVIII, 'From Miss A. B. to the Rev. J. Wesley,'" *AM* (December 1788), 663–64. Banks notes the following assessment by Ann Bolton written on the occasion of her thirty-seventh birthday in 1780: "'Seventeen years have I known his fear, and ten years have I known Him as my reconciled God and Savior.'" Banks, *Nancy Nancy*, 83.

43. This is clearly the case, for example, in Wesley's letter dated December 15, 1770. Wesley, *Letters*, 5:213.

44. Ibid., 6:219–20.

45. Ibid., 6:259–60.

> MY DEAR ALLECK,—You should read Mr. Fletcher's *Essay on Truth*. He has there put it beyond all doubt that there is a medium between a child of God and a child of the devil—namely, a servant of God. This is *your* state. You are not yet a son, but you are a servant; and you are waiting for the Spirit of adoption, which will cry in your heart, "Abba, Father." You have "received the Spirit of grace," and in a measure work righteousness. Without being pained for what you have not, you have cause to bless God for what you have, and to wait patiently till He gives the rest by revealing His Son in your heart.[46]

In this passage, Wesley's description of the attributes of a servant is consistent with distinctions made previously—the servant is one who is awaiting the Spirit of adoption and who, meanwhile, works righteousness. Furthermore, this progress is described as dependent upon Christ being revealed in Knox's heart. On his part, Knox has only "to bless God" for what he has already and "to wait patiently."

In this letter three descriptors make something of a first appearance in Wesley's mention of the servant-son metaphor. First, Wesley notes that Knox has received "the Spirit of grace." It may be that what prompts Wesley to use this phrase is his recollection of its appearance in Fletcher's *Essay on Truth*,[47] though it reflects a view already held by Wesley. The phrase appears in Zechariah 12:10. In his commentary on the verse Wesley clearly connects receiving the Spirit of grace with the divine initiative that produces repentance and mourning for sins. The verse speaks of the inhabitants of Jerusalem looking upon the one "whom they pierced" and mourning (being "in bitterness for him"). Wesley notes that such mourning is the sign of true repentance. It is in this context that Wesley, in his commentary, describes the "Spirit of grace" as the "fountain of all graces in us."[48] Second, and in relation to his assertion that Knox had received "the Spirit of grace," Wesley observed that Knox "in a measure" works righteousness. The qualifier "in a measure" is not surprising in light of Wesley's understanding that the person who labors under the

---

46. Ibid., 6:272–73.

47. Fletcher, *Essay on Truth*, 168–69.

48. Wesley, *Explanatory Notes upon the Old Testament*, 3:2599. This is similar to the Matthew Henry's commentary on the phrase. Henry, *An Exposition of All the Books of the Old and New Testaments*, 4:803. This view correlates with the accepted general meaning of the phrase, "spirit of grace." See, for example, Walter H. Wagner, "Luther and the Positive Use of the Law," 48–49; see also, Zaret, "Calvin, Covenant Theology, and the Weber Thesis," 378.

spirit of bondage is constantly thwarted in the endeavors of inward holiness despite firm resolve and occasional successes.[49]

The third descriptor identifies for Knox that there is "a medium between a child of God and a child of the devil." This was not a new idea for Wesley. In a letter to Richard Tompson in 1755, Wesley affirmed that "a man who is not assured that his sins are forgiven may yet have a kind or degree of faith which distinguishes him not only from a devil, but from an heathen; and on which I may admit him to the Lord's Supper."[50] In Wesley's view, Fletcher's essay provided an additional and sufficiently clear and persuasive explanation of what Wesley considered applicable and valuable in helping Knox to properly understand his state and to remain steadfast while waiting for Christ to be revealed in his heart.

Subsequent correspondence makes no further mention of the servant-son metaphor. On April 2, 1778, just seven months after the letter just discussed, Wesley wrote to Knox: "It is right to know ourselves, but not to stop there, as you are apt to do. This is only of use if it leads us to know Him that loves and saves sinners; and, I doubt not, He will save *you*. Trust Him, and you shall praise Him."[51] This response clearly references the fruit of the spirit of bondage—namely, the fearful experience of coming to know oneself. This apparently created a level of despondency in Knox. Wesley affirms the value of self-knowledge but works to shift Knox's focus from the spiritual destitution such self-knowledge discloses to the One that "loves and saves sinners."

This response is not what might have been expected. In fact, it is what is *missing* in Wesley's response that is perhaps most instructive with respect to the metaphor. For one thing, Wesley does *not* assuage Knox's apparent anguish by assuring him that the faith that he *does* have has secured him the favor of God. Thus, he does not assure Knox that he is a child of God, even though Fletcher in his *Essay on Truth* applies Galatians 4 in order to emphasize that those under the Law were "constituted . . . children of God" though they were "in a state of nonage and bondage."[52] Wesley does not raise the matter of assurance at all; rather, the concern is that Knox be saved.

Two months later on June 5, 1778, Wesley exhorts Knox to "Trust in God," to resist the lies of "the old murderer" and to rest assured that

---

49. Wesley is likely recalling a portion of Fletcher's essay in which he addresses the circumstance of "a penitent mourner." Fletcher, *Essay on Truth*, 218–20.

50. Wesley, *Works* (BE), 26:575.

51. Wesley, *Letters*, 6:309.

52. Fletcher, *Essay on Truth*, 230.

God is on his side. A month afterward, on July 11, 1778, Wesley counsels Knox more extensively:

> It is a natural effect of your bodily weakness and of the turn of your mind that you are continually inclined to write bitter things against yourself. Hence you are easily persuaded to believe him that tells you that you "are void of every degree of saving faith." No; that is not the case. *For salvation is only by faith; and you have received a degree of salvation.* You are saved from many outward sins—from the corruption that overspreads the land as a flood. You are saved in a degree from inward sin; from impenitence, for you know and feel yourself a sinner. You are saved in a degree from pride; for you begin to know yourself poor and helpless. You are saved from seeking happiness in the world: this is not a small thing. O praise God for all you have, and trust Him for all you want![53]

In this brief passage, Wesley looks to prove to Knox that he *does* indeed have a "degree of saving faith." This is manifested in the fact that Knox has been saved from outward sins and, "in a degree," from inward sins (namely, impenitence) and from pride and from seeking happiness in the world. The evidence of "a degree of salvation" is submitted before the skeptical jury of Knox's self-perception *not* as proof that he is a child of God but as proof that he knows and feels himself "a sinner" and as one who is "poor and helpless." Once again, Wesley makes no mention of assurance nor does he comfort the afflicted Knox with the declaration that he has been justified in the gospel sense of the term.

Almost eighteen months later, on December 23, 1779, Wesley writes yet again to Knox and identifies four aspects of Knox's "disorder": 1) "a bodily complaint"; 2) smallness of faith—"and you are fearful, because you are of little faith"; 3) the small and inconstant love for God—"You want to have [i.e., lack] the love of God fully shed abroad in your heart"; and 4) "the main cause—diabolical agency".[54] The vital sign of one who is awakened—"fear without love"[55]—remains strong in Knox, indicating that he is yet a servant groaning under the law rather than a son set at liberty.

In the cases of Ann Bolton and of Alexander Knox, it is quite clear that Wesley remains steadfast and insistent in his conviction that escape

---

53. Wesley, *Letters*, 6:315. Emphasis mine.
54. Ibid., 6:364.
55. Wesley, *ENNT*, 795.

from the legal state to the evangelical is invariably signaled by the revelation of Christ in the heart and accompanied by the work of the Spirit as the spirit of adoption (though this work of the Spirit is not always clear at first, nor always of the same intensity afterward[56]). For Wesley, the pre-eminence of sonship was accentuated and safeguarded by his unrelenting conviction that "Christ revealed" is the authenticating attribute of sonship. Though Wesley held that a *sense* of pardon could not be a *condition* of pardon, he remained convinced that it was certainly *evidence* of pardon. Holland is correct that Wesley certainly did not regard the revelation of Christ—the certainty that "Christ loved *me* and gave himself for *me*"—as merely a matter of "intellectual persuasion."[57]

On this point, it does not appear that Wesley ever changed course from what he had declared in *A Farther Appeal to Men of Reason and Religion*. Responding to the notion that "'The believers mentioned in the Acts did not receive faith in a moment,'" Wesley declared, "They might first apprehend, then assent, then confide [in the promises of God], then love, and yet receive faith in a moment; in that moment wherein their *general* confidence became *particular*, so that each could say, 'My Lord and my God!'"[58] Forty years later in his sermon, "Of the Church," written in September 1785, Wesley stated that "'[t]here is one faith,' which is the free gift of God" and that "it is the faith of St. Thomas, teaching him to say with holy boldness, 'My Lord and my God.' It is the faith which enables every true Christian believer to testify with St. Paul, 'The life which I now live I live by faith in the Son of God, who loved me and gave himself for me.'"[59]

While quick to provide encouragement and to recognize and celebrate spiritual advances, neither the passage of time nor the intensity of the desire of the person longing for escape was sufficient to persuade him to pronounce them a son rather than a servant. What *was* sufficient was the revelation of Christ to *them* with the testimony of the Spirit. For Wesley, except in exempt cases, one's escape from the legal state to the evangelical was a discernible, marked transition that was, in some sense, momentous. This is captured in Ann Bolton's recounting to Wesley the spiritual sojourn of one John Taylor on the occasion of Taylor's death:

---

56. See Wesley's brief discussion on this point in *Farther Thoughts Upon Christian Perfection*, 10.
57. Holland, "The Conversions of John and Charles Wesley," 53.
58. Wesley, *Works* (BE) §IV.6, 11:138.
59. Ibid., §11, 3:49.

I think it is now twelve years since he was first awakened to a sense of his sin and misery. Weary and heavy laden he earnestly applied himself to seek for mercy, bringing forth fruits meet for repentance. In this state he continued four months, at which time the Lord, in mercy, was found of him and gave him the oil of joy for mourning, and the garment of praise for the spirit of heaviness.[60]

Wesley's Defense of the Faith of a Servant

Undergirding Wesley's conviction of the pre-eminence of sonship was his confidence that "He is nigh that justifieth!" and that "If you are fit for hell, you are just fit for Him! If you are a mere sinner, He cannot cast you out!"[61] It is not surprising, then, that in every context where he draws the distinction between servant and son, he does so not in a fashion that condemns those who have "only the faith of a servant" but in a way that admonishes and encourages them to go on "from faith to faith."[62]

If this is the aim of this advocacy, what is its substance? What is the theological basis for Wesley's defense of the faith of a servant? What is his affirmation regarding the standing with God that persons like Ann Bolton and Alexander Knox have as those who have the faith of a servant? In what sense are they—or are they *not*—in God's favor? What does Wesley mean when he says that the one having the faith of a servant is "in a state of acceptance" and that "'the wrath of God' no longer 'abideth on him'"?[63]

Outside the correspondence in which he employs the servant-son metaphor, two of Wesley's later sermons, "On Faith" and "On the Discoveries of Faith," serve as windows into both his theological thought and his pastoral agenda with respect to the metaphor. While it is readily evident from the texts that Wesley sought to address distinct theological concerns with each sermon, it is significant that he views the metaphor as a strategic component in *both* efforts. This strengthens the case that the sermons, written within a few weeks of each other late in his life (the spring of 1788), might reasonably be understood to substantially convey the theological basis of his defense of the faith of a servant. In addition,

---

60. Bolton, "A Short Account of Mr. John Taylor," *AM* (May, 1789), 237–38.
61. "John Wesley to Thomas Davenport, December 2, 1781," Wesley, *Letters*, 7:95.
62. Wesley, "On the Discoveries of Faith," *Works* (BE) §13–14, 4:35.
63. Wesley, "On Faith," *Works* (BE) §I.10, 3:497.

considering the sermons alongside each other promotes proper regard for Wesley's "contextual selectivity"[64] and encourages scholars to resist the temptation to turn the sermons into proof texts.

In his 1788 sermon "On Faith," Wesley chooses his language carefully in his defense of those who fear God but who answer in the negative when asked whether they know their sins are forgiven. He rejects the verdict routinely pronounced on each of these persons—"'Then you are a child of the devil'"—and declares, "It might have been said (and it is all that can be said with propriety) 'Hitherto you are only a *servant*; you are not a *child* of God.'"[65] The parenthetical qualifier suggests that Wesley was sensitive to theological pitfalls surrounding his advocacy in behalf of those having the faith of a servant. On the one hand, there was the danger of minimizing the soteriological advance evident in their lives so far, thus "making sad the hearts of those whom God had not made sad."[66] On the other hand, there was the danger of overstating it, assuring them of being in the favor of God (in terms of being in the enjoyment of the divine design and provision of the gospel dispensation) when in fact they were not, thus diminishing both their expectation of and incentive for going on to the privileges of the gospel dispensation as well as robbing them of the actual enjoyment of those blessings and privileges.

Acceptance with God

In scholarly inquiries touching upon the servant-son metaphor over the past twenty-five years, Wesley's assertion that those having the faith of a servant are "in a state of acceptance" and that the wrath of God "no longer 'abideth'" on them, has been a focal point of discussion. Some have taken Wesley to mean that those having the faith of a servant are justified, and have arrived at this view having concluded that "acceptance" and "the wrath of God no longer abiding" were, for Wesley, descriptive of justification. "What can this mean," Maddox asks, "but that they are presently justified?"[67] Collins rejects this view arguing that while it is true that "all who are justified are accepted," it does not follow that "all

---

64. Zaret, "Calvin, Covenant Theology, and the Weber Thesis," 373–74. Zaret defines contextual selectivity as "variations in textual representations of a belief system that bear the imprint of diverse obstacles" being confronted, and notes that "writings by the same author, often exhibit a range of variation in textual representations that are composed in different contexts of argumentation." Ibid.

65. Wesley, "On Faith," *Works* (BE) §I.11, 3:497.

66. Ibid.

67. Maddox, "Continuing the Conversation," 237. As noted earlier in this thesis, Maddox is not alone in holding this view.

who are accepted are thereby justified."[68] In a separate critique of the matter, Collins proposes that when Wesley spoke of one having the faith of a servant as being "in a state of acceptance," he was speaking not in a "*theological* context of justification, regeneration and other normative doctrines" but strictly in terms of a "*pastoral* context" where the term ("acceptance") was applied to those who were "on the way to justification and regeneration and therefore should not be discouraged."[69]

There is no question that Wesley's declaration of acceptance was pastorally motivated, as Collins has affirmed. Yet, it would be highly uncharacteristic for Wesley—in the interest of providing a psychological-emotional safety net for those on the way of salvation—to marginalize the theological question of how it is that one might be accepted (and no longer under the wrath of God) and yet not be justified. In actual fact, there was substantial "theological context" in Wesley's clearly distinguishing between one who was "a believer in the gospel sense" and one who had the faith of a servant.[70] Furthermore, it is difficult to imagine that his readers, upon coming to this passage, would have distinguished between "pastoral" and "theological" contexts. Surely, the pastoral *value* of Wesley's assertion rested squarely upon its theological substance. Indeed, it is his covenant theology that provided a *theological* basis for his declaration of the divine acceptance of one having the faith of a servant.

On the other hand, while it is plainly evident that, with some frequency, Wesley used the term "accepted" specifically as a description of one who is justified,[71] Collins is correct in raising doubts about the assumption that either Wesley or his audience conceived of the term in this sense alone. There was, in fact, a significant interpretive history which regarded the notion of acceptance with God in a broader sense—a sense which could *include* but which did not *necessitate* the idea of being justified, in the gospel sense. William Perkins made the distinction between reconciliation "in nature" and reconciliation "in God's acceptation." The context of this distinction is Perkins' declaration that "the desire of reconciliation with God in Christ, is reconciliation it selfe."

---

68. Collins, *The Theology of John Wesley*, 183. Collins' response rests on what he sees as a theological incongruity in the view held by Maddox *et al*. Ibid. 184.

69. Collins, "Real Christianity as the Integrating Theme," 73; n. 81.

70. Wesley makes this distinction very clearly in "On Friendship with the World," a sermon he finished writing on May 1, 1786. Wesley, *Works* (BE), §12, 3:132.

71. One such clear example is found in the lyrics of Hymn XXXVIII: "The deaf hear his voice And comforting word, / It bids them rejoice In Jesus their Lord: / 'Thy sins are forgiven Accepted thou art;' / They listen, and heaven Springs up in their heart." Wesley, *A Collection of Hymns* (1780), 43.

He qualifies this assertion by noting that "A desire to be reconciled, is not reconciliation in nature"—that is, in actual fact—"(for the desire is one thing, and reconciliation, another)" but is reconciliation "in God's acceptation: for if we being touched throughly for our sinnes, doe desire to haue them pardoned, and to bee alone with God, God accepts vs as reconciled." This was not itself "a liuely faith" but was, says Perkins citing the words of Theodore Beza, "'a pledge of the Fathers will to thee'" and is in this sense "as truly in the acceptation with God, as the prayer made in liuely faith."[72] William Ames, too, spoke of a divine "acceptation" by which the mediation of the lamb slain from the foundation of the world was made effectual in all ages (i.e., in all dispensations).[73]

Wesley was certainly cognitive of the theological nuances of the notion of acceptance with God. When he asserts in his commentary on Acts 10:35 that Cornelius was accepted of God "through *Christ*, though he knows him not," he confirms the basis for this acceptance (which he declares is "express, and admits of no exception") along lines that reflect distinctions largely consistent with those made by John Guyse. Guyse had stipulated that acceptance should be understood in a broad sense:

> [Peter] cannot reasonably be supposed to have meant, that all persons who served God according to their present light, whatsoever their religion were, should be accepted of him to eternal life: And the apostle *Peter's* being sent to *Cornelius*, to *tell him words whereby he and all his house should be saved* (*chap* xi. 14.) intimates, that even *they* were not already in a state of salvation, according to the tenor of the gospel. I therefore take it, that acceptance, here spoken of, relates chiefly, if not only, to the proselytes of the gate being so far accepted of God, as to be admitted to an enjoyment of the privilege of the gospel for their own salvation; and that their fearing God, and working righteousness, as far as it went, was agreeable to the perfections and will of God, though it did not give them a claim to eternal life, any more than the penitent and becoming behaviour of a condemned rebel, which is pleasing to his prince, can entitle him to a pardon of his crime, and to high favour and honours in his kingdom; . . .[74]

Wesley likewise acknowledged the evidence that Cornelius was in the favor of God but distinguished this from his being in the enjoyment

---

72. Perkins, "A Graine of Musterd-Seede" in *The Workes of . . . William Perkins.* (1626), 1:639–41.

73. Ames, *The Marrow of Sacred Divinity*, 80–81.

74. Guyse, *The Practical Expositor*, 120–21.

of "the full Christian salvation"[75]—that is, salvation under the salvific perfection of the Christian dispensation. What clearly remained central to Wesley in the account of Cornelius was, first of all, his coming to have faith *in Christ* (as opposed to resting in any confidence in his commendably fearing God and working righteousness[76]), and second, the corroborating evidence of such faith: the descent of the Holy Spirit upon Cornelius and his household.[77]

At the heart, then, of Wesley's appropriation of the interpretive history of the notion of acceptance with God is the conviction of the salvific sufficiency of the covenant of grace from its inception. And, specifically, the question of acceptance would necessarily be considered within the context of his understanding of the salvific sufficiency of the various dispensations of the covenant of grace as *relative* and *concurrent*. That is, acceptance was relative to the dispensation one was under; and, the various dispensations were concurrent with each other *soteriologically*, though *historically* the present moment belonged only to the gospel dispensation.

It is within the context of this theological orientation that Wesley pursues a primary aim of his sermon, "On Faith": to demonstrate the breadth of "the faith which is properly saving."[78] Wesley first takes pains to show that saving faith is *not* a matter of mere assent to the truths of the gospel:

> Hitherto faith has been considered chiefly as an evidence and conviction of such or such truths. . . . But in the meantime let it be carefully observed (for eternity depends upon it) that neither the faith of a Roman Catholic nor that of a Protestant, if it contains no more than this, no more than the embracing such and such truths, will avail any more before God than the faith of a Mahometan or a heathen, yea of a deist or materialist.[79]

---

75. See Wesley's commentary on Peter's defense before the believers in Jerusalem, particularly Acts 11:14. Wesley, *ENNT*, 388.

76. In his commentary on Acts 10:43 Wesley specifically notes that faith as belief in Christ is not to be confused or equated with fearing God and working righteousness. Wesley, *ENNT*, 387.

77. In his commentary on Acts 10:44 Wesley adheres to the strict sense in which the term "accepted" is used within the salvation-historical context of Luke's presentation of the Cornelius story. Wesley, *ENNT*, 387.

78. Wesley, *Works* (BE) §10, 3:497.

79. Ibid., §9, 3:496–97. See also Wesley's commentary on 2 Cor 3:9. Wesley, *ENNT*, 570.

He then proceeds to declare that the faith that is properly saving "is such a divine conviction of God and of the things of God as even in its infant state enables everyone that possesses it to 'fear God and work righteousness.'"[80] This faith brings the person possessing it into "a state of acceptance" in which "'the wrath of God' no longer 'abideth on him.'"[81]

It does not appear that this emphasis is indicative of a new perspective by Wesley. There is, in fact, a significant amount of common ground between Fletcher's *Essay on Truth*, and Wesley's sermon, "On Faith," though Outler's footnote on Wesley's acknowledgement of Fletcher's "treatise on the various dispensations of the grace of God" suggests that Wesley is referencing Fletcher's *The Doctrines of Grace and Justice*.[82] While this may be correct, the parallels between Fletcher's *Essay on Truth* and Wesley's sermon are noteworthy.[83] In *Essay on Truth*, Fletcher, too, took up the question of identifying what saving faith is and proposed that "a definition of faith adequate to 'the everlasting Gospel'" is "'believing the saving truth with the heart unto internal and (as we have opportunity) unto external righteousness, according to our light and dispensation.'"[84] Fletcher also connects with Wesley's lament concerning the tenor of the earliest Methodist preaching and cautions against deriding the faith of those who have not entered into the privileges of the Christian dispensation: "God forbid that an *antichristian* zeal for the *Christian* gospel should make me drive into the burning lake Christ's *sheep*, which are *big with young:* I mean the sincere worshipers, that wait like pious Melchisedec, devout Lydia, and charitable Cornelius, for brighter displays of gospel-grace."[85]

In making this point, Fletcher distinguishes those who "sincerely seek the kingdom" from those who are "absolute unbelievers."[86] Before proceeding to describe that faith which is "properly saving," Wesley made essentially the same distinction in his extensive description of the various sorts of faith that, in the end, cannot save any man "either from

---

80. Wesley, *Works* (BE) §10, 3:497. For an earlier description of "the entire work of God, from the first dawning of grace in the soul till it is consummated in glory," see "The Scripture Way of Salvation," *Works* (BE) §I.1–2, 2:156–57.

81. Ibid., §10, 3:497.

82. Ibid., §2, 3:492. Outler's comment appears as fn. 2 in the text of the sermon.

83. It is not easy to discern when Wesley is borrowing from Fletcher and when Fletcher is borrowing from Wesley.

84. Fletcher, *Essay on Truth*, 144.

85. Ibid., 169.

86. Ibid., 237.

sin or from hell."[87] And when Wesley declares the divine acceptance of those having the faith of a servant and asserts that God's wrath does not abide on them, Fletcher's own declaration along the very same lines suggests that this view concerning the wrath of God was no new theological turn in the last several years of Wesley's life. The logic of Fletcher's argument may well represent—or, on the other hand, may well have provided—the basis upon which Wesley took liberty to adapt the Scripture *phrase* of John 3:36 in order to accurately represent what he felt was the Scripture *sense*.[88] Speaking of those who sincerely seek the kingdom, Fletcher cross-examined his objectors: "Ought we to keep from those who sincerely seek the kingdom of God the comfort that the Gospel allows them? Are not 'they that seek the Lord' commanded 'to rejoice?' And how can they do it, if 'the wrath of God abideth on them,' as it certainly does on all absolute unbelievers?"[89]

It is important to recognize that for both Wesley and Fletcher this lifting of wrath was neither cause for complacency nor verification of one's justification. In the case of those having the faith of a servant, the lifting of wrath must be understood in relation to the nature of the acceptance enjoyed. This is a critical point that is frequently overlooked as evidenced in the failure to address what exactly Wesley might have meant when he spoke of acceptance in a *qualified* sense: "*in some measure* accepted" or "*in a degree* . . . 'accepted with him.'"[90]

These qualifiers provide some insight into Wesley's theological thought as they suggest something of the nature of acceptance affirmed by him. His exhortation to Thomas Davenport ("He is nigh that justifieth! that justifieth the ungodly and him that worketh not!") would seem to be sufficient testimony that Wesley did not understand the divine acceptance of sincere seekers of the kingdom as equivalent to justification, a term he consistently reserved to refer to the benefits of the achievements of Christ's death *in realitor* conferred upon those exercising explicit faith in Christ. At the same time, at the heart of his

---

87. Wesley, *Works* (BE) §9, 3:496–97.

88. John 3:36 reads, "He that believeth on the Son hath everlasting life: but he that obeyeth not the Son, shall not see life, but the wrath of God abideth on him." Wesley, *ENNT*, 278. Compare Wesley's adaptation of the verse in "On Faith" to his use of the verse to describe the absolute unbeliever awakening to the reality of the "entire, universal corruption of his nature." Wesley, "Upon Our Lord's Sermon on the Mount (Sermon 21)," *Works* (BE) §I.5, 1:478.

89. Fletcher, *Essay on Truth*, 237.

90. See Wesley's commentary on Acts 10:35. Wesley, *ENNT*, 386. See also Wesley, "On the Discoveries of Faith," *Works* (BE) §13, 4:35. Emphasis mine.

defense of the faith of a servant is his defense of the *sufficiency* of this divine acceptance. How this acceptance may be regarded as sufficient and yet be distinct from justification proper can be understood only in light of Wesley's covenant theology.

It is helpful on this point to note Fletcher's assertion that the acceptance enjoyed by Cornelius and his household was "according to an inferior dispensation."[91] In making this point, Fletcher realized that his opponents (and perhaps, constituents) would argue that to defend the sufficiency of such acceptance is to endanger the spiritual welfare of true seekers by marginalizing their need of Christ: "If we see our way by the candle of Moses, as thou intimatest, what need is there that 'the Sun of righteousness' should arise upon us with 'healing in his wings?'"[92] In reply, Fletcher pointed to the biblical record of Cornelius' response to Peter's declaration of divine acceptance:

> But although St. Peter began his discourse by acknowledging that his pious hearers "were accepted with God," none of the congregation said, "Well, if we *are accepted*, we are already in a state of salvation, and therefore, we need not 'hear words whereby we shall be saved.'" On the contrary, they all "believed the word of this *fuller* salvation: for the Holy Ghost fell on all them that heard the word;" . . . Hence it is evident that the doctrine we maintain, if it be properly guarded, far from having a necessary tendency to lull people asleep, is admirably calculated to excite every penitent to faith, prayer, the improvement of their talents, and the perfecting of holiness.[93]

This became the basis for his subsequent assertion that it is characteristic of those who are genuine seekers of the kingdom to not settle into an inferior dispensation when they come to realize that the perfections of the Christian dispensation await them.[94]

Although Wesley does not explicitly describe those having the faith of a servant as enjoying an acceptance that is "according to an inferior dispensation," he implies the same—first, by specifically noting (and not disqualifying) Fletcher's description of what characterizes the Christian

---

91. Fletcher, *Essay on Truth*, 240.

92. Ibid., 239.

93. Ibid., 240.

94. Fletcher summarizes, "Thus our doctrine, instead of being dangerous to sincere seekers, will prove a Scriptural clue, in following which they will happily avoid the gloomy haunts of Pharisaic despair, and the enchanted ground of Antinomian presumption." Ibid., 242.

dispensation;[95] and second, by using the language of lesser-to-greater comparison: "he is at present only a *servant* of God, not properly a *son*."[96] In the words "not properly" Wesley seems to recall the distinction of Galatians 4 between the child in minority and the adult son where to be "properly" a son means to come into the full enjoyment of all the privileges of that sonship (i.e., the perfections of the Christian dispensation of the covenant of grace).

It should be noted that Wesley makes no mention of Cornelius in either "On Faith" or "On the Discoveries of Faith." As previously argued, all of the following point to a generally more narrow conception of the faith of a servant than what seems, on the surface, to appear in "On Faith": a) Wesley's employment of the metaphor with his correspondents, b) his particular attentiveness to the "two grand manifestations of God, the legal and the evangelical," c) the affirmation of Galatians 4 as an illustration of the pre-eminence of the Christian over the legal dispensation, d) the discussions of the early conferences and the qualifying language—distinguishing those who have heard the gospel from those who have not—of the infamous minutes of the 1770 Conference, and e) the specific contrast drawn in his sermons as early as 1746 and as late as 1788.

On the one hand, it is difficult to argue that Wesley absolutely excludes the heathen (those not having come under the sound of the gospel), such as Cornelius, when he applies the identifier "servant of God" to those whose "conviction of God and of the things of God" is "in an infant state." On the other hand, given the preponderance of the evidence, it is reckless to assume that with a single statement in a single sermon Wesley is reconfiguring the metaphor at this late date. Instead, keeping in mind Zaret's concept of contextual selectivity, a more defensible conclusion is that Wesley is underscoring the continuity of those having the faith of a servant with all those sincere seekers of the kingdom under *any* dispensation other than the Christian dispensation.

Thus, rather than expanding the purview of the servant-son metaphor in "On Faith," Wesley is locating the metaphor in its broader soteriological context. This point is substantiated by the fact that Wesley very clearly restates the purview of the metaphor in his sermon "On the Discoveries of Faith," written, as noted above, only a few weeks *after* "On Faith." In "On the Discoveries of Faith," Wesley describes in considerable detail the soteriological and existential reality of those

95. Wesley, *Works* (BE) §3, 3:492–93.
96. Ibid., §I.10, 3:497.

in whom the witnessing Spirit is the spirit of bondage. And in this description, rather than offer the consolation that the wrath of God no longer abides, Wesley emphasizes that the terror of God's wrath weighs *heavily* upon those who have the faith of a servant as they are convinced of their evil nature, evil tempers, evil words, and evil actions. Utterly guilty before God they fear his wrath, the punishment they deserve, and consignment to eternal death. They are "altogether sinful, altogether guilty, and altogether helpless."[97] As Paul Hoon has so aptly described this state of affairs, "God's love claims his soul as mysteriously as His wrath terrifies it."[98]

It is evident that Wesley has no interest in gutting his theological thought of the biblically-founded notion of the wrath of God. The fear of God experienced by those having the faith of a servant was not the filial fear of those that are children of God, but is servile fear—a fear having more than a hint of dread. This is the reason why Wesley labored to lift despairing correspondents from all doubts of God's intended purpose to deliver them from the excruciating experience of being under the spirit of bondage and into the delights administered by the spirit of adoption. In essence, then, the relationship between the assertion in his sermon "On Faith" that the wrath of God does *not* abide and his description in "On the Discoveries of Faith" of the very effects of abiding wrath, rests in his understanding that the spirit of bondage is nothing other than the witnessing work of the Holy Spirit himself.

Wesley's view might be fairly summarized in the following way: where this witnessing work is underway and where its purposes continue to be co-operantly advanced, the wrath of God does not abide *in the same sense* that it abides upon those who are unresponsive to the divine initiatives to awaken them from the slumber of their sinful estate. Conversely, it might be said that the wrath of God *abides* upon those who *are* responding to such divine initiatives (as evidenced by the continuing work of the spirit of bondage) in a way that it does *not* abide upon the *unresponsive*. That is, the unresponsive do not feel the wrath of God even though they are, in fact, under it, while the responsive are keenly sensitized to It." This double entendre of abiding wrath is actually portrayed in Wesley's commentary on the story of the jailor in Acts 16:30, who certainly was under the wrath of God prior to the earthquake but who had no sensitivity to this abiding wrath until he became responsive: "*Sirs . . . What must I do to be saved?* From the guilt I feel, and the vengeance

---

97. Ibid., §12, 4:34–35.
98. Hoon, "The Soteriology of John Wesley," 146.

I fear. Undoubtedly God then set his sins in array before him, and convinced him in the clearest and strongest manner, that the wrath of God abode upon him."[99] For Wesley, it is this distinction that serves as both a warning and as an encouragement to those having the faith of a servant. "Indeed," he declares, "unless the servants of God halt by the way, they will receive the adoption of sons."[100]

It is for this very reason that Wesley labored so insistently in defending the faith of a servant. He was theologically assured and utterly confident that "all this conviction" which the servant experienced while under the spirit of bondage, "implies a species of faith, being 'an evidence of things not seen.'"[101] This affirmation connects with the continuity noted above (and emphasized in "On Faith") and is again followed by Wesley's declaration that one having the faith of a servant is "*in a degree* (as the Apostle observes), 'accepted with him.'"[102] At the same time, and almost in the same breath, Wesley restates—perhaps in order to reconfirm for his readers—the legal and the evangelical dispensations as the purview of the metaphor when he specifically describes what passing "'from faith to faith'" means: "Exhort [the one having the faith of a servant] to press on by all possible means, till he passes 'from faith to faith,' from the faith of a *servant* to the faith of a *son*; from the spirit of bondage unto fear, to the spirit of childlike love."[103] This passing from "faith to faith" was of utmost importance to Wesley and drove his ardent defense of the validity and worth of the faith of a servant. As he once declared to Ann Bolton, "[A]lthough as yet you are rather in the state of a servant than a child. . . . it is a blessed thing to be even a servant of God!"[104]

The Promise of the Metaphor

His confidence in the value of the faith of a servant notwithstanding, Wesley was unmoved from his conviction that obedience out of love is the capacity and privilege peculiar to those who have the faith of a son—those in whose hearts Christ has been revealed and who, from this revelation, are enabled to testify, "The life I now live in the flesh I live

---

99. Wesley, *ENNT*, 409.
100. Wesley, *Works* (BE) §I.12, 3:497–98.
101. Ibid., §12, 4:34–35. See also Fletcher, *Essay on Truth*, 232–33.
102. Wesley, *Works* (BE) §13, 4:35. Emphasis mine.
103. Ibid., §14, 4:35–36.
104. Wesley, *Letters*, 5:207.

by faith in the Son of God, who loved *me*, and gave himself for *me*."[105] Consequent with the revelation of Christ in their hearts, these have also come to know the work of the witnessing Spirit as the spirit of adoption who has shed abroad in their hearts the love of God.[106]

In each of the 1788 sermons touching upon the metaphor, Wesley composes his closing argument regarding the pre-eminence of sonship by packing into one paragraph every primary scriptural descriptor of those having the faith of a son. In "On Faith" that paragraph first collects verses from the Pauline epistles of Galatians and Romans:

> And, indeed, unless the servants of God halt by the way, they will receive the adoption of sons. They will receive the faith of the children of God by his revealing his only-begotten Son in their hearts. Thus the faith of a child is properly and directly a divine conviction whereby every child of God is enabled to testify, "The life that I now live, I live by faith in the Son of God, who loved me, and gave himself for me." And whosoever hath this, "the Spirit of God witnesseth with his spirit that he is a child of God." So the Apostle writes to the Galatians, "Ye are the sons of God by faith." "And because ye are sons, God hath sent forth the Spirit of his Son into your hearts, crying, Abba, Father"; that is, giving you a childlike confidence in him, together with a kind affection toward him. This then it is that (if St. Paul was taught of God, and wrote as he was moved by the Holy Ghost) properly constitutes the difference between a servant of God and a child of God.[107]

To punctuate, he adds a descriptor of the person having the faith of a son taken from 1 John 5:10, "'He that believeth,' as a child of God, 'hath the witness in himself.' This the servant hath not."[108] Wesley's conviction of the pre-eminence of sonship is unmistakable.

The metaphor provided Wesley a means of communicating this conviction with pastoral sensitivity and theological integrity by emphasizing faith as a *gift* of God to be *stewarded* by its recipients. While a comprehensive study of Wesley's understanding of faith is outside the

---

105. Wesley, *Works* (BE) §14, 4:35–36.

106. Ibid.

107. Ibid., §I.12, 3:497–98. In this paragraph, Wesley strings together portions of Gal 4:5, 1:16 (actually, a combination of v. 16 with the familiar phrase from John 3:16, "only-begotten"), 2:20; Rom 8:16; Gal 3:26, 4:6. In the parallel passage in "On the Discoveries of Faith" Wesley adds Rom 1:17, 5:5; 1 John 3:9; Phil 2:5. Ibid., §14, 4:35–36.

108. Ibid., §I.12, 3:497. The verse is adapted similarly in "On the Discoveries of Faith." Ibid., §14, 4:35–36.

scope of this investigation, it is important to observe that when Wesley distinguished between servants and sons, he distinguished not simply between the attributes of each (such as servile fear or filial fear, or the spirit of bondage and the spirit of adoption) but between the faith of each: the *faith* of a servant, the *faith* of a son. And in each case, he emphasized faith as a *gift* of God.

The Gift of Faith: A Divine Prerogative and Invitation

In *An Earnest Appeal to Men of Reason and Religion*, Wesley emphasized the divine power and provision in responding to the question of why all persons do not have the faith that saves: "We answer, . . . 'it is the gift of God.' No man is able to work it in himself. It is a work of omnipotence. . . . You not only do not, but cannot, by your own strength, thus believe. . . . No merit, no goodness in man precedes the forgiving love of God. . . . God freely gives faith, for the sake of Him in whom he is always 'well pleased.'"[109]

Almost forty years later, in 1787, he fielded the same question in relation to the metaphor: Why do not all have the faith of a son? Why is it that some have "only the faith of a servant"? Wesley's explanation in a letter to Theophilus Lessey bears repeating: "To believe the being and attributes of God is the faith of an heathen. To believe the Old Testament and trust in Him that was to come was the faith of a Jew. To believe Christ gave Himself for me is the faith of a Christian. This faith He did give to you, and I hope does still; hold it fast without any philosophical refinement. When we urge any to believe, we mean, 'Accept that faith which God is now ready to give.'"[110]

In stating these affirmations to Lessey, Wesley clearly brings the gift of faith into relationship with the structure of his covenant theology by asserting the concurrence *soteriologically* (not historically) of the various dispensations of the covenant of grace. But more than that, he is moving beyond the emphasis of his response in the *Appeal* by grounding the gift of faith not only in the divine power and provision, but in the divine *prerogative* as well: "Accept that faith which *God is now ready* to give."

This was not a new position for Wesley as is evident from a careful survey of the language of his sermons, essays, and correspondence.[111] He

---

109. Ibid., §9–11, 11:47–49.

110. Wesley, *Letters*, 7:361.

111. Quoting from the minute record of the 1758 Conference, Wesley notes in *A Plain Account of Christian Perfection*: "God's usual method is one thing, but his sovereign pleasure is another. He has wise reasons both for hastening and retarding his work.

was certainly cognizant of the well-observed mystery of the divine prerogative, as evidenced by his including in the first volume of *A Christian Library* Macarius' homily on God's execution of his grace:

> The wisdom of God being infinite and incomprehensible: He executes the dispensations of his Grace upon mankind after an unsearchable manner with great variety; . . . Some are prevented with the favours and gifts of the Holy Spirit, immediately, as soon as they ask, without toil, and sweat, and fatigue; . . . On others, (though they have withdrawn from the world, and persevere in prayer, and fasting and diligence) God does not immediately bestow his grace and rest and the gladness of the Holy Spirit, but he withholds the gift, that he may see whether they thought him the faithful and true God, who has promised, *to give to them that ask, and to open to them that knock*, the door of life; that he may observe whether they endure to the end, asking and seeking; or whether through remissness, they fall off, not holding on to the end.[112]

In a letter dated November 9, 1777, Wesley confirmed what had become for him an underlying principle regarding the "unsearchable manner and great variety" of God's dealings with humanity in the matter of faith: "That every man may believe *if* he will I earnestly maintain, and yet that he can believe *when* he will I totally deny. But there will always be more to the matter which we cannot well comprehend or explain."[113] This is captured vividly in a hymn entitled "Looking Unto Jesus, the Author and Finisher of our Faith":

> Lord, I despair Myself to heal,
> I see my Sin, but cannot feel:
> I cannot, till the Spirit blow,
> And bid th'obedient Waters flow
>
> . . .
>
> With simple Faith, to Thee I call,
> My light, my Life, my Lord, my All:
> I wait the Moving of the Pool;
> I wait the Word that speaks me whole.[114]

Sometimes he comes suddenly and unexpected; sometimes, not till we have long looked for him." Wesley, *A Plain Account of Christian Perfection*, 91. See also "On the Spirit of Bondage and of Adoption," *Works* (BE) §II.10, 1:260.

112. Wesley, *ACL*, §1–2, 1:136–37. Note: the word "dispensations" is used here, as it is with some frequency by Wesley, in its more generic sense and not as the technical term of covenant theology.

113. Wesley, *Letters*, 6:287. Emphasis mine.

114. Wesley, *A Collection of Hymns* (1743), 11–12.

The matter of the divine prerogative seemed to be of increasing interest to Wesley. On four occasions in 1783 he preached from 1 Cor 13:9—"For we know in part, and we prophesy in part"—and in March 1784 wrote and published a sermon on the text entitled "The Imperfection of Human Knowledge" in which he commented extensively on the question:

> 3. . . . [T]here are still many circumstances in his dispensations which are above our comprehension. We know not why he suffered us so long to go on in our own ways before we were convinced of sin. Or why he made use of this or the other instrument, and in this or the other manner. And a thousand circumstances attended the process of our conviction which we do not comprehend. We know not why he suffered us to stay so long before he revealed his Son in our hearts; or why this change from darkness to light was accompanied with such and such particular circumstances.
>
> 4. It is doubtless *the peculiar prerogative of God* to reserve the "times and seasons in his own power." And we cannot give any reason why of two persons equally athirst for salvation one is presently taken into the favour of God and the other left to mourn for months or years. One, as soon as he calls upon God, is answered, and filled with peace and joy in believing. Another seeks after him—and it seems with the same degree of sincerity and earnestness—and yet cannot find him, or any consciousness of his favour, for weeks, or months, or years. We know well this cannot possibly be owing to any absolute decree, consigning one before he was born to everlasting glory, and the other to everlasting fire. But we do not know what is the reason for it: it is enough that God knoweth.[115]

Earlier that same year, on January 4, 1784, Wesley had written along similar lines to Isaac Andrews. In this letter he emphasized faith not only as a gift but as an *invitation*:

> Undoubtedly faith is *the work of God*; and yet it is *the duty of man* to believe. And every man may believe *if* he will, though not *when* he will. If he seek faith in the appointed ways, sooner or later the power of the Lord will be present, whereby (1) God works, and by *His* power (2) man believes. In order of thinking God's working goes first; but not in order of time. Believing

---

115. Wesley, *Works* (BE), III.3–4, 2:583–84. Emphasis mine. Note: Wesley here uses the term "dispensations" in the generic sense of "God's ways."

is the act of the human mind, strengthened by the power of God.[116]

In light of the foregoing, three pastoral affirmations come into view to which the metaphor serves as host:

1. *A person's response to God cannot exceed the extent of the faith given him or her to that point in time.* That is, one cannot exercise the faith of a Christian if God has been "ready to give" that person only "a Jewish faith."
2. *It is incumbent upon every person to believe in accordance with the faith given.* That is, each one is to believe to the full extent of the "reach" of the faith he or she has been given.
3. *It is the duty of every person to seek that faith which they do not yet have but which they have become apprised awaits them.*[117] There is, after all, a promise—validated by the divine goodness—that attends the divine prerogative.

The Certainty of Divine Response: "When the fullness of the time was come"

In specific relation to the metaphor, the one having the faith of a servant is to seek the faith of a son in the confidence that "sooner or later the power of the Lord will be present":[118]

> Even one who has gone thus far in religion [i.e., who has the faith of a servant], who obeys God out of fear, is not in any wise to be despised, seeing "the fear of the Lord is the beginning of wisdom." Nevertheless he should be exhorted not to stop there; not to rest till he attains the adoption of sons; till he obeys out of love, which is the privilege of all the children of God.[119]

While Wesley is clear that it is first God who works and then, "by *His* power . . . man believes," he shunned any vestige of the Stillness doctrine as a perversion of the notion of the divine prerogative. He affirmed

---

116. Wesley, *Letters*, 7:202–3.

117. It is on the basis of this last affirmation that Wesley distinguished, as noted earlier in this investigation, between the heathen and those who have come under the sound of the gospel.

118. Ibid.

119. Wesley, "On the Discoveries of Faith," *Works* (BE) §13, 4:35. Bracketed inserts mine. Likewise, those having the faith of a son are to "go on to perfection." Ibid., §16, 4:37.

the Anglican value of sincerity in the sense expressed by the admonition of Thomas Boston: "Will ye do nothing for your selves, because ye cannot do *all?* Lay down no such impious Conclusion against your own Souls. Do what you *can*; and it may be, while ye are doing what ye *can* for your selves, God will do for you what ye *cannot.*"[120] As Wesley had pointed out, while "in order of thinking God's working goes first," "in order of time" (i.e., in terms of appearances, experientially, on the human side of co-operancy) a person's believing is "first." It is on this basis that Wesley could declare to Ann Bolton in a letter from London on February 4, 1769: "A blessing is ready for many; for *you* in particular. I say still, Dare to believe, and feel Him near! Put forth your hand and touch Him! Is He not standing at the door of your heart?"[121]

Yet, his confidence that "he is nigh that justifieth," his calls to faith, and his certainty that those having the faith of a servant were "in a measure" accepted with God, did not diminish Wesley's conviction that this acceptance did not signify their enjoyment of the privileges and soteriological provisions that belong to the gospel dispensation alone. Rather, he remained steadfast in the conviction that the soteriological privileges unique to the gospel dispensation were the work of the Holy Spirit whose coming was conjoined with "the fullness of the time" set by the Father for the revelation of the Son. *This appointed time was as certain with respect to the individual believer as was the historical moment when the gospel dispensation itself was inaugurated in accordance with the time set by the Father.* Thus, Wesley's encouragement to Alexander Knox was "you are not yet a son, but you are a servant; and *you are waiting* for the Spirit of adoption. . . . Without being pained for what you have not, you have cause to bless God for what you have, and to *wait patiently till He gives the rest* by revealing His son in your heart."[122] In the words of Wesley's contemporary, John Green,

> Ye that are at last convinced . . . Ye who are so brought under the Thunder and Lightning of *Sinai*'s Mount, that ye exceedingly quake and tremble . . . Your Faith in Distress shall shortly be triumphant. . . . Heaviness shall be turned into Joy. Yea, ye shall rejoyce with Joy unspeakable and full of Glory. . . . Yea, wait ye patiently . . . the Promise is for an appointed Time. Oh! wait ye

---

120. Boston, *Fourfold State*, 172.
121. Wesley, *Letters*, 5:125.
122. Ibid., 6:28. Emphasis mine.

for it, so shall there be great Joy in the Heaven above, and also in the Heaven in you.[123]

While Wesley consistently held servant and son in contrasting relation to each other, there were relatively few contexts in which Wesley employed the metaphor in order to address both those having the faith of a servant and those having the faith of a son. Most often, the metaphor functioned as a definitive narrative of his soteriology specifically in relation to those awakened to their need of Christ and brought to a place of being convinced of sin, mourning over sin, and longing for reconciliation with God. These are the persons he aimed to advance "from faith to faith" and whom he identified as ones having the faith of a servant.[124] Thus, while Wesley was confident that the redemptive achievements of Christ's death and resurrection were intended for all persons, he did not understand the purview of the metaphor itself to be so all-encompassing as to include those who, like Cornelius, had never heard of Christ.

The driving force behind Wesley's use of the metaphor was his conviction of the pre-eminence of sonship as the divine intention for all of humankind. He was unrelenting in his insistence on this point, as evidenced in the counsel offered his correspondents. At the same time, Wesley defended those who longingly awaited the revelation of Christ in their hearts, assuring them of a measure of divine acceptance in light of his confidence in the relative salvific sufficiency of each dispensation of the covenant of grace. Yet, he maintained rather than diminished the distinction between servant and son and retained an emphasis on divine wrath, underscoring it as a reality encountered by those waiting and longing for the faith of a son. Above all, Wesley was unflagging in his confidence that the gift of faith necessary to move one from the faith of a servant to the faith of a son was most certainly on its way and would be given "when the fulness of the time was come"—that is, in a time and manner befitting the prerogative of God. Nonetheless, at the same time, he was constant in his admonition that this faith was not only to be anticipated but also to be sought after earnestly.

---

123. Green, *Grace and Truth Vindicated*, 192–97.
124. See the discussion above regarding the operative purview of the metaphor.

CHAPTER 10

Epilogue

IN A SERMON WRITTEN just three years before his death, Wesley spoke about a distinction between what he called "species of faith." He emphasized that this was "a point of no small importance" and was worthy of his ongoing effort to make the distinction and its implications "a little plainer."[1] The distinction he was highlighting was that between "the faith of a servant" and "the faith of a son." It is significant not only that Wesley viewed the distinction as important but that he was convinced that the biblical contrast between servant and son most adequately conveyed the dynamic of the distinction. And conveying this *dynamic* was his ultimate aim. Rather than a tome explaining the nuances of his appropriation of classic covenant theology, his interest was in providing those gathered into the scores of Methodist Societies the coordinates by which they might both locate themselves on the way of salvation and navigate their way forward.

For Wesley, the value of the servant-son metaphor lay in its capacity to provide a concise summary of what he considered to be the centerpiece of the story-line of covenant theology's account of God's redeeming work in and for the world. It is, in fact, Wesley's covenant theology that oversees his use of the metaphor, that is replicated in his soteriology, and that is reflected in his pastoral initiatives over the course of his years as a leader of the Evangelical Revival. Lamentably, by and large, the Wesley corpus has been read and researched with little if any attention given to the influence of covenant theology on his theological thought. Consequently, rather than making things "a little plainer," his theological thought—and his soteriology, in particular—has been obscured in some measure.

This is not to say that knowing the story-line of covenant theology would clear up any and all confusion over Wesley's soteriology. The fact

---

1. Wesley, "On the Discoveries of Faith," *Works* (BE) §12–14, 34–35.

that he himself felt compelled to make things "a little plainer" indicates that his own best efforts to communicate "the Successive Conquests of Grace"[2] were not always crystal clear or needed to be freshly articulated in order to answer some competing point of view that had gained a hearing in the Societies. A case in point is his stern response to James Morgan twenty years before his late sermons on the servant-son metaphor. As previously noted, Morgan had reportedly asserted that "'all who mourn after God are in the favour of God.'" Wesley unequivocally rejected this assertion declaring it to be "unscriptural and unsafe" and "contrary to what we have always taught."[3]

Yet, in Morgan's defense, it is conceivable that he may have thought himself to be defending a central feature of Wesley's appropriation of covenant theology: namely, that each dispensation is "live" (or active) simultaneously, soteriologically and existentially, though not historically.[4] And given the conviction that each dispensation is salvifically sufficient, the assertion may have seemed the logical conclusion: that a mourning penitent would surely be "in the favour of God."

While Morgan may have intended to fairly represent Wesley's soteriology, he nonetheless missed a turn, so to speak, in Wesley's thinking on this important point. It is true that affirming the soteriological and existential concurrence of the various dispensations provided to Wesley and, he hoped, to his Methodists a way of preserving and expressing the biblical witness to the magnanimity of the grace of God toward all of humankind. On this point, paramount for his soteriology was his conviction that, while no one had lived under the covenant of works since Adam in the time of his innocency, all persons since the fall lived within the reach of the redemptive initiatives of the covenant of grace. And further, the magnanimity of God's grace was demonstrated by the extension of divine favor wherever there was response to these redemptive initiatives,[5] however little or much these initiatives may be recognized or understood as such. Cornelius was an example of one having such favor.

For Wesley, response was critical; for grace was not only to be received but stewarded. In concert with Christian orthodoxy, he

2. Wesley and Wesley, *Hymns and Sacred Poems* (1740), iv.

3. Wesley, *Letters*, 5:103–5.

4. Since Christ's death *in realitor*, only the gospel dispensation is "live" *historically-*speaking. See Chapter 7 for the discussion on Wesley's conception of the salvific sufficiency of the various dispensations of the covenant of grace.

5. The term "initiative" is intended here to preserve Wesley's understanding of the prevenient grace of God extended to all. Any capacity on the part of humanity is the God-given capacity to elect to respond to divine initiative.

understood that the only response compatible with *any* of the various dispensations of the covenant of grace was faith, for without faith there was no life ("believe, and live"). The reach of this faith was in accordance with the divine prerogative, and was to be affirmed and celebrated on the basis of the salvific sufficiency of each dispensation of the covenant of grace secured by Christ as "the lamb slain from the foundation of the world." Wesley could therefore assert, for example, that one having died while under the Jewish dispensation soteriologically was "darkly safe with God."

Wesley's view on the interplay of the divine prerogative and the obligation to steward that grace is well-expressed by Robert South in his sermon on the first chapter of Titus:

> It highly concerns us so to discourse of God . . . that his prerogative of being the first cause of all things, and both the author and finisher of man's salvation, be not infringed by such assertions as of necessity infer the contrary. And yet, on the other side, this prerogative of God is to be defended with such sobriety, as not in the mean time to leave the creature no scope of duty, or to render all exhortations and threatnings, and other helps of action, absurd and superfluous.[6]

As Wesley had pointed out, while "in order of thinking God's working goes first," "in order of time" (i.e., experientially, on the side of grace-assisted human agency) a person's believing is "first." So then, these two pastoral affirmations, noted earlier in this study, are foundational for Wesley: 1) a person's response to God cannot exceed the extent of the faith given to that point in time; and 2) it is incumbent upon every person to believe in accordance with the faith he or she has been given.

Yet, Wesley was neither inclined nor permitted by his understanding of Scripture and of covenant theology to rest content in the notion of the soteriological and existential concurrence of the various dispensations of the covenant of grace. And for good reason: these dispensations are not only concurrent but relative. There is a progression from lesser to greater. And this progression represents a difference that is not only quantitative (i.e., an increase in light, or an increase in clarity) but qualitative, too.[7] In other words, with the dawning of each dispensation

---

6. South, "Sermon V," *Five Additional Volumes of Sermons*, 1744), 93. This admonition stood in firm agreement with that of Thomas Boston as noted above. See Boston, *Fourfold State* (1735), 172.

7. The Coeccian distinction between *parēsis* (the divine forbearance) and *aphēsis* (the divine forgiveness) highlighted this qualitative difference between the dispensations

of the covenant of grace the stage is reset as the redemptive activity of God progresses. As a result, while the previous dispensation remains "live" soteriologically and existentially, it is no longer *normative*. What is soteriologically and existentially *normative* is determined wholly by whatever dispensation is "live" *historically*.

This understanding formed the basis of Wesley's strong response to James Morgan. There was certainly a sense in which Wesley could agree with Morgan that the penitent is in the favor of God. This had been affirmed by the 1746 Conference in its conclusions regarding the experience of Jonathan Reeves. And, in his sermon "On Faith," Wesley underscored this in his assertion that there was a sense in which the wrath of God does not abide upon the person having the faith of a servant, and that such a one is accepted of God. But what Wesley was safeguarding in correcting Morgan was the fact that the dispensations previous to the gospel dispensation are not to be regarded as normative. And consequently, being in the favor of God is *redefined* in light of the new norm (i.e., the new standard) of the gospel dispensation. Morgan had overlooked this fact. Alarmed, Wesley countered: "We have always taught that a penitent mourned or was pained on this very account, because he felt he was 'not in the favour of God,' having a sense of guilt upon his conscience and a sense of the divine displeasure at the same time."[8] Wesley similarly described the state of the one having the faith of a servant in his 1788 sermon, "On the Discoveries of Faith."

What is unique about the gospel dispensation is that it is the culmination and crown of every previous dispensation. It is not only that the gospel dispensation surpasses the dispensation just previous to it as a greater revelation of God's redemptive activity (just as the legal or Jewish dispensation surpassed the dispensation from Abraham to Moses), but that there is a salvific perfection to the gospel dispensation that is unique and unsurpassable. This salvific perfection resides in the revelation of Christ—the lamb slain *in realitor*—and the accompanying work of the Spirit of Adoption. These are the inaugurating and defining events of the gospel dispensation of the covenant of grace. In this dispensation, the ever-increasing light of every previous dispensation reaches its fullest intensity, never to wane.

An important point with respect the inauguration of the gospel dispensation is that since the revelation of Christ, all of humankind lives

---

of the covenant of grace prior to the gospel dispensation. See the discussion on successive, relative sufficiency in Chapter 7 of this volume.

8. Wesley, *Letters*, 5:103–5.

in the historic moment of the gospel dispensation, whatever may be the individual responses to the grace of God. And this means that the divine intentions for every person are now calibrated to the divine provisions of the *gospel* dispensation. Thus, while the various dispensations of the covenant of grace remain soteriologically and existentially concurrent, the gospel dispensation is alone definitive of the divine intentions and constitute that to which all are called. This is the basis of the third pastoral affirmation noted earlier in this study: it is the duty of every person to seek that faith which they do not yet have but which they have become apprised awaits them. It is on this basis that Wesley could declare to Ann Bolton in a letter from London on February 4, 1769: "A blessing is ready for many; for *you* in particular. I say still, Dare to believe, and feel Him near! Put forth your hand and touch Him! Is He not standing at the door of your heart?"[9] And in his 1788 sermons concerning the servant-son metaphor, Wesley called upon those having the faith of a servant to not "halt by the way"[10] but "to press on by all possible means, till he passes 'from faith to faith'; from the faith of a *servant* to the faith of a *son*."[11]

The way of salvation, then, by divine design and divine enabling, is intended to culminate in coming into possession of all the provisions of the gospel dispensation. And the defining "moment" wherein one enters *soteriologically* into the provisions of the gospel dispensation is that moment when Christ is "'. . . revealed in his heart,' enabling him to testify, 'The life that I now live in the flesh I live by faith in the Son of God, who loved *me*, and gave himself for *me*." This, says Wesley, is "the proper voice of a child of God."[12]

It is important to understand that this new norm is definitive for Wesley's understanding of justification (and sanctification, for that matter). As he says in his commentary on Hebrews 7:18–19, the Mosaic Law is abrogated "*for the weakness and unprofitableness thereof*—For its insufficiency either to justify or to sanctify. . . . *For the law*—Taken by itself, separate from the gospel, *made nothing perfect*—Could not perfect its votaries, either in faith or love, in happiness or holiness."[13] In light of so much of the contemporary discussion over whether or not Wesley believed those having the faith of a servant were justified, we have noted

9. Wesley, *Letters*, 5:125.
10. Wesley, "On Faith," *Works* (BE) §12, 498.
11. Wesley, "On the Discoveries of Faith," *Works* (BE) §14, 35–36.
12. Ibid.
13. Wesley, *ENNT*, 721.

Epilogue

that Wesley never once describes one having the faith of a servant as justified. The reason is that, for him, the Reformation doctrine of Justification is to be understood solely in terms of the salvific perfection of the gospel dispensation of the covenant of grace. *This* is the new standard soteriologically because it is the present dispensation of the covenant of grace. Therefore, while there is a sense in which he could speak of someone who was—soteriologically—under the legal or Jewish dispensation as being, in a real and significant sense, in God's favor, he did not conceive that anyone could be *justified* except upon the revelation of Christ in them; that is, having soteriologically come into the provisions of the gospel dispensation. In a sense, then, the question of whether the person having the faith of a servant is justified was, for Wesley, not up for discussion.

Wesley's focus was on inviting and encouraging his reading and listening audience into all the blessings of the gospel dispensation. He was particularly interested in God's redemptive activity concentrated in the two last dispensations, the legal (or Mosaic or Jewish) and the gospel (or Christian or evangelical). Both of these dispensations had been inaugurated in dramatic fashion: in the Pentecost of Sinai and the Pentecost of Jerusalem, respectively.

While well aware and affirming of dispensations of the covenant of grace previous to the Mosaic, Wesley's attention was concentrated on these two for two reasons. First, the giving of the Law to Moses brought sin to light, and, as Ames put it, incited the responsive to "flie unto Christ." And second, this biblical and historical act of the giving of the Law (followed by the revelation of Christ in the gospel dispensation) was understood by Wesley as a pattern for the stewarding of grace. For the minister of the gospel, the worthy proclamation of the gospel would entail the preaching of the Law so that the Law might bring sin to light in the hearts and lives of those who had yet to come to know Christ. This proclamation was sure to be accompanied by the work of the Holy Spirit as the spirit of bondage, enabling those who once had considered themselves under no danger spiritually to now be fully alerted to their spiritual state and desirous of its remedy.

This might be all that such persons could expect were it not for the fact that a new dispensation, the gospel dispensation, had been ushered in by Christ's death *in realitor*. And since Christ has been revealed, the pre-eminence of the Christian over the legal dispensation is not in doubt; and neither is the fact that this is the divine invitation to one and all. Just as Christ was revealed in history by his death *in realitor* so it is the divine intention that each individual might experience Christ's death *in realitor* and be able to declare, "The life that I now live in the flesh I live by faith in the Son of God, who loved me, and *gave himself for me*."[14] Thus, for those hearing the law-to-gospel proclamation the servant-son metaphor served as an impetus to the stewardship of grace. It apprised them not only of their present state but deposited hope by unveiling the divine intention that servants become sons and assured them that "in the fulness of the time" Christ will be revealed and the Spirit of Adoption given.

This coming into the reality of Christ revealed was not something mild and matter-of-fact for Wesley. His description is not of a mere advance in maturity or simply a movement from lacking assurance to having assurance. Rather, it is a description of complete transformation:

> He will then be "born of God," inwardly changed by the mighty power of God from 'an earthly, sensual, devilish' mind to "the mind which was in Christ Jesus." He will experience what St. Paul means by those remarkable words to the Galatians, "Ye are the sons of God by faith"; "and because ye are sons, God hath sent forth the Spirit of his Son into your hearts, crying, Abba, Father." "He that believeth" as a son (as St. John observes) "hath the witness in himself." "The Spirit itself witnesses with his spirit that he is a child of God." "The love of God is shed abroad in his heart by the Holy Ghost which is given unto him."[15]

For Wesley, the servant-son metaphor was not a sidebar of his theological thought but functioned instead as a definitive narrative of his soteriology, by which he called his hearers forward into the divinely-granted benedictions of the Christian dispensation. With so much at stake, Wesley was not reticent in highlighting the urgency and significance of the disparity between servant and son. In fact, rather than *downplay* the distinction, his objective in using the metaphor was to *accentuate* the contrasting spiritual realities between the faith of a servant and the faith of a son. He accomplished this by upholding the standard of sonship as a discernible, transformative reality accompanying the revelation of Christ in the heart and the witnessing work of the Spirit as the spirit of adoption.

At the same time, he purposed to come quickly to the defense and encouragement of those who have "only the faith of a servant."[16] The earliest, most elementary level of receptivity to the initial (and normally

---

14. Wesley, "On the Discoveries of Faith," *Works* (BE) §14, 35. Emphasis mine.
15. Ibid.
16. Wesley, "On the Discoveries of Faith," *Works* (BE) §13, 4:35.

troubling) awakening work of the Spirit is affirmed, celebrated, and wed to the promise of the certainty of a benevolent divine response. This measure of divine acceptance is underscored yet without minimizing the reality of the desperation of those who, having the faith of a servant, find themselves to be "so fast in prison that they cannot get forth"[17] and who have only a "wavering sight" of Christ who alone is able to take away the veil from their hearts.[18] At the same time, while the co-operant nature of grace is emphasized, it is allowed neither to dictate nor to abridge the mystery of the divine prerogative in the giving of faith.

It is important to remember that Wesley was adamant that advancing in the way of salvation was not merely a preference or a worthy aim for those having the faith of a servant. Instead, it was *essential* to holy living, the calling given to all of humankind. Nor was the witness of the Spirit, as the hallmark of entry into the privileges and blessings of the gospel dispensation, simply an enhancement; it was, rather, the confirmation of a new reality soteriologically. The privileges and provisions of the Christian dispensation were the divine design, guaranteed by the divine promise and certified by the witnessing work of the Spirit, first as the spirit of bondage and then as the spirit of adoption. Those who progressed from the faith of a servant to the faith of a son were those who, *because* of this new reality in their lives, Wesley admonished to "go on to perfection."[19]

Above all, Wesley was intent on providing a way for Methodists to identify and affirm the working of God's grace, and to confirm and honor the work of the Holy Spirit. It was to this end that he appealed to the servant-son metaphor to communicate the dynamic of his appropriation of covenant theology, and thus to engage the hearer in an unfolding and hope-filled story—the story of a servant, the story of a son; indeed, the story of the hearer's own encounter with the God of all grace.

---

17. Ibid., §12, 4:34–35. Wesley uses this same description more than forty years earlier in his sermon, "The Spirit of Bondage and of Adoption," *Works* (BE) §II.7, 1:258.

18. 2 Cor 3:6–15. Wesley, *ENNT*, 470–71.

19. See Wesley's admonition to those having the faith of a son in his sermons "On Faith" and "On the Discoveries of Faith," Wesley, *Works* (BE) §II.5, 3:500–501 and §16, 4:498.

Bibliography

Primary Sources

Ambrose, Isaac. "Looking Unto Jesus in His Life. The Fourth Book, Part Second." In *Looking Unto Jesus: A View of the Everlasting Gospel; Or, the Soul's Eying of Jesus, As Carrying on the Great Work of Man's Salvation, From First to Last. Volume I*, 205–302. London: Printed by Edward Mottershed, 1658.

Ames, William. *The Marrow of Sacred Divinity Drawne Out of the Holy Scriptures, and the Interpreters Thereof, and Brought Into Method*. London: Printed by Edward Griffin for Henry Overton, 1642.

The Arminian Magazine: Consisting of Extracts and Original Treatises on Universal Redemption. Edited by John Wesley. 14 vols. London, 1778–91.

Arminius, James. *The Works of James Arminius*. Translated by James Nichols. 3 vols. London: Longman, Rees, Orme, Brown, and Green, 1828.

Barclay, Robert. *An Apology for the True Christian Divinity, As the Same Is Held Forth, and Preached, by the People Called, in Scorn, Quakers: Being A Full Explanation and Vindication of Their Principles and Doctrines, by Many Arguments, Deduced From Scripture and Right Reason, and the Testimonies of Famous Authors, Both Ancient and Modern: With a Full Answer to the Strongest Objections Usually Made Against Them*. 7th English ed. Dublin: Printed and Sold by Mary Fuller, 1737.

Baxter, Richard. *Aphorismes of Justification, with Their Explication Annexed Wherein Also Is Opened the Nature of the Covenants, Satisfaction, Righteousnesse, Faith, Works, &C.: Published Especially for the Use of the Church of Kederminster in Worcestershire*. The Hague: printed by Abraham Brown, 1655.

———. *An Extract of Mr. Richard Baxter's Aphorisms of Justification*. Edited by John Wesley. Originally published as *Aphorisms of Justification*. Newcastle-Upon-Tyne, UK: Printed by John Gooding, 1745.

Bennet, John. *John Ben[n]et's Manuscript Minutes of the Early Methodist Conferences, 1744–48* (1746 manuscript minutes not included). Methodist Archives of The John Rylands University Library of Manchester, England.

Bengel, John Albert. *Gnomon of the New Testament*. Edited by J. C. F. Steudel. Translated by William Fletcher. 6th ed. 5 vols. Edinburgh: T. & T. Clark, 1866.

———. *Gnomon of the New Testament, Pointing Out From the Natural Force of the Words, the Simplicity, Depth, and Harmony and Saving Power of Its Divine Thoughts*. Edited by Charlton T. Lewis. Translated by Charlton T. Lewis and Marvin R. Vincent. 2 vols. Philadelphia: Perkinpine & Higgins, 1862, 1864.

Beveridge, William. *Private Thoughts Upon Religion, Digested Into Twelve Articles; With Practical Resolutions Form'd Thereupon. By the Right Reverend Father in God. William*

Bibliography

Beveridge, D. D. Late Lord Bishop of St. Asaph. Written in His Younger Years, for the Settling of His Principles, and Conduct of His Life. 9th ed. London: printed for W. Taylor, 1719.

Bolton, Ann. *Ann Bolton Journal.* John Banks Research Collection, Methodist Archives of The John Rylands University Library of Manchester, England.

Boston, Thomas. *Human Nature in Its Four-Fold State of Primitive Integrity, Entire Depravation, Begun Recovery, and Consummate Happiness or Misery. Subsisting in The Parents of Mankind in Paradise, The Irregenerate, The Regenerate, All Mankind in the Future State. In Several Practical Discourses: By a Minister of the Gospel in the Church of Scotland.* 4th ed. Edinburgh: printed by R. Drummond and Company, 1744.

Bulkeley, Peter. *The Gospel-Covenant, or, The Covenant of Grace Opened.* 2nd ed. London: printed by Matthew Simmons, 1651.

Bunyan, John. *The Doctrine of the Law & Grace Unfolded: Or, a Discourse Touching the Law and Grace. The Nature of the One, and the Nature of the Other: Shewing What They Are, As They Are the Two Covenants; And Likewise Who They Be, and What Their Conditions Are, That Be Under Either of These Two Covenants. Wherein, For the Better Understanding of the Reader, There Is Several Questions Answered Touching the Law and Grace, Very Easie to Be Read, and As Easie to Be Understood, by Those That Are the Sons of Wisdom, the Children of the Second Covenant. Also, Several Titles Set Over the Several Truths Contained in This Book, for Thy Sooner Finding of Them; Which Are Those At the Latter End. By John Bunyan, Author of the Pilgrims Progress.* 2nd ed. London: Printed for William Marshall, the Bible in Newgate-Street, 1701.

Burk, John Christian Frederic. *A Memoir of the Life and Writings of John Albert Bengel, Prelate in Würtemberg.* Translated by Robert Francis Walker. London: William Ball, Aldine Chamgers. Paternoster Row, 1837.

Burkitt, William. *Expository Notes with Practical Observations on the Remaining Part of the New Testament.* London: printed for Thomas Parkhurst, 1703.

Burnet, Gilbert. *An Exposition of the Thirty-Nine Articles of the Church of England Written by Gilbert Bishop of Sarum.* 3rd ed. London: printed for Ri. Chiswell, 1705.

Charnock, Stephen. "A Discourse of the Knowledge of God." In *The Works of the Late Learned Divine Stephen Charnock, B.D. being several discourses upon various divine subjects,* 2:381–473. London: printed by A. Maxwell and R. Roberts, 1684.

Church of England. *The Book of Common Prayer, and Adminsitration of the Sacraments, and Other Rites and Ceremonies of the Church, According to the Use of the Church of England: Together with the Psalter or Psalms of David, Pointed As They Are to Be Sung Or Said in Churches.* Oxford: printed by John Baskett, printer to the University, 1732.

———. "Of Good Works Annexed unto Faith." In *Certain Sermons or Homilies Appointed to Be Read in Churches in the Time of Queen Elizabeth of Famous Memory,* 27–36. London: printed for S.K.J.T. and E.P., 1713.

———. "A Sermon of the Salvation of Mankind, by Only Christ Our Saviour, From Sin and Death Everlasting." In *Certain Sermons or Homilies Appointed to Be Read in Churches in the Time of Queen Elizabeth of Famous Memory,* 12–19. London: printed for S.K.J.T. and E.P., 1713.

———. "A Short Declaration of the True, Lively, and Christian Faith." In *Certain Sermons or Homilies Appointed to Be Read in Churches in the Time of Queen Elizabeth of Famous Memory,* 19–27. London: printed for S.K.J.T. and E.P., 1713.

Bibliography

Cotton, John. *The Way of the Churches of Christ in New-England. Or The Way of Churches Walking in Brotherly Equalitie, or Co-Ordination, Without Subjection of One Church to Another. Measured and Examined by the Golden Reed of the Sanctuary. Containing a Full Declaration of the Church-Way in All Particulars.* London: printed by Matthew Simmons, 1645.

Davenant, John and Josiah Allport. *A Treatise on Justification, or the Disputatio De Justitia Habituali Et Actuali. Published First in the Year 1631, and Now Translated From the Original Latin, Together with Translations of the "Determinationes" By the Rev. Josiah Allport.* London: Hamilton, Adams, & Co., 1844.

Doddridge, Philip. *The Family Expositor: Or, a Paraphrase and Version of the New Testament. With Critical Notes.* 6 vols. London: printed by John Wilson, 1739–56.

Downame, George. *A Treatise of Iustification, by George Downame, Doctor of Divinity and Bishop of Dery.* London: printed by Felix Kyngston, 1633.

Dunton, John and Samuel Wesley. "Q. 2: What Are the Opinions of the Remonstrants, As to Matters of Faith?" *The Athenian Gazette: Or, Casuistical Mercury, Resolving All the Most Nice and Curious Questions Proposed by the Ingenious of Either Sex* 16 (February 16, 1695). London, 1695. np.

Finch, Sir Henry. *The Sacred Doctrine of Diuinitie Gathered Out of the Worde of God, Togither with an Explication of the Lordes Prayer.* Middelburg, VA: Printed by Richard Schilders, 1589.

Fisher, Edward and Thomas Boston. *The Marrow of Modern Divinity: In Two Parts.* London: printed for Thomas Tegg and Son, 1837.

Fletcher, John. *The Doctrines of Grace and Justice Equally Essential to the Pure Gospel: With Some Remarks on the Mischievous Divisions Caused Among Christians by Parting Those Doctrines. Being An Introduction to a Plan of Reconciliation Between the Defenders of the Doctrines of Partial Grace, Commonly Called Calvinists; And the Defenders of the Doctrines of Impartial Justice, Commonly Called Arminians.* London: printed by R. Hawes, 1777.

———. "An Essay on the Doctrine of the New Birth." *Asbury Theological Journal* 53 (1998) 35–56.

———. "An Essay on Truth, Being a Rational Vindication of the Doctrine of Salvation by Faith." In *The First Part of An Equal Check to Pharisaism and Antinomianism*, 137–264. London: printed by J. Eddowes, 1774.

———. "The Language of the Father's Dispensation." *Asbury Theological Journal* 53 (1998) 64–78.

———. *Letters of John Fletcher: Selected and Edited by Edward Cook.* Edited by Edward Cook. Shoals, IN: Old Paths Tract Society, 1999.

———. "Salvation by the Covenant of Grace: A Discourse on Rom xi. 5,6. In *The Works of the Rev. John Fletcher with a life by the Rev. Abhaham Scott*, 1:493-535. London: printed for Thomas Allman, 1836.

———. "Second Part Containing Answers to the Objections Made to This Essay." *Asbury Theological Journal* 53 (1998) 57–64.

———. *A Vindication of the Rev. Mr. Wesley's Last Minutes: Occasioned by a Circular, Printed Letter, Inviting Principal Persons, Both Clergy and Laity, As Well of the Dissenters As of the Established Church, Who Disapprove of Those Minutes, to Oppose Them in a Body, As a Dreadful Heresy: And Designed To Remove Prejudice, Check Rashness, Promote Forbearance, Defend the Character of an Eminent Minister of Christ, and Prevent Some Important Scriptural Truths From Being Hastily Branded*

Bibliography

As Heretical. In Five Letters, to the Hon. And Rev. Author of the Circular Letter. By a Lover of Quietness and Liberty of Conscience. Bristol, UK: printed by W. Pine, 1771.

Furley, Samuel. "To John Wesley, November 21, 1759." Alfred James Derrick Album, Sugden Heritage Collection, Queens University, Melbourne. Courtesy of Ted A. Campbell.

Goodwin, John. *A Treatise on Justification: Extracted From Mr. John Goodwin; With a Preface, Wherein All That Is Material, in Letters Just Published, Under the Name of the Rev. Mr. Hervey, Is Answered.* Bristol, UK: printed by William Pine, 1765.

Green, John. *Grace and Truth Vindicated, or the Way to Heaven Manifested, From Scripture and Experience.* London: printed by H. Cock, 1752.

Guyse, John. *A Practical Exposition of the Epistle to the Galatians, And From Thence Forward to the End of the Revelation, In the Form of a Paraphrase: With Occasional Notes In Their Proper Places for Further Explication, and Serious Recollections At the Close of Every Chapter. To Which Is Added, An Alphabetical Table of the Principal Things Contained in the Paraphrase, Especially in the Notes, of This, and the Two Former Volumes. For the Use of the Family and the Closet.* London: printed for John Oswald, at the Rose and Crown in the Poultry, 1752.

———. *The Practical Expositor: Or, an Exposition of the New Testament, in the Form of a Paraphrase; With Occasional Notes.* 3rd ed. 6 vols. Edinburgh: printed by W. Darling, 1775.

———. *The Practical Expositor: Or, an Exposition of the New Testament, in the Form of a Paraphrase; With Occasional Notes.* 4th ed. 6 vols. Glasgow: printed by W. Darling, 1792–94.

Hall, Joseph. "Via Media: The Way of Peace in the Five Busy Articles, Commonly Known by the Name Arminius." In *The Works of the Right Reverend Joseph Hall, D.D., Bishop of Exeter and afterward of Norwich*, edited by Philip Wynter, 9:488–519. Oxford: at the University Press, 1863.

Hare, Edward. *Remarks on Two Sermons, on Jusification by Faith, and The Witness of the Spirit, Lately Published by Mr. Joseph Cooke, in Five Letters, Addressed to the Author.* Rochdale, UK: printed and sold by J. Harltey, 1806.

Hammond, Henry. *A Practical Catechism.* 5th ed. London: printed for R. Royston, 1649.

Henry, Matthew. *An exposition of all the books of the Old and New Testament: wherein the chapters are summ'd up in contents; the sacred text inserted at large, in paragraphs, or verses; and each paragraph, or verse, reduc'd to its proper heads; the sense given, and largely illustrated, with practical remarks and observations.* 3rd ed. 6 vols. London: Printed for J. Clark and R. Hett, J. Knapton, J. and B. Sprint, J. Darby, D. Midwinter [and 13 others in London], 1721–25.

Herbert, George. "The Church-Porch. Perirrhanterium." In *The Temple: Sacred Poems and Private Ejaculations*, 1-17. 4th ed. Cambridge: Printed by Thom. Buck, and Roger Daniel, printers to the Universitie of Cambridge, 1635.

Hervey, James. *Theron and Aspasio: Or, a Series of Dialogues and Letters, Upon the Most Important and Interesting Subjects.* 2 vols. Dublin: printed by S. Powell, 1756.

Heylyn, John. *Theological Lectures At Westminster-Abbey. With an Interpretation of the Four Gospels. To Which Are Added, Some Select Discourses Upon the Principal Points of Reveal'd Religion.* London: printed for J. and R. Tonson and S. Draper, 1749.

Hooker, Thomas. *A Survey of the Summe of Church-Discipline. Wherein the Vvay of the Churches of New-England Is Warranted Out of the Vvord, and All Exceptions of Weight, Which Are Made Against It, Answered : Whereby Also It Will Appear to*

Bibliography

the Judicious Reader, That Something More Must Be Said, Then Yet Hath Been, Before Their Principles Can Be Shaken, or They Should Be Unsetled in Their Practice. London: Printed by J.M. for John Bellamy, 1648.

Horne, George. *Works Wrought Through Faith a Condition of Our Justification. A Sermon Preached Before the University of Oxford, At St. Mary's, on June 7, 1761.* Oxford: printed at the Clarenden-Press, 1761.

Horne, Melvill. *An Investigation of the Definition of Justifying Faith, the Damnatory Clause Under Which It Is Enforced, and the Doctrine of A Direct Witness of the Spirit, Held by Dr. Coke, and Other Methodist Preachers, in a Series of Letters.* London: J. Wilson, 1809.

Ingham, Benjamin. *Diary of an Oxford Methodist, Benjamin Ingham, 1733–1734.* Edited by Richard P. Heitzenrater. Durham, NC: Duke University Press, 1985.

———. Manuscript Diary, 1733–1734. Oxford Diaries X (Colman Collection). The Methodist Archives of The John Rylands Library of Manchester, England.

———. "To [Charles Wesley], 1740." The Methodist Archives of The John Rylands University Library of Manchester, England (DDPr 1/50).

Knox, Alexander. "Remarks on the Life and Character of John Wesley." In *The Life of Wesley; and Rise and Progress of Methodism*, 2:338-410. 2nd American ed. New York: Harper & Brothers, 1847.

Law, William. *The Second Part of The Spirit of Prayer: Or, the Soul Rising Out of the Vanity of Time, Into the Riches of Eternity. Being Several Dialogues Between Academicus, Rusticus, and Theophilus. At Which Humanus Was Present.* London, 1750.

Minutes of the Methodist Conference From the First, Held in London, by the Late Rev. John Wesley, A.M. In the Year 1744. In *Minutes of the Methodist Conferences, 1744–1877.* Wesleyan Methodist Church. Vol 1. London: Printed at the Conference Office, 14, City Road, 1812.

Norris, John. *Christian Blessedness: Or, Practical Discourses Upon the Beattitudes of Our Lord and Saviour Jesus Christ; With Three Other Volumes of Practical Discourses.* 10th ed. London: printed for Edmund Parker, 1724.

Pemble, William. *Vindiciæ Fide, or A Treatise of Iustification by Faith Wherein the Truth of That Point Is Fully Cleared, and Vindicated From the Cavills of Its Adversaries Delivered At Magdalen Hall in Oxford.* 2nd ed. Oxford: printed by John Lichfield, 1629.

Perkins, William. *A Commentarie upon the Epistle to the Galatians.* London: Iohn Legatt, printer to the University of Cambridge, 1617.

———. *The First Part of The Cases of Conscience Wherein Specially, Three Maine Questions Concerning Man, Simply Considered in Himselfe, Are Propounded and Resolued, According to the Word of God. Taught and Deliuered, by M. William Perkins in His Holy-Day Lectures, by Himselfe Revised Before His Death, and Now Published for the Benefit of the Church.* 2nd ed. Cambridge: printed by Iohn Legat, 1604.

———. *A Golden Chaine: Or The Description of Theologie Containing the Order of the Causes of Saluation and Damnation, According to Gods Word. A View Whereof Is to Be Seene in the Table Annexed. Hereunto Is Adioyned the Order Which M. Theodore Beza Vsed in Comforting Afflicted Consciences.* Printed by Iohn Legat, printer to the Vniuersitie of Cambridge, 1600.

———. "A Graine of Musterd-Seede: Or, the Least Measure of Grace That Is or Can Be Effectual to Saluation." In *The Workes of That Famous and Vvorthy Minister of Christ in the Vniuersitie of Cambridge, M. VVilliam Perkins. The Second Volume. Newly Corrected According to His Owne Copies. VVith Distinct Chapters, And Contents of*

Bibliography

    Every Booke Prefixed: And Two Tables of the Whole Adjoyned; One of the Matters and Questions, the Other of Choice Places of Scripture, 1:635–44. London: Printed by Iohn Legatt, 1631.

Poole, Matthew. *Annotations Upon the Holy Bible. Wherein the Sacred Text Is Inserted, and Various Readings Annex'd, Together with Parallel Scriptures, the More Difficult Terms in Each Verse Are Explained, Seeming Contradictions Reconciled, Questions and Doubts Resolved, and the Whole Text Opened / by the Late Reverend and Learned Divine Mr. Matthew Poole.* 2 vols. London: Printed by John Richardson, 1683.

Preston, John. *The New Covenant, or, The Saints Portion a Treatise Vnfolding the All-Sufficiencie of God, Mans Vprightnes, and the Covenant of Grace: Delivered in Fourteene Sermons Vpon Gen. 17.1.2: Wherevnto Are Adioyned Foure Sermons Vpon Eccles. 9.1.2.11.12.* 2nd ed. London: Printed by I.D. for Nicolas Bourne, 1629.

Rimius, Henry. *A Candid Narrative of the Rise and Progress of the Herrnhutters, commonly Call'd Moravians or Unitas Fratrum, with a Short Account of Their Doctrines, Drawn From Their Own Writings, To Which Are Added, Observations on Their Politics in General, and Particularly on Their Conduct Whilst in the County of Budingen in the Circle of the Upper-Rhine in Germany.* Catherine-streeet *in the* Strand: A. Linde, 1753. Repr. London, n.d.

Robertson, J. "From J. Robertson at Pitcomb near Bruton, Somerset, to the Foundery (Rev. Charles Wesley), London, September 23, 1747." The Methodist Archives of The John Rylands University Library of Manchester, England (DDPr 1/67).

Rollock, Robert. *A Treatise of Gods Effectual Calling.* Second edition. London: Felix Kyngston, 1603.

Salvard, Jean Francois and Simon Goulart. *Harmonium Confessionum Fidei, Orthoxarum Et Reformatarum Ecclesiarum (An Harmony of the Confessions of the Faith of the Christian and Reformed Churches, Which Purely Professe the Holy Doctrine of the Gospell in All the Chief Kingdoms, Nations, and Provinces of Europe).* 1581. Repr. London: Iohn Legatt, 1643.

Scougal, Henry. *The Life of God in the Soul of Man.* 1st ed. 1691. Reprint. London: Inter-Varsity Fellowship, 1961.

Shepard, Thomas. *The Sound Beleever, or, A Treatise of Evangelicall Conversion Discovering the Work of Christs Spirit in Reconciling of a Sinner to God.* London: printed for R. Dawlman, 1645.

Sibbes, Richard. "Lydia's Conversion." In *The Complete Works of Richard Sibbes*, edited by Alexander Balloch Grosart, 6:517–34. Edinburgh: James Nichol, 1864.

———. "The Witness of Salvation." In *The Complete Works of Richard Sibbes*, edited by Alexander Balloch Grosart, 7:367–85. Edinburgh: James Nichol, 1864.

Smith, John. "Select Discourse Treating Of the Difference Between the Legal and the Evangelical Righteousness, the Old and the New Covenant, &C." In *Select Discourses Treating . . . As Also a Sermon Preached by Simon Patrick . . . At the Author's Funeral with a Brief Account of His Life and Death*, edited by John Worthington, 283–346. London: J. Flesher for W. Morden, bookseller, 1660.

South, Robert. "Sermon V." In *Five Additional Volumes of Sermons Preached Upon Several Occasions. By Robert South, D. D. Late Prebendary of Westminster, and Canon of Christ-Church, Oxon. Now First Printed From the Author's Manuscripts. With the Chief Heads of the Sermons Prefix'd to Each Volume: And A General Index of the Principal Matters*, 7:88–112. London: Printed for Charles Bathurst, 1744.

Southey, Robert. *The Life of John Wesley; And the Rise and Progress of Methodism.* 2 Vols, London: printed for Longman, Hurst, Rees, Orme, and Brown, 1820.

Taylor, Jeremy. "Faith Working by Love." In *The Whole Works of the Right Rev. Jeremy Taylor*, 6:267–300 London: printed by W. Clowes, 1828.

———, "How Far an Unregenerate Man May Go in the Ways of Piety and Religion." In *The Doctrine and Practice of Repentance; Deus Justificatus; And the Real Presence of Christ in the Holy Sacrament*, edited by Reginald Heber, 9:139–55. London: W. Clowes, 1828.

———. *Unum Necessarium: Or, the Doctrine and Practice of Repentance. Describing the Necessities and Measures of a Strict, a Holy, and a Christian Life. And Rescued From Popular Errors.* 4th ed. London: printed for the Executor of Luke Meredith, 1705.

Wesley, Charles, and Kenneth G. C. Newport. *The Sermons of Charles Welsey—A Critical Edition with Introduction and Notes.* Oxford: Oxford University Press, 2001.

Wesley, Charles. *Hymns and Sacred Poems. In Two Volumes. By Charles Wesley, M.A. Student of Christ-Church, Oxford.* Bristol: printed by Felix Farley, 1749.

———. *The Journal of the Rev. Charles Wesley, M.A. Sometime Student of Christ Church, Oxford to Which Are Appended Selections From His Correspondence and Poetry with an Introduction and Occasional Notes by Thomas Jackson.* Edited by Thomas Jackson. London: John Mason, 14, City-Road, 1849.

———. *The Manuscript Journal of the Reverend Charles Wesley, M.A.* Edited by S. T. Kimbrough, Jr. and Kenneth G. C. Newport. 2 vols. Nashville: Kingswood, 2008.

Wesley, John and Charles Wesley. *A Collection of Hymns, Extracted From the First Volume of Hymns and Sacred Poems.* London: Printed by W. Strahan, 1743.

———. *A Collection of Psalms and Hymns.* Second ed. London: Printed by W. Strahan, 1743.

———. *Hymns and Sacred Poems. Published by John Wesley, M. A. Fellow of Lincoln College, Oxford; And Charles Wesley, M.A. Student of Christ-Church, Oxford.* London: printed by W. Strahan, 1740.

———. *Hymns and Sacred Poems. Published by John Wesley, M.A. Fellow of Lincoln College, Oxford; And Charles Wesley, M.A. Student of Christ-Church, Oxford.* Bristol, UK: printed by Felix Farley, 1742.

Wesley, John. *The Bicentennial Edition of the Works of John Wesley.* General editors Frank Baker and Richard P. Heitzenrater. Nashville: Abingdon, 1976–.

———. *Cautions and Directions, Given to the Greatest Professors in the Methodist Society.* London: no printer identified, 1762.

———. *A Christian Library: Consisting of Extracts from, and Abridgements of, the Choicest Pieces of Practical Divinity which have been Published in the English Tongue*, 50 vols. Bristol, UK: F. Farley, 1749–55.

———. *A Collection of Hymns for the Use of the People Called Methodists.* London: printed by J. Paramore, 1780.

———. *The Complete English Dictionary, Explaining Most of Those Hard Words, Which Are Found in the Best English Writers.* 2nd ed. Bristol, UK: printed by William Pine, 1764.

———. *The Doctrine of Original Sin, Extracted From a Late Author.* London: J. Paramore, at the Foundry, Moorfields, 1784.

———. *Explanatory notes upon the New Testament. By John Wesley, M.A. Late Fellow of Lincoln-College, Oxford.* London: printed by William Bowyer, 1755.

———. *Explanatory notes upon the New Testament. By John Wesley, M.A. Late Fellow of Lincoln-College, Oxford.* 2nd ed. London, 1757.

———. *Explanatory notes upon the New Testament. By John Wesley, M.A. Late Fellow of Lincoln-College, Oxford.* London: publisher unnamed, 1788.

Bibliography

———. *Explanatory notes upon the Old Testament. By John Wesley, M. A. Late Fellow of Lincoln-College, Oxford.* 3 vols. Bristol, UK: printed by William Pine, 1765.

———. *A Farther Appeal to Men of Reason and Religion.* London: printed by W. Strahan, 1745.

———. *Farther Thoughts on Christian Perfection.* London: no printer identified, 1763.

———. *The Journal of the Rev. John Wesley, A.M.* Edited by Nehemiah Curnock. Standard ed. 7 vols. Originally published as *The Journal of the Rev. John Wesley, A.M.: Enlarged From Original Mss., With Notes From Unpublished Diaries, Annotations, Maps, and Illustrations.* London: C. H. Kelly, 1909. Reprint. London: Epworth, 1938.

———. *A Letter to the Reverend Dr. Conyers Middleton, Occasioned by His Late Free Enquiry.* London: printed by G. Woodfall, 1749.

———. *A Letter to the Rev. Mr. Horne: Occasioned by His Late Sermon Preached Before the University of Oxford.* London: printed by W. Flexney, 1762.

———. *A Letter to the Reverend Mr. Law: Occasioned by Some of His Late Writings. By John Wesley, M.A. Late Fellow of Lincoln College, Oxford.* London: [printed by W. Strahan], 1756.

———. *The Letters of the Rev. John Wesley, A.M., Sometime Fellow of Lincoln College.* Edited by John Telford. Standard ed. 8 vols. London: Epworth, 1931.

———. *The Manuscript Diary of John Wesley.* Colman Collection OD IV. The Methodist Archives of the John Ryland University Library of Manchester, England.

———. *The New Testament with an Analysis of the Several Books and Chapters.* London: printed and sold at the New-Chapel, City-Road; and at the Rev. J. Wesley's Preaching-Houses in town and country, 1790.

———. *A Plain Account of Christian Perfection As Believed and Taught by Rev. John Wesley From 1725 to 1765.* Bristol, UK: printed by William Pine, 1766.

———. *A Plain Account of Christian Perfection As Believed and Taught by Rev. John Wesley From 1725 to 1777.* 4th ed. London: printed by R. Hawes, 1777.

———. *A Plain Account of Christian Perfection As Believed and Taught by Rev. John Wesley From 1725 to 1777.* 1777 ed. New York: The Methodist Book Concern, n.d.

———. *A Plain Account of the People Called Methodists In a Letter to the Rev. Mr. Perronet, Vicar of Shoreham in Kent.* London: printed by W. Strahan, 1749.

———. *Predestination Calmly Considered.* London: printed by W.B., 1752.

———. *The Principles of a Methodist; Occasion'd by a Late Pamphlet, Intitled, A Brief History of the Principles of Methodism.* Bristol: printed by Felix Farley, 1742.

———. *Sermons on Several Occasions: In Three Volumes. By John Wesley, M.A. Fellow of Lincoln-College, Oxford. Vol. I.* London: printed by W. Strahan, 1746.

———. "Unpublished Letters of John Wesley." *Methodist History* 1 (April 1963) 38–60.

———. *Wesley's Veterans: Lives of Early Methodist Preachers Told by Themselves.* Edited by John Telford. London: Robert Culley, n.d.

———. *The Works of the Rev. John Wesley.* Edited by Joseph Benson. 17 vols. London: Conference Office at City-Road, 1809–1813.

———. *The Works of the Rev. John Wesley, A.M. Sometime Fellow of Lincoln College, Oxford. With the last corrections of the Author.* Edited by Thomas Jackson. 14 Vols. London: Methodist Publishing House, 1831.

Wesleyan Methodist Church Conference. *Minutes of Several Conversations Between The Reverend Mr. John and Charles Wesley, and Others. From the Year 1744, to the Year 1780.* London: printed by J. Paramore, at the Foundry, Moorfields, (1780).

Wesleyan Methodist Church Conference. *Minutes of Several Conversations Between the the [Sic] Reverend Messieurs John and Charles Wesley, and Others.* London, 1770.

Westminster Assembly (1643–52). *The Confession of Faith, and The Larger and Shorter Catechism, First Agreed Upon by the Westminster Assembly of Divines At Westminster, And Now Approved by the General Assembly of the Kirk of Scotland, to Be a Part of Uniformity in Religion Between the Kirks of Christ in the Three Kingdomes*. Edited by David Dickson. 2nd ed. Edinburgh: Printed by Evan Tyler, 1660.

Whitehead, John. *The Life of the Rev. John Wesley, M.A. Some Time Fellow of Lincoln College, Oxford. Collected From His Private Papers and Printed Works; And Written At the Request of His Executors. To Which Is Affixed Some Account of His Ancestors and Relations*. 1845 reprint ed. London: printed by Stephen Couchman, 1793.

Wilson, Thomas. *A Christian Dictionarie, Opening the signification of the chiefe wordes dispersed generally through Holie Scriptures*. London: printed by W. Iaggard, 1612.

Witsius, Herman. *Animadversiones Irenicae Ad Controversias, Quæ, Sub Infaustis, Antinomorum Et Neonomorum Nominibus, in Britannia Nunc Agitantur (Conciliatory, or Irenical Animadversions, on the Controversies Agitated in Britain, Under the Unhappy Names of Antinominans and Neonomians)*. Translated by Thomas Bell. Glasgow: W. Lang, 1807.

———. *The Oeconomy of the Divine Covenants: Book III*. Vol. 1 of *The Oeconomy of the Covenants Between God and Man, Comprehending a Complete Body of Divinity. By Herman Witsius, D.D. Professor of Divinity in the Universities of Franeker, Utrecht, and Leyden; And Also Regent of the Divinity College of the States of Holland and West-Friesland. Faithfully Translated From the Latin, and Carefully Revised, by William Crookshank, D.D. To Which Is Prefixed The Life of the Author*. 3 vols. Dublin: printed by R. Stewart, 1774.

Secondary Sources

Abraham, William J. "The Epistemology of Conversion." In *Conversion in the Wesleyan Tradition*, edited by Kenneth J. Collins and John H. Tyson, 175–91. Nashville: Abingdon, 2001.

———. "Keeping Up with Jones on Wesley's Conception and Use of Scripture." *Wesleyan Theological Journal* 33 (Spring 1998) 5–13.

Aikens, Alden. "Wesleyan Theology and the Use of Models." *Wesleyan Theological Journal* 14 (Spring 1979) 64–76.

Allison, C. F. *The Rise of Moralism: The Proclamation of the Gospel From Hooker to Baxter*. London: SPCK, 1966.

Armstrong, Brian G. *Calvinism and the Amyraut Heresy: Protestant Scholasticism and Humanism in Seventeenth-Century France*. Milwaukee, WI: Wisconsin University Press, 1969.

Balzer, Cary. "John Wesley's Developing Soteriology and the Influence of the Caroline Divines." Ph.D. Thesis, The University of Manchester (Nazarene Theological College), 2005.

Banks, John. *Nancy Nancy*. Wilmslow, UK: Penwork, 1984.

Beach, James Mark. *Christ and the Covenant: Francis Turretin's Federal Theology as a Defense of the Doctrine of Grace*. Reformed Historical Theology 1. Göttingen: Vandenhoeck & Ruprecht, 2007.

Berlin, Isaiah. *The Age of Enlightenment: The 18th Century Philosophers*. New York: The New American Library, 1956.

Blacketer, Raymond A. "Arminius' Concept of Covenant in Its Historical Context." *Nederlands Archief Voor Kerkgeschiedenis* 80 (2000) 193–220.

Bibliography

Blankenship, Paul F. "The Significance of John Wesley's Abridgement of the Thirty-Nine Articles as Seen From His Deletions." *Methodist History* 2 (April 1964) 35–47.

Blevins, Dean G. "The Means of Grace: Toward a Wesleyan Praxis of Spiritual Formation." *Wesleyan Theological Journal* 32 (Spring 1997) 69–83.

Booty, John E. "Contrition in Anglican Spirituality: Hooker, Donne, & Herbert." In *Anglican Spirituality*, edited by William J. Wolf, 25-48. Wilton (Conn): Morehouse-Barlow Co., Inc., 1982.

Borgen, Ole E. "John Wesley and Early Swedish Pietism: Carl Magnus Wrangel and Johan Hinric Liden." *Methodist History* 38 (January 2000) 71–81.

Brown, W. Adams. "Covenant Theology." In *Encyclopedia of Religion and Ethics*, 12 vols., edited by James Hastings, 6:216–24. 1908–22. Reprint. Edinburgh: T. & T. Clark, 1981.

Bryant, Barry Edward. "John Wesley's Doctrine of Sin." Ph.D. Thesis, King's College, The University of London, 1992.

Bultmann, Rudolf. "Aphemi, Aphesis, Pariemi, Paresis." In *Theological Dictionary of the New Testament*, edited by G. Kittel and G. Friedrich. Translated by Geoffrey W. Bromiley, 1:509–12. Grand Rapids: Eerdmans, 1964.

Carter, Henry. *The Methodist Heritage*. London: Epworth, 1961.

Cell, George Croft. *The Rediscovery of John Wesley*. Lanham, MD: University Press of America, 1935.

Chamberlain, Jeffrey S. "Moralism, Justification, and the Controversy over Methodism." *The Journal of Ecclesiastical History* 44 (October 1993) 652–78.

Clifford, Alan C. *Atonement and Justification: English Evangelical Theology 1640–1790, An Evaluation*. Oxford: Clarendon, 1990.

Coffey, John. "Puritanism, Evangelicalism and the Evangelical Protestant Tradition." In *The Advent of Evangelicalism: Exploring Historical Continuities*, edited by Kenneth J. Stewart, Michael A. G. Haykin, and Timothy George, 252–77. Nashville: B & H, 2008.

Cohen, Charles L. "Two Biblical Models of Conversion: An Example of Puritan Hermeneutics." *Church History* 58 (June 1989) 182–96.

Colie, Rosalie L. *Light and Englightenment: A Study of the Cambridge Platonists and the Dutch Arminians*. Cambridge: Cambridge University Press, 1957.

Collins, Kenneth J. "The Motif of Real Christianity in the Writing of John Wesley." *Asbury Theological Journal* 49 (1994) 49–62.

———. "Real Christianity As the Integrating Theme in Wesley's Soteriology: A Critique of a Modern Myth." *Wesleyan Theological Journal* 40 (Fall 2005) 52–87.

———. "Recent Trends in Wesleyan/Holiness Scholarship." *Wesleyan Theological Journal* 35 (Spring, 2000) 67–86.

———. *The Scripture Way of Salvation: The Heart of John Wesley's Theology*. Nashville: Abingdon, 1997.

———. *The Theology of John Wesley: Holy Love and the Shape of Grace*. Nashville: Abingdon, 2007.

Collins, Kenneth Joseph. "John Wesley's Theology of Law." Ph.D. Diss., Drew University, 1984.

Cornwall, Robert. "The Rite of Confirmation in Anglican Thought during the Eighteenth Century." *Church History* 68 (June 1999) 359–72.

Cragg, G. R. *From Puritanism to the Age of Reason: A Study of Changes in Religious Thought within the Church of England, 1660–1700*. Cambridge: Cambridge University Press, 1966.

Bibliography

Creed, J. M. "*Paresis* in Dionysius of Halicarnassus and St. Paul." *Journal of Theological Studies* 41 (1940) 28–30.
Cubie, David L. "Placing Aldersgate in John Wesley's Order of Salvation." *Wesleyan Theological Journal* 24 (1989) 32–53.
Cubie, David Livingstone. "John Wesley's Concept of Perfect Love: A Motif Analysis." Ph.D. Diss., Boston University Graduate School, 1965.
Davies, Horton. *Worship and Theology in England: From Watts and Wesley to Maurice, 1690–1850*. Princeton: Princeton University Press, 1961.
Davies, William Rhys. "John William Fletcher of Madeley as Theologian." Ph.D. Thesis, University of Manchester, 1965.
Dayton, Donald W. "The Use of Scripture in the Wesleyan Tradition." In *The Use of the Bible in Theology: Evangelical Options*, edited by Robert K. Johnston, 121–36. Atlanta: John Knox, 1985.
Del Colle, Ralph. "John Wesley's Doctrine of Grace in Light of the Christian Tradition." *International Journal of Systematic Theology* 4 (July 2002) 172–89.
Deschner, John. *Wesley's Christology: An Interpretation*. Dallas: Southern Methodist University Press, 1960.
Dreyer, Frederick. "Faith and Experience in the Thought of John Wesley." *The American Historical Review* 88 (February 1983) 12–30.
———. "John Wesley: *Ein Englischer* Pietist." *Methodist History* 40 (January 2002) 71–84.
Ehmer, Hermann. "Johann Albrecht Bentel (1687–1752)." In *The Pietist Theologians*, edited by Carter Lindberg, 224–38. Oxford: Blackwell, 2005.
Emerson, Everett H. "Calvin and Covenant Theology." *Church History* 25 (June 1956) 136–44.
English, John C. "John Wesley and Francis Rous." *Methodist History* 6 (July 1968) 28–35.
———. "John Wesley and His 'Jewish Parishioners': Jewish-Christian Relationships in Savannah, Georgia, 1736–1737." *Methodist History* 36 (July 1998) 220–27.
Erb, Peter C. "Introduction." In *Pietists: Selected Writings*, edited by Peter C. Erb, 1–27. New York: Paulist, 1983.
Evans, Richard W. "The Relations of George Whitefield and Howell Harris, Fathers of Calvinistic Methodism." *Church History* 30 (June 1961) 179–90.
Fee, Gordon D. *Galatians*. Pentecostal Commentary Series. Blandford Forum (UK): Deo, 2007.
Felleman, Laura Bartels. "Degrees of Certainty in John Wesley's Natural Philosophy." In *Divine Grace and Emerging Creation*, edited by Thomas Jay Oord, 58–80. Eugene, OR: Pickwick, 2009.
———. "John Wesley and the 'Servant of God'." *Wesleyan Theological Journal* 41 (Fall 2006) 72–86.
Forsaith, Peter S. *Unexampled Labours: Letters of the Revd John Fletcher to Leaders in the Evangelical Revival*. Werrington, UK: Epworth, 2008.
Fujimoto, Mitsuru Samuel. "John Wesley's Doctrine of Good Works." Ph.D. Thesis, Drew University, 1986.
Ganske, Karl Ludwig. "The Religion of the Heart and Growth in Grace: John Wesley's Selection and Editing of Puritan Literature for *A Christian Library*." Ph.D. Thesis, The University of Manchester (Nazarene Theological College), 2009.
Gerlach, Sandra. "John Wesley, Inquirer Seeking Grace." *Methodist History* 45 (July 2007) 223–31.

Bibliography

Graham, William [william.graham80@ntlworld.com]. "Publishing History of *A Christian Library*, August 18, 2010.

Green, J. Brazier. *John Wesley and William Law*. London: Epworth, 1945.

Greig, Martin. "Burnet, Gilbert (1643–1715)." In *Oxford Dictionary of National Biography*, edited by H. C. G. Matthew and Brian Harrison, n.p. (online). Oxford: Oxford University Press, 2004. Online edition, 2008. http://www.oxforddnb.com/view/article/4061.

Gunter, W. Stephen. "The Quadrilateral and the 'Middle Way.'" In *Wesley and the Quadrilateral: Renewing the Conversation*, edited by W. Stephen Gunter, Scott J. Jones, Ted A. Campbell, Rebekah L. Miles, Randy L. Maddox, 17–38. Nashville: Abingdon, 1997.

Guttenplan, Samuel. *Objects of Metaphor*. Oxford: Oxford University Press, 2005.

Halliday, F. E. *A Concise History of England*. London: Book Club Associates, 1974.

Hammond, Geordan. "High Church Anglican Influences on John Wesley's Conception of Primitive Christianity, 1732–1735." *Anglican and Episcopal History* 78 (June 2009) 174–207.

Hampton, Stephen. *Anti-Arminians: The Anglican Reformed Tradition From Charles II to George I*. Oxford: Oxford University Press, 2008.

Heitzenrater, Richard Paul. "John Wesley and the Oxford Methodists, 1725–35", Ph.D. Diss., Duke University, 1972.

———. *Mirror and Memory: Reflections on Early Methodism*. Nashville: Kingswood, 1989.

Helmbold, Andrew. "J. A. Bengel—'Full of Light.'" *Bulletin of the Evangelical Theological Society* 6 (1963) 73–81.

Hempton, David. "The People Called Methodists: Transitions in Britain and North America." In *The Oxford Handbook of Methodist Studies*, edited by William J. Abraham and James E. Kirby, 67–84. Oxford: Oxford University Press, 2009.

Heppe, Heinrich. *Reformed Dogmatics*. Edited by Ernst Bizer. Translated by G. T. Thomson. London: George Allen & Unwin, 1950.

Hillman, Robert John. "Grace in the Preaching of Calvin and Wesley: A Comparative Study." Ph.D. Thesis, Fuller Theological Seminary, 1978.

Hindmarsh, D. Bruce. *The Evangelical Conversion Narrative: Spiritual Autobiography in Early Modern England*. Oxford: Oxford University Press, 2005. Online: http://dx.doi.org/10.1093/0199245754.001.0001.

———. "'Let Us See Thy Great Salvation': What Did It Mean to Be Saved for the Early Evangelicals?" In *What Does It Mean to Be Saved?: Broadening Evangelical Horizons of Salvation*, edited by John G. Stackhouse, Jr., 43–66. Grand Rapids: Baker Academic, 2002.

Hindson, Edward, editor. *Introduction to Puritan Theology: A Reader*. Grand Rapids: Baker, 1976.

Holland, Bernhard G. "The Conversions of John and Charles Wesley and Their Place in Methodist Tradition." *Proceedings of the Wesley Historical Society* 38 (August 1971) 46–53; 38 (December 1971) 65–71.

Hoon, Paul W. "The Soteriology of John Wesley." PhD Thesis, Edinburgh University, 1936.

Horton, Michael. *God of Promise*. Grand Rapids: Baker, 2009.

Horton-Parker, H. S. "John Wesley and the Roots of Contemporary Orthopathy: A Modest Proposal." *Journal of Renewal Studies* (n.d.) 1–22.

Ingersol, Stan, Floyd Timothy Cunningham, Harold E. Raser, and D. P. Whitelaw. *Our Watchword and Song: The Centennial History of the Church of the Nazarene*. Kansas City: Beacon Hill, 2009.

Ireson, Roger W. "The Doctrine of Faith in John Wesley and the Protestant Tradition: A Comparative Study." Ph.D. Thesis, Manchester University, 1973.

Jeon, Jeong Koo. *Covenant Theology: John Murray's and Meredith G. Kline's Response to the Historical Development of Federal Theology in Reformed Thought*. Lanham, MD: University Press of America, 2004.

Jinkins, Michael. "Perkins, William (1558–1602)." In *Oxford Dictionary of National Biography*, edited by H. C. G. Matthew and Brian Harrison, n.p. (online). Oxford: Oxford University Press, 2004. Online edition, 2008. http://www.oxforddnb.com/view/article/21973.

Jones, David Ceri. "Calvinistic Methodism and the Origins of English Evangelicalism." In *The Emergence of Evangelicalism: Exploring Historical Continuities*, edited by Kenneth J. Stewart, Michael A. G. Haykin, and Timothy George, 103–28. Nottingham, UK: Apollos, 2008.

———. "*A Glorious Work in the World*': Welsh Methodism and the International Evangelical Revival, 1735–1750. Cardiff: University of Wales Press, 2004.

Jones, Scott J. *John Wesley's Conception and Use of Scripture*. Nashville: Kingswood, 1995.

Karlberg, Mark W. "Covenant Theology in Reformed Perspective." N.p. (online), November 30, 2008. http://www.ntslibrary.com/PDF%20Books/Covenant%20Theology%20in%20Reformed%20Perspective.pdf.

Keddie, Gordon J. "'Unfallible Certenty of the Pardon of Sinne and Life Everlasting': The Doctrine of Assurance in the Theology of William Perkins (1558–1602)." *The Evangelical Quarterly* 48 (1976) 230–44.

Keefer, Luke L., Jr. "John Wesley and English Arminianism." *Evangelical Journal* 4 (1986) 15–28.

Kendall, R. T. *Calvin and English Calvinism to 1649*. Oxford Theological Monographs. Oxford: Oxford University Press, 1979.

Kisker, Scott. "Justified But Unregenerate? The Relationship of Assurance to Justification and Regeneration in the Thought of John Wesley." *Wesleyan Theological Journal* 28 (1993) 44–58.

Larminie, Vivienne. "Davenant, John (*bap.* 1572, *d.* 1641)." In *Oxford Dictionary of National Biography*, edited by H. C. G. Matthew and Brian Harrison, n.p. (online). Oxford: Oxford University Press, 2004. Online edition, 2008. http://www.oxforddnb.com/view/article/7196.

Langford, Paul. *Eighteenth-Century Britain: A Very Short Introduction*. Very Short Introductions originally published as The Oxford Illustrated History of Britain. 1984. Reprint. New York: Oxford University Press, 2000.

Leclerc, Diane. *Discovering Christian Holiness: The Heart of Wesleyan-Holiness Theology*. Kansas City: Beacon Hill, 2010.

Lee, Umphrey. *John Wesley and Modern Religion*. Nashville: Cokesbury, 1936.

Leffel, G. Michael. "Prevenient Grace and the Re-Enchangment of Nature: Toward a Wesleyan Theology of Psycholtherapy and Spiritual Formation." *Journal of Psychology and Christianity* 23 (2004) 130–39.

Lettinga, Neil. "Covenant Theology Turned Upside Down: Henry Hammond and Caroline Anglican Moralism 1643–1660." *The Sixteenth Century Journal* 24 (Autumn 1993) 653–69.

Bibliography

Lillback, Peter A. "The Continuing Conundrum: Calvin and the Conditionality of the Covenant." *Calvin Theological Journal* 29 (1994) 72–74.

Lindstrom, Harald. *Wesley and Sanctification: A Study in the Doctrine of Salvation.* London: Epworth, 1946.

Long, Stephen D. *John Wesley's Moral Theology: The Quest for God and Goodness.* Nashville: Kingswood, 2005.

Luby, Daniel Joseph. "The Perceptibility of Grace in the Theology of John Wesley: A Roman Catholic Consideration." Ph.D. Thesis, University of St. Thomas, 1994.

Maddox, Randy L. "Continuing the Conversation." *Methodist History* 30 (July 1992) 235–241.

———. "John Wesley's Reading: Evidence in the Book Collection at Wesley's House, London." *Methodist History* 41 (April 2003) 118–33.

———. "John Wesley's Reading: Evidence in the Kingswood School Archives." *Methodist History* 41 (January 2003) 49–67.

———. "Kingswood School Library Holdings (CA. 1775)." *Methodist History* 41 (October 2002) 342–70.

———. "Prelude to a Dialog". *Wesleyan Theological Journal* 35 (2000) 87–98.

———. "Remnants of John Wesley's Personal Library." *Methodist History* 42 (January 2004) 122–28.

———. *Responsible Grace: John Wesley's Practical Theology.* Nashville: Kingswood, 1994.

Manchester, Eric. "Why Is Evangelism Important If One Can Be Saved Without the Gospel?" *Wesleyan Theological Journal* 37 (2002) 158–70.

Martin, Ralph P. "'The Almost Christian': John Wesley's Sermon and a Lukan Text (Acts 26:28)." In *Holiness as a Root of Morality: Essays on Wesleyan Ethics (Essays in Honor of Lane A. Scott)*, edited by John S. Park, 17–24. Lewiston, NY: Mellen, 2006.

Matthews, Rex Dale. "'Religion and Reason Joined': A Study in the Theology of John Wesley." Th.D. Thesis, Harvard University, 1986.

McCoy, Charles S. and J. Wayne Baker. *Fountainhead of Federalism: Heinrich Bullinger and the Covenantal Tradition.* Louisville: Westminster/John Knox, 1991.

McGiffert, Michael. "Bulkeley, Peter (1583–1659)." In *Oxford Dictionary of National Biography*, edited by H. C. G. Matthew and Brian Harrison, n.p. (online). Oxford: Oxford University Press, 2004. Online edition, 2008. http://www.oxforddnb.com/view/article/3901.

———. "From Moses to Adam: The Making of the Covenant of Works." *The Sixteenth Century Journal* 19 (Summer, 1988) 131–55.

McGonigle, Herbert Boyd. *Sufficient Saving Grace: John Wesley's Evangelical Arminianism.* Studies in Evangelical History and Thought. Carlisle, UK: Paternoster, 2001.

McGowan, A. T. B. *The Federal Theology of Thomas Boston.* Rutherford Studies in Historical Theology. Edinburgh: Rutherford House, 1997.

Møller, Jens G. "The Beginnings of Puritan Covenant Theology." *The Journal of Ecclesiastical History* 14 (April 1963) 46–67.

Monk, Robert C. *John Wesley: His Puritan Heritage.* London: Epworth, 1966.

Moore, Jonathan D. "Preston, John (1587–1628)." In *Oxford Dictionary of National Biography*, edited by H. C. G. Matthew and Brian Harrison, n.p. (online). Oxford: Oxford University Press, 2004. http://www.oxforddnb.com/view/article/22727.

More, Ellen. "John Goodwin and the Origins of the New Arminianism." *Journal of British Studies* 22 (Autumn 1982) 50–70.

Morgan, Edmund Sears. *Visible Saints: The History of a Puritan Idea.* Ithaca: Cornell University Press, 1963.

Bibliography

Muller, Richard A. "The Federal Motif in Seventeenth Century Arminian Theology." *Nederlandsch Archief Voor Kerkgeschiedenis* 62 (1982) 102–22.

Noble, Thomas A. "John Wesley As a Theologian: An Introduction." Center for Evangelical and Reformed Theology, Free University of Amsterdam, April 5, 2007.

O'Donovan, Oliver. *On the Thirty Nine Articles: A Conversation with Tudor Christianity.* Exeter, UK: Paternoster, 1986.

Olson, Mark K. *John Wesley's Theology of Christian Perfection: Developments in Doctrine and Theological System.* Fenwick, MI: Truth in Heart, 2007.

———. "The Roots of John Wesley's Servant Theology." *Wesleyan Theological Journal* 44 (Fall 2009) 120–41.

Outler, Albert C., editor. *John Wesley.* New York: Oxford University Press, 1964.

Patrides, C. A. *The Cambridge Platonists.* Cambridge: Harvard University Press, 1970.

Pelikan, Jaroslav. *Reformation of Church and Dogma (1300–1700).* Vol. 4 of *The Christian Tradition: A History of the Development of Doctrine.* Chicago: University of Chicago, 1984.

Pettit, Norman. *The Heart Prepared: Grace and Conversion in Puritan Spiritual Life.* New Haven: Yale University Press, 1966.

Podmore, C. J. "The Fetter Lane Society, 1738." *Proceedings of the Wesley Historical Society* 46 (May 1988) 125–53.

Podmore, Colin. *The Moravian Church in England, 1728–1760.* Oxford: Clarendon, 1998.

Prest, Wilfrid. "Finch, Sir Henry (C.1558–1625)." In *Oxford Dictionary of National Biography*, edited by H. C. G. Matthew and Brian Harrison, n.p. (online). Oxford: Oxford University Press, 2004. Online edition, 2008. http://www.oxforddnb.com/view/article/9436.

Rack, Henry D. *Reasonable Enthusiast: John Wesley and the Rise of Methodism.* Philadelphia: Trinity, 1989.

———. "Wesley, John." In *Oxford Dictionary of National Biography*, edited by H. C. G. Matthew and Brian Harrison, 60 vols., 58:182–93. Oxford: Oxford University Press, 2004.

Reay, B. "Radicalism and Religion in the English Revolution: An Introduction." In *Radical Religion in the English Revolution*, edited by J. F. McGregor and B. Reay, 1–21. Oxford: Oxford University Press, 1984.

Ricoeur, Paul. *Figuring the Sacred: Religion, Narrative, and Imagination.* Edited by Mark I. Wallace. Translated by David Pellauer. Minneapolis: Fortress, 1995.

———. *The Rule of Metaphor: The Creation of Meaning in Language.* Translated by Robert Czerny. Reprint. London: Routledge, 2003.

Rivers, Isabel. "John Wesley and the Language of Scripture, Reason and Experience." *Prose Studies* 4 (1981) 252–86.

———. *Reason, Grace, and Sentiment: A Study of the Language of Religion and Ethics in England, 1660–1780, I. Whichcote to Wesley.* Cambridge: Cambridge University Press, 1991.

Rogers, Charles Allen. "The Concept of Prevenient Grace in the Theology of John Wesley." Ph.D, Diss., Duke University, 1967.

Runyon, Theodore. *The New Creation: John Wesley's Theology Today.* Nashville: Abingdon, 1998.

Rupp, Ernest Gordon. *Religion in England 1688–1791.* Edited by Henry Chadwick and Owen Chadwick. Oxford History of the Christian Church. Oxford: Clarendon Press, 1986.

Bibliography

Rupwate, Daniel. "The Covenant Theology of John Wesley." *Canadian Methodist Historical Society* 9 (1991–92) 79–89.

Scholtz, Gregory F. "Anglicanism in the Age of Johnson: The Doctrine of Conditional Salvation." *Eighteenth-Century Studies* 22 (Winter 1988–1989) 182–207.

Schwarz, Suzanne. "The Legacy of Melvill Horne." *International Bulletin of Missionary Research* 31 (April 2007) 88–94.

Scott, Lane A. "Experience and Scripture in John Wesley's Concept of Saving Faith." In *Holiness as a Root of Morality: Essays on Wesleyan Ethics (Essays in Honor of Lane A. Scott)*, edited by John S. Park, 245–58. Lewiston, NY: Mellen, 2006.

Scroggs, Robin. "John Wesley As Biblical Scholar." *Journal of the American Academy of Religion* 28 (November 4, 1960) 415–22.

Sell, A. P. F. *The Great Debate: Calvinism, Arminianism, and Salvation*. Grand Rapids: Baker, 1982.

Sledge, Robert W. "What Böhler Got From Wesley." *Methodist History* 45 (July 2007) 214–22.

Smith, Harmon L. "Wesley's Doctrine of Justification: Beginning and Process." *The London Quarterly and Holborn Review* (April 1964) 120–28.

Snyder, Howard A. "John Wesley and Macarius the Egyptian." *The Asbury Theological Journal* 45 (1990) 55–60.

Song, Young Jae Timothy. *Theology and Piety in the Reformed Federal Thought of William Perkins and John Preston*. Lewiston, NY: Mellen, 1998.

Spellman, W. M. *The Latitudinarians and the Church of England, 1660–1700*. Athens, GA: University of Georgia Press, 1993.

Spieler, Robert F. "The Theological Significance of Johann Albrecht Bengel." Th.D. Thesis, Concordia Seminary, May 1957.

Sprunger, Keith L. "Ames, William (1576–1633)." In *Oxford Dictionary of National Biography*, edited by H. C. G. Matthew and Brian Harrison, n.p. (online). Oxford: Oxford University Press, 2004. Online edition, 2008. http://www.oxforddnb.com/view/article/440,

Spurr, John. "'Latitudinarianism' and the Restoration Church." *The Historical Journal* 31 (1988) 61–82.

Stead, Geoffrey and Margaret Stead. *The Exotic Plant: A History of the Moravian Church in Great Britain, 1742–2000*. Peterborough, UK: Epworth, 2003.

Stoeffler, F. Ernest. *German Pietism during the Eighteenth Century*. Leiden: Brill, 1973.

———. *The Rise of Evangelical Pietism*. Studies in the History of Religions (Supplements to Nvmen) IX. Leiden: Brill, 1965.

———. "The Wesleyan Concept of Religious Certainty—Its Pre-History and Significance." *The London Quarterly and Holborn Review* (April 1964) 128–39.

Tipson, Baird. "Invisible Saints: The 'Judgment of Charity' in the Early New England Churches." *Church History* 44 (December 1975) 460–71.

Towlson, Clifford W. *Moravian and Methodist: Relationships and Influences in the Eighteenth Century*. London: Epworth, 1957.

Tracey, Wesley D. "John Wesley, Spiritual Director: Spiritual Guidance in John Wesley's Letters." *Wesleyan Theological Journal* 23 (Spring-Fall 1988) 148–62.

Tripp, David H. "John Wesley's Letters of Orders as Deacon (1725) and as Priest (1728) Translated." *Methodist History* 41 (July 2003) 192–96.

Tyson, John H. "Essential Doctrines and Real Religion: Theological Method in Wesley's *Sermons on Several Occasions*." *Wesleyan Theological Journal* 23 (1988) 163–79.

———. "Interdependence of Law and Grace in John Wesley's Teaching and Preaching." Ph.D. Thesis, University of Edinburgh, 1991.

Van Asselt, W. J. *"Amicitia Dei* As Ultimate Reality: An Outline of the Covenant Theology of Johannes Cocceius (1603–1669)." *Ultimate Reality and Meaning* 21 (1998) 35–47.

———. "The Doctrine of the Abrogations in the Federal Theology of Johannes Cocceius (1603–1669)." *Calvin Theological Journal* 29 (1994) 101–16.

Van Asselt, Willem J. *The Federal Theology of Johannes Cocceius (1603–1669).* Translated by Raymond Andrew Blacketer. Leiden: Brill, 2001.

Van den Brink, Gert. "Calvin, Witsius (1636–1708), and the English Antinomians." *Church History and Religious Culture* 91 (2011) 229–40

Vickers, Jason E. "Wesley's Theological Emphases." In *The Cambridge Companion to John Wesley,* edited by Randy L. Maddox and Jason E. Vickers, 190–206. New York: Cambridge University Press, 2010.

Visser, Derk. "The Covenant in Zacharias Ursinus." *The Sixteenth Century Journal* 18 (Winter 1987) 531–44.

Von Rohr, John. "Covenant and Assurance in Early English Puritanism." *Church History* 34 (June 1965) 195–203.

———. *The Covenant of Grace in Puritan Thought.* Studies in Religion (American Academy of Religion) 45. Atlanta: Scholars, 1986.

Vorlander, H. "Forgiveness." In *The New International Dictionary of New Testament Theology,* edited by Colin Brown. 4 vols., 1:697–703. Exeter, UK: Paternoster, 1975.

Wagner, Walter H. "Luther and the Positive Use of the Law." *Journal of Religious History* 11:1 (1980) 45–63.

Wallace, Charles. *Susanna Wesley: The Complete Writings.* New York: Oxford University Press, 1997.

Wallace, Dewey D. *The Spirituality of the Later English Puritans: An Anthology.* Macon, GA: Mercer University Press, 1987.

Walls, Jerry L. "John Wesley on Predestination and Election." In *The Oxford Handbook of Methodist Studies,* edited by William J. Abraham and James E. Kirby, 619–32. Oxford: Oxford University Press, 2009.

Walsh, John. "'Methodism' and the Origins of English-Speaking Evangelicalism." In *Evangelicalism: Comparative Studies of Popular Protestantism in North America, the British Isles, and Beyond,* 1700–1990, edited by David W. Bebbington, Mark A. Noll, and George A. Rawlyk, 19–37. Oxford: Oxford University Press, 1994.

Ward, W. R. *The Protestant Evangelical Awakening.* Cambridge: Cambridge University Press, 1992.

Ward, W. Reginald. "John Wesley and His Evangelical Past." *Asbury Theological Journal* 59 (Spring, Fall 2004) 5–15.

Watson, Richard. "The Life of the Rev. John Wesley, A.M. Sometime Fellow of Lincoln College, Oxford, and Founder of the Methodist Societies." In *A Christian Library. A Reprint of Standard Religious Works.* Edited by Jonathan Going, 3–102. New York: Thomas George, 1835.

Weir, David A. *The Origins of the Federal Theology in Sixteenth-Century Reformation Thought.* New York: Oxford University Press, 1990.

Wesley, John and George C. Cell. *John Wesley's New Testament: Compared with the Authorized Version.* Philadelphia: Winston, 1938.

Bibliography

Wheeler, Henry. *History and Exposition of the Twenty-Five Articles of Religion of the Methodist Episcopal Church.* New York: Eaton & Mains, 1908.

White, Charles Edward. "'From Strength to Strength Go On': Images of Growth in the Hymns of Charles Wesley." *Proceedings of the Charles Wesley Society* 12 (2008) 49–64.

White, Peter. "The Rise of Arminianism Reconsidered." *Past & Present* 101 (1983) 34–54.

Williams, Colin W. *John Wesley's Theology Today.* Nashville: Abingdon, 1960.

Wolsterstorff, Nicholas. "The Assurance of Faith." *Faith and Philosophy* 7 (October 1990) 396–417.

Wood, Laurence. "John Fletcher as the Theologian of Early American Methodism." In *Religion, Gender, and Industry: Exploring Church and Methodism in a Local Setting,* edited by Geordan Hammond and Peter S. Forsaith, 189–204. Cambridge: James Clarke, 2011.

———. "The Rediscovery of Pentecost in Methodism." *Asbury Theological Journal* 53 (Spring 1998) 7–34.

Wright, Stephen. "Alleine, Richard (1610/11–1681)." In *Oxford Dictionary of National Biography*, edited by H. C. G. Matthew and Brian Harrison, n.p. (online). Oxford: Oxford University Press, 2004. Online edition, 2008. http://www.oxforddnb.com/view/article/367.

Wynkoop, Mildred Bangs. "Theological Roots of Wesleyanism's Understanding of the Holy Spirit." *Wesleyan Theological Journal* 14 (1979) 77–98.

Yates, Arthur S. *The Doctrine of Assurance: With Special Reference to John Wesley.* London: Epworth, 1952.

Young, B. W. "William Law and the Christian Economy of Salvation." *The English Historical Review* 109 (April 1994) 308–22.

Zaret, David. "Calvin, Covenant Theology, and the Weber Thesis." *The British Journal of Sociology* 43 (September 1992) 369–91.

Name Index

Abel, 137–38, 175
Abraham, 56n, 136, 138, 142, 145, 175, 219
Adam, 6, 19, 37, 43–50, 60, 62, 65–72, 100, 135–36, 141–42, 145, 217
Alleine, Richard, 171
Amama, Sixtinus, 51
Ambrose, Isaac, 97, 167–68
Ames, William, 12, 39–42, 46–49, 51, 53, 58, 63–65, 68–70, 74n, 77, 79, 105, 136–37, 140n, 141–42, 144–45, 147, 153, 201, 221
Amyraut, Moïses, 36, 50
Andrews, Isaac, 212
Annesley, Samuel, 41
Aristotle, 16
Armstrong, Brian G., 49n, 50n
Arndt, Johann, 92
Atlay, Joseph, 158n

Baker, J. Wayne, 44n, 46n, 51n, 52, 74n
Ball, John, 7
Banks, John, 4n, 145n, 190, 193n
Baxter, Richard, 29, 44n, 98, 106–7, 122, 125–27
Bayley, Cornelius, 41n

Note: Each page listing followed immediately by the letter "n" indicates that the name indexed appears only among the footnotes on that particular page.

Bengel, J. A., 21–23, 31–32, 52–53, 77, 81–82, 84, 144–45, 171, 177
Bennet, John, 32n
Bennis (Mrs.), 177
Benson, Joseph, 24n, 120n, 177
Beveridge, William, 60n, 120n
Beza, Theodore, 56, 201
Blacketer, Raymond A., 9n, 56n
Blankenship, Paul F., 100n
Böhler, Peter, 5
Bolton, Ann, 4–5, 23, 27n, 130n, 145n, 148–49, 172, 187n, 189–93, 196–98, 208, 214, 220
Bolton, Robert, 97, 158–59, 168
Bosanquet, Mary, 177
Boston, Thomas, 49n, 160, 165n, 214, 218n
Brenz, Johannes, 52
Briggs, Philothea, 127n
Bulkeley, Peter, 139, 150n
Bull, George, 127
Bullinger, Henry (Heinrich), 7, 44, 45n, 134
Bunyan, John, 50
Burk, J. C. F., 152n
Burkitt, William, 160
Burnet, Gilbert, 78

Calvin, John, 7, 113
Cameron, John, 49
Cennick, John, 41n, 42n

Name Index

Chamberlain, Jeffrey, 40n
Charnock, Stephen, 135, 137–38
Clifford, A. C., 102n
Cloppenburg, Johannes, 56, 143
Cocceius, Johannes, 7, 36, 42,
    51–58, 59n, 77, 140, 143–45,
    153
Coffey, John, 94n, 95, 96n, 98n
Cohen, Charles L., 107n
Coke, Thomas, 2n
Colie, Rosalie, 94
Collins, Kenneth, 3, 10n, 17n,
    131n, 157n, 199–200
Cooke, Mary, 188
Cornelius, 29–30, 105–8, 110,
    117, 120–22, 132, 174, 176,
    183–84, 201–3, 205–6, 215,
    217
Cotton, John, 59n, 113–14, 124
Cragg, G. R., 94–96
Creighton, James, 186
Crisp, Tobias, 102n
Cubie, David L., 178n

Davenant, John, 101–2
Davenport, Thomas, 163–64,
    186–87, 198n, 204
Davies, W. R., 11
Davis, Richard, 93
Del Colle, Robert, 182
Deschner, John, 63
Doddridge, Philip, 84, 86n
Downame, George, 101

Edwards, Jonathan, 39n, 93
Erb, Peter, 52, 144n
Eve, 141

Fee, Gordon, 88
Felleman, Laura, 4, 5n, 30n, 35n
Fenner, Dudley, 45, 46n
Fisher, Edward, 49n
Fletcher, John, 10–12, 126, 135,
    155n, 178, 194–95, 203–5,
    208n

Foard, Ann, 130
Forsaith, Peter, 11
Francke, August Hermann, 91, 92n,
    105
Frei, Hans, 53
Frelinghuysen, T. J., 93
Fujimoto, M. S., 5n
Furley, Samuel, 138, 145n

Ganske, Karl Ludwig, 43n
Gomarus, Franciscus, 46n
Goodwin, John, 9–10, 63n, 64n,
    87n, 94
Goodwin, Thomas, 66
Green, John, 214
Guttenplan, Samuel, 16
Guyse, John, 38, 51, 66n, 69n,
    81–82, 84, 86, 88, 201

Halévy, Elie, 97
Hall, Joseph, 102
Hall, Martha, 166
Hall, Westley, 114, 166
Hammond, Henry, 40–41, 60n
Hampton, Stephen, 96
Heitzenrater, Richard, 4, 19n, 41n,
    60n, 95–96, 178n
Henry, Matthew, 51, 83–84, 160,
    194n
Heppe, Heinrich, 72n
Hervey, James   10n, 64, 87n
Hindmarsh, D. Bruce, 104, 105n,
    106n, 133–34, 181n
Hindson, Edward, 43n
Holland, Bernard, 2, 197
Hooker, Thomas, 114, 124, 131
Hoon, Paul, 207
Horne, George, 129, 130n, 149–50,
    159
Horne, Melvill, 2n
Horton, Michael, 6–7
Hulsius, Antonius, 57

Ingham, Benjamin, 114–16

244

Name Index

Jäger, Wolfgang, 52
John (the Apostle), 116, 155
John (the Baptist), 86, 135
Jones, David Cari, 91n, 93n, 95, 97, 131n
Jones, Griffith, 93

Keddie, Gordon J., 41n
Keefer, Luke, 93, 95, 97
Kendall, R. T., 42n
Kisker, Scott, 3n
Knox, Alexander, 16–18, 25–26, 186, 189, 193–96, 198, 214

Larminie, Vivienne, 101n
Laud, William, 18n
Law, William, 98, 125, 161
Lee, Umphrey, 4
Lessey, Theophilus, 150, 210
Lettinga, Neil, 9n, 40
Lillback, Peter, 6
Lydia, 107, 203

Macarius, 211
Maccovius, Johannes, 51
Maddox, Randy, 2–3, 10n, 17n, 22n, 35n, 41n, 134n, 182n, 199, 200n
Marshall, Walter, 97
Martini, Matthias, 51–52
McCoy, Charles S., 44n, 46n, 51n, 52, 74n
McGiffert, Michael, 45, 46n, 139n
McGonigle, Herbert, 9, 10n, 98n, 117, 126n
Melchizedek (Melchisedec), 203
Møller, Jans, 40, 43, 44n, 46n
Molther, Philip, 104
Moltmann, Jürgen, 6
Monk, Robert, 8, 41n
Moore, Jonathan D., 59n
More, Ellen, 9, 10n
Morgan, James, 188–89, 217, 219

Moses, 37, 45, 47, 49–50, 56n, 60–61 65–67, 69, 79, 81–86, 136, 139, 142, 146, 155n, 156, 205, 219, 221
Musculus, Andreas, 56

Noble, Thomas A., 8n
Norris, John, 115

Olevianus, Caspar, 7
Origen, 94
Outler, Albert, 7–8, 12, 28n, 31, 32n, 39, 41n, 58, 79n, 110n, 137n, 169n, 203

Packer, J. I., 6–7
Patrides, C. A., 94n, 95
Paul (or "the Apostle" i.e., Paul), 20, 37–38, 61, 65–67, 73, 81, 100, 106, 112–13, 150, 156, 160, 163, 171, 174, 179, 197, 209, 222
Pelikan, Jaroslav, 49n
Pemble, William, 49
Perkins, William, 12, 39–46, 58, 63, 65, 68, 69n, 70, 74n, 77, 79, 107, 112, 118n, 142, 153, 200–201
Peter (or "the Apostle" i.e. Peter), 23, 27, 121, 128n, 130, 149–50, 176, 191, 201, 202n, 205, 208
Pettit, Norman, 106n, 107n, 113n, 114n, 131n
Podmore, Colin, 92n
Polanus, Amandus, 49
Poole, Matthew, 83
Preston, John, 7, 41n, 59–61

Rack, Henry, 91–93, 109, 124n, 131
Raser, Harold, 11n
Reeves, Jonathan, 20, 85, 111, 120n, 149, 219
Ricoeur, Paul, 14, 16–17

Name Index

Rijssenius, Leonard, 72n
Rivers, Isabel, 91, 95n, 96
Rollock, Robert, 7, 49
Runyon, Theodore, 3
Rupp, Gordon, 97, 110
Rutherford, Samuel, 113n
Rutherford, Thomas, 152, 170n, 173n, 174–75, 185n

Sell, A. P. F., 99n
Shirley, Walter, 126n
Sibbes, Richard, 97, 107, 113n, 159
Smith, John, 28n, 78, 118–19, 122, 139n, 157, 173n
Song, Young Jae Timothy, 49n, 141n, 142n, 143n
South, Robert, 218
Southey, Robert, 30n
Spellman, W. M., 94n
Spener, Philipp Jakob, 91–92
Sprunger, Keith L., 46n
Spurr, John, 95n
Stoeffler, Ernest, 52, 144n

Taylor, Jeremy, 112–13
Taylor, John, 197
Taylor, John, non-conformist minister (1694–1761), 121n
Throgmorton, George, 159n
Tipson, Baird, 113n
Tompson, Richard, 173n, 184n, 187n, 195
Tracy, Wesley, 4
Tucker, Josiah, 100
Tyerman, Luke, 12, 126n
Tyndale, William, 106

Ursinus, Zacharias, 7, 46

Van Asselt, Willem J., 53–56, 57n, 85n, 143n, 144n
Van den Brink, Gert, 102n, 103n, 104n
Vickers, Jason, 8

Visser, Derk, 46n
Vitringa, Campegius, 52
Voetius, Gisbertus, 56, 58
Von Rohr, John, 44n

Wagner, Walter H., 194n
Wallace, Charles, 167n
Walls, Jerry, 98n
Walsh, John, 95–97
Ward, Samuel, 102
Ward, W. R., 92, 124n
Warr, John, 110
Watson, Richard, 11, 12n
Weir, David A., 6n
Wesley, Charles, 2, 11, 18n, 30n, 31–32, 99, 114–16, 119, 122, 149n, 156, 165, 167, 170n
Wesley, Sarah, 187–88
Wesley, Susanna, 164–67
Westley, Bartholomew, 41
Whichcote, Benjamin, 94n, 95
White, John, 41
Whitefield, George, 16, 95, 97, 129
Whitehead, John, 120n
Whitehead, Thomas, 148n
Whitgift, John, 44n
Williams, Colin, 2, 3n
Wilson, Thomas, 47
Witsius, Herman, 6n, 102–4
Wood, Laurance, 12n
Wynkoop, Mildred, 3n

Zaret, David, 194n, 199n, 206
Zinzendorf, Nikolaus Ludwig von, 92, 105
Zwingli, Huldreich, 7, 143

Scripture Index

Old Testament

Genesis

3:15   44, 57, 62, 138, 141, 154

Exodus

39:1	74

Deuteronomy

13:4	121
30:11–14	65
34:12	83

Joshua

1:1	83

Job

2:3	121

Psalms

40:7–8	86

Proverbs

9:10	122

Note: Page listings not associated with a particular verse or passage indicate occurrences where that book of the Bible is referenced in general.

Ecclesiastes

12:13	121

Isaiah

1:16–17	121
50:10	120–21

Zechariah

12:10	194

New Testament

Matthew

3:2	86

John

1:12	171
1:14	139
1:17	81
3:16	209
3:36	204
5:46	155
17:24	21, 23

Acts

2:1	71
10:1—11:18	29
10:34–35	29–30, 120–22, 124, 128, 130, 176, 204

Scripture Index

Acts (*cont.*)

10:2	30, 183
10:4	120, 175–76
10:22	183
10:36	176
10:43	176, 202
10:44	202
11:14	202
16:30	207

Romans

	29, 31, 156, 189, 209
1:7	22, 23, 144
1:17	81, 209
1:19	80
3:19	80
3:20	69
3:31	73
4:15	71
5:5	209
6:14	75
7	156, 163–64, 170, 183, 187
7:4	54
7:9	80
7:12	72
7:14	163
8:15–16	22, 29, 32, 157, 159, 209
10:5–8	37, 65
10:4	67, 69
11	75

1 Corinthians

3:1	172

2 Corinthians

	61
3:6–15	223
3:9	202
3:13	87
5:15	54
5:21	54
6:14	131

Galatians

	88
1:16	169, 209
2:19	54
2:20	209
3:10	61
3:24	184
3:26	209
4	19, 87–89, 195, 205, 209, 222
4:1–7	18, 22, 29, 38, 74, 87–89, 170–72, 178–79, 209
4:24–25	45

Philippians

2:5	209

Colossians

4:12	1

Hebrews

	51, 74, 84, 107
3:5–6	82
7:18–19	84, 220
8:6–8	84, 86
8:5	74
9:23	74
10:7–9	86
10:11–12	83
10:1	74, 87

James

2:24	129

1 Peter

1:10	87
4:11	78

1 John

2:12–13	172
2:8	86
2:18	80
3:9	209

1 John (*cont.*)

3:14	115
3:24	121
4:18	172, 177
5:7	32
5:10	173, 209

Jude

1	17, 22–23, 29, 32, 88

Revelation

11:19	74
13:8	57, 62–64

www.ingramcontent.com/pod-product-compliance
Lightning Source LLC
Chambersburg PA
CBHW050346230426
43663CB00010B/2007